Acquiring, Processing, and Deploying

Voice *of the* Customer

M. Larry Shillito

S^t_L

St. Lucie Press
Boca Raton • London
New York • Washington, D.C.

Library of Congress Cataloging-in-Publication Data

Shillito, M. Larry.
    Acquiring, processing, and deploying voice of the customer / M. Larry Shillito
      p. cm.
      Includes bibliographical references and index.
      ISBN 1-57444-290-2 (alk. paper)
      1. Customer services--Management. I. Title.

HF5415.5 .S545 2000
658.8′12--dc21
                                        00-055358
                                            CIP

© 2001 by CRC Press LLC
St. Lucie Press is an imprint of CRC Press LLC

No claim to original U.S. Government works
International Standard Book Number 1-57444-290-2
Library of Congress Card Number 00-055358
Printed in the United States of America   2 3 4 5 6 7 8 9 0
Printed on acid-free paper

CONTENTS

PREFACE

First and foremost, this is not a book about market research or market research techniques. The content herein is a supplement and a precursor to market research (MR) and not a replacement of many already excellent and useful MR techniques. This is not to say that they are used in the absence of the MR community. The process described requires interdisciplinary teams in which marketing and/or MR must be one of the team members.

The VOC process and techniques are used to raise questions with both product development and MR. Although the VOC tools described are to be a bridge between the development community and MR, there may be times when established ways of doing things are challenged. This may be upsetting or intimidating to some people. However, it is best if these controversies are surfaced and addressed early in the commercialization process rather than midway through when it may be too late or too costly to turn back or make course corrections.

This book is about qualitative processes that are generally precursors to the more formal and traditional quantitative MR type processes. It describes a process for a product development team to get early focus and communication. MR is part of this process by being a member of the development team.

Total Quality Management (TQM), in whatever form, is still alive and well today. It may have different names in different companies. Regardless of the name it is still part and parcel of a company's commercialization process. My interpretation of a commercialization process is a phases–and–gates process where you cannot advance to the next phase until you pass the previous gate. In any form of commercialization process, most people have experienced that the front end is not very clear and there can be considerable confusion in the initial phases. This has commonly been referred to as "the fuzzy front end." Due to time and schedule pressures, many gates are used as speed bumps in order to keep forward momentum. Cutting the first phases short is almost a guarantee that it will protract the development cycle and eventually cost more money and time.

The first phase is where the company focus, market segment, and customer are defined. This, in turn, provides the structure for collecting the voice of the customer (VOC). A poor or cursory job here increases the chances of being off course from the beginning.

Project leaders are nervous to spend much time in the front end. They want to quickly lead to product specifications and get to manufacturing because that is what is familiar to them and that is what they are paid for. I believe the reason is that they don't understand it that well, and the data that they do have is not in a form that makes it easy to use and understand. I believe that if market planning and commercialization teams had a structured VOC process in place there would not be this subconscious reluctance to short cut the crucial front end of the commercialization cycle. A template is needed to guide teams in structuring and processing VOC data, a sort of paint by numbers. Chapter 1 describes the world of VOC as a customer-function-feature system. When a customer buys a product, he is buying the functions that the product provides which, in turn, allows him to accomplish his intended task. Functions are provided or accomplished through features and features lead to customer needs (VOC).

How we provide the functions can directly affect what the customer wants in the product. Therefore, VOC becomes critical input to the study and design of product and service functions. Vertical VOC within the company and where VOC fits in the company commercialization process are also discussed.

Chapter 2 describes how to set the stage for company and customer focus. Too often, VOC activity is started without a clear vision of the company direction and the customer playing field. The chapter contains a set of boiler plate questions to initiate VOC activity, several profiling matrices for describing customers and products, and a morphology to help in segmentation and VOC focus.

Chapter 3 discusses the collection process and the many activities involved in preparing, collecting, and debriefing the customer visits and data collection.

Chapter 4 involves the process of interpreting what we think we heard the customer say, both during and after the collection process.

Chapter 5 shows how to structure the collected and processed VOC verbatims. It involves affinity diagrams and trees and interrelationship diagrams. The purpose for structuring is to show the relationship and interconnects among the verbatims. This allows us to look for patterns and use our creativity to react to signals within the patterns.

Chapter 6 is a collection of value measurement techniques. The tools are used to quantify the VOC for importance. This is done by the team and/or customer but must eventually be verified with the customer. It is necessary to know what the VOC hierarchy looks like so we can design to the more important things the customer wants.

Chapter 7 is where we look at vertical VOC within the company at the strategic, tactical and operational levels. It involves the voice of management, voice of the company, voice of the engineer, in addition to voice of the customer. Developing processed understanding and politically connecting the vertical VOC's is paramount to forming the basis for the all important information highway to company success in the future.

Chapter 8 is where the rubber hits the road and involves the deployment of VOC into the system, product, and company. The deployment mechanisms are Customer Oriented Product Concepting (COPC) for product design and/or Quality Function Deployment (QFD) for problem solving, product technical requirements, and specifications. Unfortunately VOC changes with time. When we collect it we actually take a static slice in time.

Chapter 9 shows how to extend and track VOC into the future and how to monitor it once it is there.

Chapter 10 takes all the perspectives and variables in the front end of the commercialization process and shows how they all relate from a VOC perspective. The interrelationship model emphasizes all the variables that must be considered to do a good job in building VOC. Everything needs to be in sync to do the job right.

The appendices include a treatise on the Kano VOC collection and interpretation method and a step–by–step description of Customer Oriented Product Concepting (COPC), a VOC deployment mechanism. Also included is a completed VOC template showing all of the VOC tools filled out in a running example in order of execution.

It is my intent in this book to provide a sequential process for defining company focus, defining market and customer focus, and describe a set of tools that can be used to collect VOC within the focus window. Many books discuss VOC within the confines of QFD. I have chosen to make the VOC a separate independent process that integrates and triggers the dependent deployment mechanisms. I want to emphasize that a poor or quick fix in the VOC process can spell disaster in subsequent deployment. The sequential listing of the chapters form a template for doing VOC right the first time.

This book does assume the reader is already familiar with the Quality Function Deployment Process (QFD).

M. Larry Shillito

THE AUTHOR

Larry Shillito is retired from the Eastman Kodak Company where he provided internal quality management technology consulting to company units worldwide. He is a consultant, educator, author, and speaker.

His 30 years' industry experience has been in Industrial Engineering, Value Engineering, Voice of the Customer, Technology Forecasting, and Quality Function Deployment. He has used these skills in products, services, systems, procedures, and organizations across all lines of business in many countries.

He is a consultant in Value Management (VM), Quality Function Deployment (QFD), Voice of the Customer (VOC), and Customer Oriented Product Concepting (COPC). Larry developed the Technology Roadmap used in Value Engineering (VE) and target costing and the COPC process used in product and service development.

He has co-authored two chapters on Value Engineering and Techno-logical Forecasting in *The Handbook of Industrial Engineering* by John Wiley & Sons. He has co-authored a book also through Wiley, titled *Value, Its Measurement Design and Management*. This is one of the first books on value. It discusses how value management, value planning, target costing, VOC, COPC, and Strategic Intent are used to design products and services consistent with customer and company needs. He published a second book through Wiley, *Advanced QFD Linking Technology to Market and Company Needs*. This book advances the state of the art and includes Technological Forecasting and value graphing to project QFD and VOC data into the future. It also presents a unique method of cost deployment for QFD.

He has given over 50 presentations and papers at many international symposiums and universities. As an adjunct lecturer, he also teaches seminars on VOC, QFD, and VE at the Rochester Institute of Technology.

Mr. Shillito graduated from Duke University with a BA in Chemistry and West Virginia University with a Masters in Industrial Engineering. He is a member of Alpha Pi Mu Industrial Engineering Honorary and Sigma Xi Scientific Research Honorary.

INTRODUCTION

VOC TEMPLATE: FORMAT FOR THE BOOK

The format for this book is illustrated by the template shown in Figure 0.1. Each chapter is devoted to a template phase at a how-to level of detail where possible. The template consists of the following steps:

1.	Company/Customer Focus	Chapter 2
2.	Collection	Chapter 3
3.	Interpretation	Chapter 4
4.	Structure	Chapter 5
5.	Quantification	Chapter 6
6.	Verification	Chapter 7
7.	Deployment	Chapter 8
8.	Monitor (Tracking)	Chapter 9

If a team performs these functions in this order they will in fact acquire, process, and deploy VOC. The above model is not ratcheted in one direction. It is iterative and looping. Documents produced at each phase are living and dynamic. As new information is obtained or changes occur, they are entered into the process template for updating.

Chapter 8 only briefly discusses actual deployment. It mostly concerns how to prepare for it. I consider full scale deployment to be in the realm of Quality Function Deployment (QFD). Many books have already been written that cover this subject well and I do not feel it is necessary to cover it in detail here. I have included in Appendix C, however, a special deployment mechanism, Customer Oriented Product Concepting (COPC). It is an improved hybrid version of QFD, developed by the author, that more quickly integrates VOC into product design through function analysis

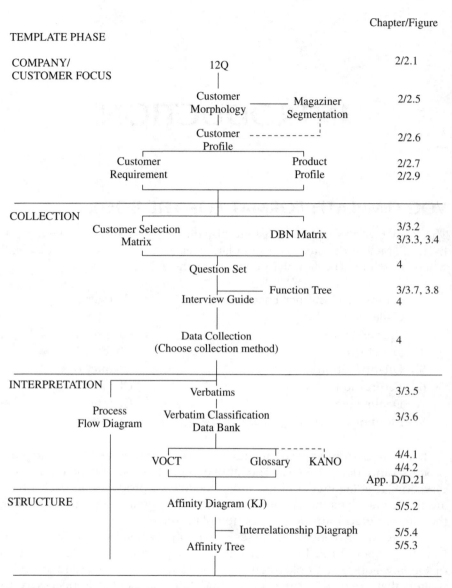

TEMPLATE PHASE

Chapter/Figure

Figure 0.1a VOC templates and tools.

borrowed from value engineering. The process will provide the reader with an alternative deployment tool and complete the VOC process template within the confines of this book. For those who want more background on QFD, I have listed several books on the subject in Appendix E.

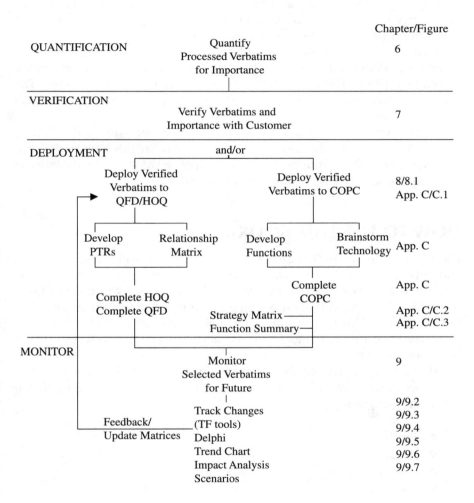

Figure 0.1b VOC templates and tools.

WHO SHOULD READ THIS BOOK?

The book is useful for product, process, and service developers at all levels of an organization. Because it concerns VOC it is useful for individuals and teams in the fuzzy front end of a commercialization process or product life cycle. The steps of the VOC process are too often given too little attention. Many times they and the VOC information that are to be developed are taken for granted and the development project quickly gets into trouble. The focus is always changing and there is always a moving target for product and service design. Consequently, cycle time gets extended and unit manufacturing cost goes up. This results in too many good projects and services being canceled.

Too often a good documented VOC process is missing in many companies. Perhaps if one existed, more VOC activity and documentation would take place. The chapters in this book give the basic elements. The reader will have to connect those elements and tools to develop a process that works for them.

As we begin the new millenium, the next decade will be the decade of the customer and the information revolution. In this movement into the future, we will go from the traditional *caveat emptor* to *caveat vendator*! VOC will be the engine to drive this movement.

HOW TO USE THIS BOOK

Use the VOC template (Figure 0.1) to learn what has to be done to obtain and deploy good VOC. The corresponding chapters are used as a process guide and a set of tools that may be used. The reader will have to tailor his own VOC process by combining and using those tools that will work best for him and his projects and company. In this respect the book serves as a reference to allow the reader to develop his own VOC plan from beginning to end.

Although the book mostly refers to hardware examples, the tools and processes apply equally well to many areas. In this respect the following words are interchangeable:

- Product.
- Process.
- Service.
- Procedure.
- Training.
- Hardware.
- Software.
- Organization.
- Building.
- Structure.

So, welcome to the world of VOC!

1

THE WORLD OF VOC

INTRODUCTION

The backbone of a commercialization process is the Voice of the Customer (VOC). It is also the basis for product design. It is what started the Quality Function Deployment (QFD) movement in Japan and the rest of the world. A poor job defining the VOC up front will create problems through the rest of the product life cycle. The problems are poor design, over-design, value mismatch, inflated unit manufacturing costs, excess redesign cycles, problems in the field, and the list goes on!

VOC can also be elusive. How do you know when you really have it? What is the VOC? How many different types are there? When do you use which type? Where and when do you start to collect it? Who should be involved in collecting and structuring the data?

Just as difficult to define is the customer. Who is the customer? Is there more than one customer? Which one(s) should we use to collect VOC? To make matters more complex, the VOC changes with time. How does the importance of customer verbatims change with time? Can we track the direction of change? Can we estimate the magnitude of change?

Let us address all of these concerns one topic at a time.

FUNCTIONS, FEATURES, AND VOC — A SYSTEMS APPROACH

When designing a product/service, it is helpful to think in terms of a customer-product system. My reason for describing such a system is to show how VOC relates to a product. That is VOC is tied to a product through functions.

When a customer purchases a product or service he is buying the functions that the product or service provides. Features pertain to functions and describe how the functions should perform. For example, one function of a three hole punch is "pierce sheet." Some features describing the function are "can pierce multiple sheets" and "does not jam." One function of a bank is to "engage transaction." Some features describing it are "don't want to wait in line" and "can make deposit quickly." As we will see later, customers often talk in terms of features.

Therefore, product manufacturers and service providers provide and design functions which, in turn, can considerably affect those features and performance attributes that the customer would like to have in the product or service. The VOC, then, becomes the driving force to define functions, features, and performance attributes of products and services.

The customer-need product-fulfillment system works as any other system. All the elements are linked together. If one element is changed the entire system reacts. It is similar to a mobile hanging from a ceiling. If we touch one element the mobile moves or jiggles, maybe slightly. Whereas we could touch another part of the mobile and it could shake terribly, perhaps even fall from the ceiling. The system can be described in terms of the customer task, the overall basic function of the product, the operational functions that support the basic function, and product features (which are short term solutions to long term customer needs).

For example, the customer (user) has a task that he wants to perform. (See Figure 1.1.) This task, in turn, is accomplished through the basic function of the product. That is, the basic function (the reason for existence of the product) allows the customer to accomplish his task. The basic function is accomplished through a series of operational functions which we can group into work functions (the basic nuts and bolts), sell functions (performance attributes that differentiate ours from other products and attract the user), and perk functions (those that excite the user and make the product more attractive above the sell functions). Product features fulfill customer needs for each function. They are the physical fulfillment of a need. These are the traditional customer needs and are often labeled as VOC. The groupings of functions (basic, sell, and perk) are akin to the three plots on the now widely familiar Kano graph (Appendix B Figure B1). That is, work functions aggregate "table stakes" and "must be" quality items. Sell functions collect the "one-dimensional satisfiers" and perk functions contain the "exciters." Basic features pertain to its work functions and are the company's ticket to play the game. "I expect my car to start. I expect my car to be safe." Basic features are expected by the customer and the manufacturer gets little credit if they are there. Conversely, you can lose big if they are not there. The producer also gets no credit if the basic threshold is exceeded. The best you can do is break even. Basic needs are unspoken and nonmeasurable; they are either satisfied or they're not.

Customer–Function–Feature System

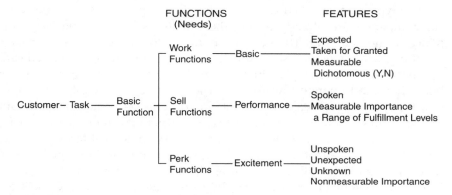

Feature = A physical fulfillment of a function (need)

Figure 1.1   Customer–function–feature. (From Shillito, M. L., *Advanced QFD Linking Technology to Market and Company Needs,* John Wiley & Sons, New York, 1994. With permission.)

Performance features pertain to the sell functions. They are spoken desires. They can be measured for importance as well as for a range of fulfillment levels. The customer tells us or answers our question about what they want. "I want a car that accelerates quickly. I want a car with good gas mileage." The measure may be 0 to 60 in 12 seconds or 24 mpg. This is where it is best to bring in Business Research for assistance. The manufacturer who best consistently supplies these features will get the sales. These are differentiating features that cater to differentiating needs. This is where marketing comes into play. This is where advertising spends its time. This is the battlefield.

Excitement features are future–oriented and many times high-tech. They can also be as simple as cup holders. They pertain to the perk functions. These are features that the customer is not always aware of. They come from the R&D shelf. Air conditioning in a car in the middle '50's is a good example. Today we have ABS brakes, air bags, voice-activated phones. They are exciting but are not quite to the point of being standard equipment. Very soon manufacturers will introduce a satellite auto-navigation system or a global positioning system. High-tech, but still on the development shelf. These needs are unspoken and unexpected because the customer does not know they exist other than in science-type magazines. Boaters are already using them, and some rental car companies are already testing these features which came to prominence in the Gulf War. They are too futuristic to measure for importance. Another exciter is night vision, already being offered in higher priced cars.

The perk functions contain the signals for the future. New features begin here and migrate toward the basic function features. For example, in a few years ABS breaks will be standard items on certain lines of cars. In the 1940's, cars did not have turn signals; today they are taken for granted as standard equipment. The tools of technological forecasting can be used to look into the future to see what is on the horizon for perk functions. Products will track technology. The company that goes public first with excitement features sets the trend and in many cases sets the international standards such as in cassette tape and CD formats.

Figure 1.2 illustrates the customer-function-feature system for a 3-hole punch. The customer task is to organize papers, not to punch holes as most people believe. The basic function of the punch is "register holes." In order to register holes, the fundamental functions of "locate sheet" and "pierce sheet" must be performed. These are assumed by the user. How we design the product to provide these functions can affect customer VOC like "easy to insert paper" and "paper stays in place once I insert it." We also have some sell functions such as being able to relocate the punch assembly to accommodate other paper-hole formats. "Collect waste" is a convenience function especially if our design prevents holes from falling all over my office. Finally, a perk function might be "pierce other material," such as overhead transparency material which is difficult to punch, and "punch without jamming." The company who makes a 3-hole punch that will punch this tough material may just have an edge.

Looking at the next two columns, "requirements" and "specifications" we see that VOC will influence these as well. What the customer wants drives the technology to provide the necessary functions, the requirements within the functions, and the specifications within the requirements.

If viewed as a system (Figure 1.2) we can see that if the provider changes a feature or a function in the product or the customer develops new needs or new uses for the product or changes his VOC, the system reacts. Things change. Companies must be alert to these changes. Their antenna must always be raised to catch new signals. Many of these signals, but not all, are contained in the VOC. Therefore, if any item under any of the columns is changed, the world — the entire system — changes. Unfortunately too many company projects start with requirements and specifications and crash forward with little regard to customer task,

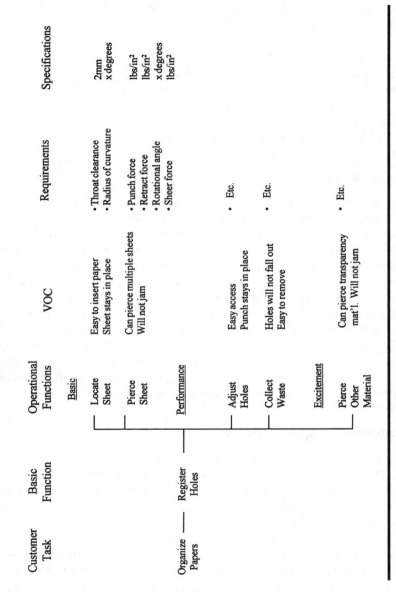

**Customer-Product System
3-Hole Punch**

Customer Task	Basic Function	Operational Functions	VOC	Requirements	Specifications
		<u>Basic</u>			
		Locate Sheet	Easy to insert paper Sheet stays in place	• Throat clearance • Radius of curvature	2mm x degrees
		Pierce Sheet	Can pierce multiple sheets Will not jam	• Punch force • Retract force • Rotational angle • Sheer force	lbs/in² lbs/in² x degrees lbs/in²
Organize Papers	Register Holes	<u>Performance</u>			
		Adjust Holes	Easy access Punch stays in place	• Etc.	
		Collect Waste	Holes will not fall out Easy to remove	• Etc.	
		<u>Excitement</u>			
		Pierce Other Material	Can pierce transparency mat'l. Will not jam	• Etc.	

Figure 1.2 Customer-function-feature system for a 3-hole punch. (From Shillito, M. L., *Advanced QFD Linking Technology to Market and Company Needs*, John Wiley & Sons, New York, 1994. With permission.)

functions, and VOC. Technological forecasting discussed later may be used to capture signals of technological change to improve design.

VOC is where the action is. The company that does a good job capturing the VOC and delivering the product the fastest is the one who is going to win. Notice that quick to market is a key issue. Incorporating VOC into the product alone will not guarantee success.

Where does quality fit into the picture? I am afraid that today quality is quickly becoming a hygiene factor. Either you have it or you don't and if you have it, it must be the best. As we begin the 21st century, quality is being taken more for granted. Quality will not be a differentiator because all competitive companies will have it. Time and VOC will be where the battle will be won.

So, let's talk more about VOC.

Supply and Demand

Figure 1.3 is a supply-demand function diagram[1] that describes broad functions involved in obtaining and using VOC data. The demand side of the diagram, shown on the left-hand side of the center scope line, answers why the VOC is obtained. It is company– and future–oriented. Methods for meeting the demand are presented on the right-hand side of the diagram and show how the VOC can be obtained. This side is meth-ods–oriented and deals basically with the present. Qualitative methods are shown at the upper right of the diagram and indicate that they are the first tools to be used. Notice that the methods become more quanti-tative as one progresses down the list of functions. The entire diagram is based on how-why logic; how is asked from the left to right side of the diagram, and why is asked in the opposite right to left direction. The answers should check in both directions.

Customer–Company Balance

The supply-demand model reveals that there are two VOCs that must be in balance; the voice of the customer and the voice of the company. Before starting any VOC activity, there are two questions that must be answered: (1) what are we trying to do for the customer and (2) what are we trying to do for the company? Figure 1.4 depicts this balance.

On the customer side are marketing, sales, product development, and market development activities. These organizations are concerned about features and selling price. On the company side are R/D, product design, manufacturing, and delivery organizations. They are concerned about scale-up, process, and unit manufacturing cost. Both sides must work in tandem with each other. The only way to do this is with interdisciplinary design/commercialization teams. The fulcrum for the balance is based on the strategic plan and business plan. The whole balance is a system that must be addressed equally to derive a quality functional product with a price/cost ratio that is affordable to both customer and company.

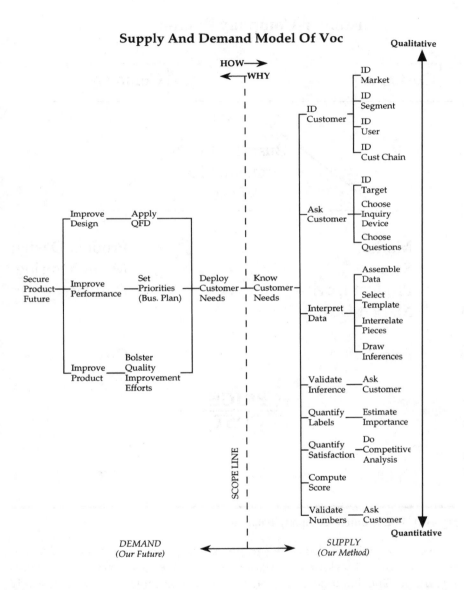

Figure 1.3 Supply and demand model of VOC. (From Shillito, M. L., *Advanced QFD Linking Technology to Market and Company Needs*, John Wiley & Sons, New York, 1994. With permission.)

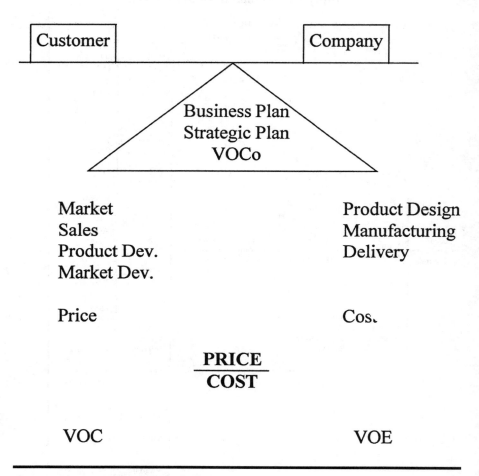

Figure 1.4 Customer--company balance.

We must invite the customer to become a partner in our business, and part of product development. Marketing will have to act more as a systems integrator. The battlefield is time to product acceptance not necessarily time to market. Customer needs will have to be included into design. This is certainly a paradigm shift for product development. The balanced approach to VOC neutralizes the traditional product/technology push or executive driven "We know what the customer wants better than the customer" decisions.

VERTICAL VOC

Based on large companies, the Voice of the Company consists of four levels of detail. The top level is the strategic level and represents the Voice of the Company (VOCo). Use of this voice shapes participation and technology strategies. Voice of Management (VOM) is the tactical level and provides the creative focus needed for selecting and shaping product concepts, product families, and services. At the operational level is the Voice of the Engineer (VOE) that deals with implementation and impacts product commercialization through specific requirements (specs, volumes, market programs, etc.). Finally, VOC is actual feedback from the customer using our product in the field. This feedback drives corrective action to current and future products and services, and improves and modifies the value proposition and market programs. Figure 1.5 depicts this vertical relationship. In reality the boundaries are not discrete — there is much overlapping. It is important to note that one VOC level cannot be completed until data is received from the next higher level. For example, implementation VOC cannot be completed without creative focus data from the tactical level. More often than not, design and commercialization teams operate at the VOE level with little or no VOM tactical data. In this situation the design team must derive such data and carry it up the decision-making chain for course correction. It is this situation that forms the bases for the 12 questions discussed in Chapter 2. It takes focused dialogue and interdisciplinary teams to make good connections. Too often the connections are taken for granted.

Smaller companies may not have these four distinct levels of VOC. Because they are smaller, some of these levels may be combined into a very flat organization structure. In some cases the owner/president may be on the design/commercialization team such that there is only one level. Aren't these companies so fortunate not to have to go through all the levels of politics, road blocks, and protective "good ole boys?" But they, too, have their problems and paradigms like, "But this is the way we have always done it," variety.

To operate in this fast paced dynamic world of customer focus will require some major paradigm shifts. Companies will have to shift to more customer–oriented plans. We will need market focused organizations.[2] Rather than traditional segmentation by similarity of products, socioeconomic status, etc., the future may require companies to segment by customer and use of our product or the net end result benefit the customer expects from our product. We will find that customers segment themselves. Vertical VOC will be discussed further in a later chapter.

Vertical VOC

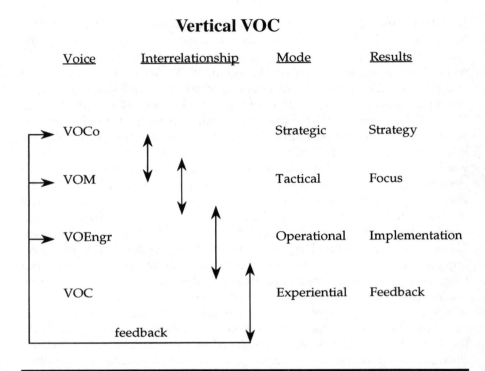

Figure 1.5 Vertical VOC.

EVOLUTIONARY AND REVOLUTIONARY PRODUCTS AND VERTICAL VOC

An evolutionary product is defined as an upgrade to an existing product. A revolutionary product is one that the company never made before. Revolutionary may or may not exist in the commercial world. In any case a revolutionary product is a new venture for a company.

Is the VOC similar for both type of products? Is collection and interpretation the same? The nature of VOC is the same for both types of products. VOC should be readily available for evolutionary products. However, VOC for a revolutionary product may or may not exist in the company or in the customer world.

Consequently, the collection process for the two products begins at different levels of the vertical VOC hierarchy. For evolutionary products, VOC starts at the lower level of the hierarchy through customer feedback and prior databases. See Figure 1.6. The collection process for revolutionary products begins at the top of the hierarchy with little feedback from

Evolutionary and Revolutionary VOC

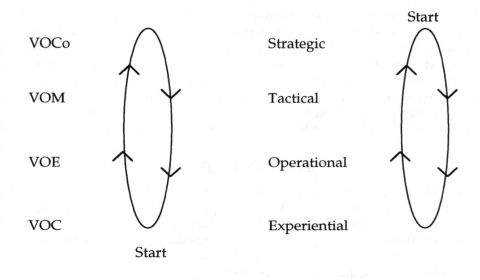

VOCo Strategic Start

VOM Tactical

VOE Operational

VOC Experiential

Start

Figure 1.6 Evolutionary and revolutionary VOC.

the outside world. VOC at this level is at a macro level of detail based on signals from competitive intelligence and scouting firms and reports.

THE INFLUENCE AND POWER OF PARADIGMS

A paradigm is a mental model of how we view the world and make decisions. Joel Barker, the futurist, describes paradigms as "a set of rules and regulations that (1) define boundaries and (2) tells you what to do to be successful within those boundaries."[3,4]

Paradigms constantly filter incoming information. They influence the way we do things and the way we make decisions. Based on past experience, they can block our vision of the future. If we are aware of our paradigms we can take measures to reduce their effect.

What does this have to do with VOC? Simply, paradigms can influence the way we collect and process VOC. The worst case scenario is when your paradigm becomes *the* paradigm, the only way to see things. The classic example of this paradigm is borne out by the all too familiar phrase, "We know what the customer wants better than the customer." This happens often in many companies and more than enough have gotten into trouble because of it.

So, throughout the rest of this book we must constantly be aware of paradigms — ours, others, and the company. The tools described can help us reduce the influence of paradigms but the burden is on us to act accordingly.

Other classic paradigms are disguised in situations like "not invented here," parochialism, turf protection, politics, and fawning. These are typical models that have worked for many people to advance in their profession. They cling to them until they retire. The aftermath of these paradigms is well known to many. Because VOC is a front end process, the effects of the paradigms can have long term implications and steer us off course very early on. Correcting VOC paradigms early in the commercialization process can result in significant savings and cycle time compression.

GLOSSARY OF TERMS

The following glossary of terms will be helpful for future references.

Want: Something a person believes will fulfill a known need; short-term orientation and temporary; quick fix. Can quickly change with time.

Need: What a customer wants; a lack of something; future–oriented; lead to *tomorrow's* dominant product; long term. Cannot always be recognized or described by the customer.

Solution: Fulfillment of a customer problem or a need.

Feature: Physical solution (fulfillment) to a customer problem; lead to *today's* dominant product. A short-term solution to a long-term need.

Benefit: A way in which one or more features of the product provide a definable advantage, improvement, or satisfaction for the buyer/user/customer.

Requirement: Engineering (producers) technical solution to meet a customers need.

Spec: Quantitative engineering measure, limit, or range developed to meet a requirement.

Problem: Wants/needs stated in negative terms.

VOC: Customers' needs, expressed in the customers' terms. They are both spoken and observed. Be aware that the customer speaks in wants, needs, solutions, and features. We must identify which is which. Aggregated together they are VOC.

Verbatim: The exact words of a customer. Usually a sentence or part of a sentence.

Task: What the customer wants to accomplish; the reason for buying/using your product. Too often not defined. Leads to purchasing drivers.

Basic Function: The reason for existence of the product; allows the customer to accomplish the task.

Work Function: Functions that permit a product to work; the basic elementary building blocks.

Sell Function: Functions that supply performance attributes that differentiate our product and attract the users.

Perk Functions: Functions that excite the user and make the product more attractive beyond the sell and basic functions.

VOC AND THE COMMERCIALIZATION PROCESS

VOC is a front end process to any commercialization process. That is, before we design a product or service we have to know who the customers are and what they want. Figure 1.7 represents a generic commercialization process (CP). It is a typical phases–and–gates process where one cannot advance to the next phase until the requirements at each gate are passed or satisfied. There is a review at each gate with a review– or gate–enabling committee.

VOCo, including VOM, represents information on company overall strategy, technology/service strategy, business plan, and product concepts and families. The shaping and focus must take place in the first two phases of the CP. VOC is a parallel process also occurring in Phases 0 and 1. The overlap of VOCo and VOC provides the structure to form the business plan. 99% of the information and plans are obtained and set in the first two phases. They are, however, living processes and are verified and updated through the CP. The most common problem with many companies is that they do not do a good job producing VOCo and VOC in the front end of the CP. Thus, they are always changing them throughout the CP. This merely protracts cycle time and drives up unit manufacturing cost. Perhaps one of the reasons companies do not do VOCo and VOC in the fuzzy front end of the CP is that they do not have a formalized structured VOC process in place. If a VOC template were in place it would increase the chances of *doing* VOC. In many companies VOC does not have a home. Responsibility is too often assumed and left up to each business unit or department for execution and format. In a large company, the focus or home for VOC could reside in corporate quality, or business research. In smaller companies with only one line of business, it is the responsibility of the business unit or company management. You will have to find a home for VOC, this book cannot help you do that. The contents of this book can help you design your VOC process, though.

Customer Value Hierarchy

Woodruff and Gardial provide yet another unique model of customer value.[5] They discuss a hierarchical representation of how customers view

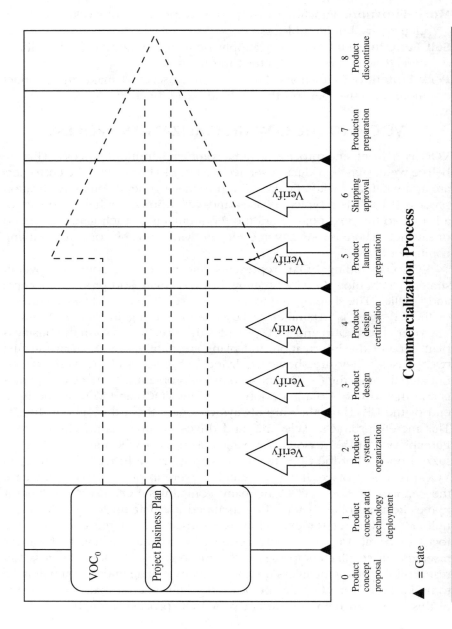

Figure 1.7 Commercialization process.

products, which they term the customer value hierarchy. There are three levels; attributes, consequences, and desired end-states. They become increasingly more abstract and macro in scope as you ascend the hierarchy.

Attributes are the most basic level. These are the terms and words a customer uses to describe a product or service (i.e. the camera has a 3X zoom lens, auto focus, auto exposure, redeye reduction, etc., or, the service has a 24-hour hotline, home delivery, in-house maintenance, etc.). Attributes are short term, unstable, and lead to incremental change (Figure 1.8).

Consequences are the results and possession of the product. For example, "The camera is simple and easy to use, it is dependable, it gives me confidence, I feel relaxed to use it." The words express what the customer wants to have happen and are more feeling and emotional (dependable, confidence, relaxed, etc.). Designing products around consequences opens the door to creativity and more dramatic change than designing at the lower attribute table stakes level.

Desired end-states are the customer's purposes and goals. They are stable and long term. Designing products at this level of the hierarchy results in creative and sometimes radical change compared to change developed at the lower level of the spectrum.

The higher levels of the Woodruff/Gordial hierarchy are more future oriented and suggests a top-down approach to product design.

SUMMARY

I have tried to describe VOC as a customer-product system. The system is dynamic and is connected by functions and features. The balance of the system is affected by the law of supply and demand. This balance also affects another balance — the one between customer and company. Like any system, if you change one variable there are ripple effects (both positive and negative) which ultimately create tradeoffs to maintain balance. These ripples should be viewed as concentric emanating circles rather than simple linear spoke-like events. Within the company there are vertical VOC levels that represent the strategic, tactical, operational, and experiential levels of operation. All levels must be in sync in order to deal with the horizontal VOC systems which deal with this customer/product would. Vertical VOC concerns the company's ability to deliver the right product to the right customer at the right time at the right price and the right company profit. The power of paradigms can influence the way we view and operate in the world of VOC.

Although I have used several points of view to describe the VOC system which the reader may or may not agree with, one thing is certain, all points of view emphasize the need for a structured process to acquire, process and deploy VOC.

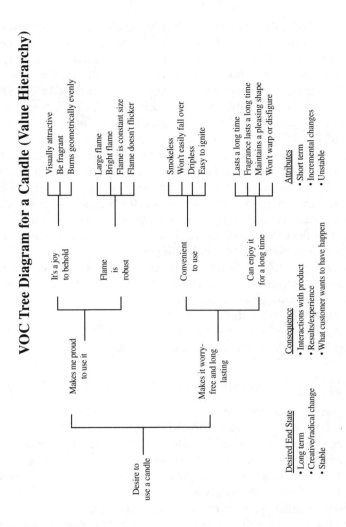

Figure 1.8 VOC tree diagram for a candle (value hierarchy).

Figure 1.9 illustrates how all parts of the VOC system interface with one another. I have used a Venn diagram for this purpose. The intersection of function and VOC involves features and solutions. The interface of VOC and voice of the engineer/designer (VOE) involves requirements. And finally the interface of functions and VOE involves specifications. The intersection of all three areas represent the Voice of the Product. I have placed the three sets inside an arrow to indicate that if all of the sets are linked together properly they will create a forward vector that delivers benefit and value to the customer and company.

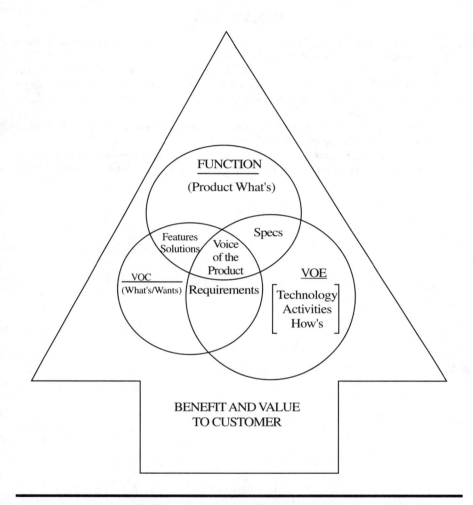

Figure 1.9 VOC, function, and product design relationship.

BIBLIOGRAPHY

Barnard, W. and Wallace, T. F., *The Innovation Edge, Creating Strategic Breakthroughs Using the Voice of the Customer*, Oliver Wight Publications, Essex Junction, VT, 1994.

Daetz, D., Barnard, W., and Norman, R., Customer Integration. *The Quality Function Deployment (QFD) Reader's Guide for Decision Making*, Oliver Wight Publications, Essex Junction, VT, 1994.

Shillito, M. L., *Advanced QFD, Linking Technology to Market and Company Needs*, John Wiley & Sons, New York, 1994.

Shillito, M. L., "VE In Project Definition," *Proc., Soc. Am. Value Eng.*, 29, 1994, 238-242.

REFERENCES

1. Shillito, M. L. and DeMarle, D. J., *Value: Its Measurement, Design and Management*, John Wiley & Sons, New York, 1992.
2. Lanning, M. J. and Phillips, L. W., *Building Market Focused Organizations*, unpublished manuscript, Lanning-Phillips and Associates, Atlanta, GA, 1994.
3. Barker, J. A., *Discovering the Future: The Business of Paradigms*, ILI Press, St. Paul, MN, 1985.
4. Barker, J. A., *Future Edge: Discovering the New Paradigms of Success*, William Morrow and Company, New York, 1992.
5. Woodruff, R. B. and Gardial, S. F., *Know Your Customer: New Approaches to Understanding Customer Value and Satisfaction,* Blackwell Publishers, Cambridge, MA, 1996.

2

COMPANY AND CUSTOMER FOCUS*

SETTING THE STAGE FOR VOC — THE 12 QUESTIONS

Before VOC and best practices such as QFD can be used it is necessary to answer some basic, up front, preparation questions to provide focus for the team. The questions are designed to elicit Voice of Management data. Figure 2.1 is an outline of 12 such questions needed to initiate a VOC or QFD study. The questions are reviewed by the VOC or commercialization team to develop a "strawman" document of the best answers available at this time. The questions will very quickly establish what is known and what is not known about the subject of the study. Once the team derives its answers they should be reviewed with management (VOM) or at least with the first person in the decision chain for course correction.

Developing answers to these questions is especially important because VOC activity and later best practices like QFD are structured around the effective use of people in teams. Once we add people, teams, organization structure, emotions, and power to the process, the process becomes more complex. Consider the following circumstances and roadblocks usually encountered in these processes.

1. VOC and QFD are always performed with interdisciplinary teams. Teams can waste time, be overly conservative, avoid decisions, and prematurely solve unclear problems.

---

* Please note that all tools and techniques discussed from this chapter forward have a corresponding example of use in the running example (a 3-hole punch) in Appendix D, "VOC Example."

QFD STARTING QUESTIONS*

1. Purpose
   a. Why are we doing this study?
   b. What is the team mission?
2. Completion Date
   a. When MUST this study be finished?
3. Decision Maker
   a. Who is the decision maker?
   b. Who is the first person in the decision chain that can say "no"?
4. Scope
   a. What is included in this study?
   b. What is not included in this study?
5. Product
   a. What product? Model? Generation?
   b. World class? Revolutionary?
6. Market/Customer
   a. Who is the customer we are trying to satisfy?
   b. Country?
   c. Market?
   d. Segment?
   e. User?
   f. Chief buying influence?
7. Time Horizon for the Product
   a. This year? Next year? When?
8. Assumptions
   a. Product
   b. Market
   c. Company
   d. Manufacturing — Who? Location?
   e. Distribution
   f. Customer
   g. Other
9. Organization Business Plan
   a. Do the answers to the questions above fit the organizations' business plan?
   b. Do we (the team) have a copy of the business plan?
   c. Are there spinoffs that will apply to other organizations?
10. Team Members
    a. Based on the answers to the questions above, do we still have the right people on the core team?
    b. The core team remains for the life of the project; who are the members? What background do we need? What geography represented?
    c. Ad hoc members? Who? What? Background/expertise/information? When do we need them? how long do we need them for?

2. Individuals involved in this activity usually have other full-time jobs and are already busy.

QFD STARTING QUESTIONS (cont.)

11. Buying/Purchasing Drivers (Influences)
    a. Economics
    b. Produt performance
    c. Safety
    d. Ease of use
    e. Workforce capability
    f. Environment
12. Task/Deliverable/Function
    a. What task is the customer/user trying to accomplish through buying our product?
    b. What is the deliverable or output from using this product?
    c. What is the basic function of the product? Why does it exist?

* This set of questions is used to initiate a QFD project. Discussing and documenting these subjects is one of the most important parts of the QFD process. A poor job here can cause teams to be off-course, lose time and develop excellent recommendations on the wrong thing.

Figure 2.1 QFD starting questions. (From Shillito, M. L., *Advanced QFD Linking Technology to Market and Company Needs,* John Wiley & Sons, New York, 1994. With permission.)

3. Strong parochial interests are common.
4. The output of a VOC study may be threatening, especially to designers, planners, and decision makers.
5. Emotional as well as rational conflicts of interest are often generated.
6. The purpose of the VOC/QFD project is not always clear.
7. The final decision maker is not always obvious.

The success of the VOC project is enhanced if organizational, political, and behavioral aspects of the project are addressed early in the project. Roadblocks can be anticipated and planned for before they occur. The process facilitator should emphasize to the team that it should consider the first team meeting as the first day of implementation. The following "getting started" topics are particularly germane to the process.

Discussing and documenting these topics is one of the most important parts of the VOC/QFD process. A poor job here can cause teams to be off course, lose time, and develop excellent recommendations on the wrong thing. The team should take as much time as needed to do a good job documenting these topics. Each topic will now be discussed separately. (Also see Example D.2 in Appendix D.)

Question 1. Purpose

1. Why are we doing this project?
    - ◼ To produce a revolutionary design?
    - ◼ To produce an evolutionary design?
    - ◼ To redesign an existing product to:
      Reduce costs?
      Increase productivity?
    - ◼ Increase customer perceived value?
    - ◼ Improve manufacturability? Assembly? Setup?
    - ◼ Reduce cost only?
    - ◼ Improve quality? Reliability?

Answers to these questions are not always obvious or are taken for granted. Considerable amounts of time have been consumed by teams in generating a purpose statement. Sometimes it is necessary to recheck again with the requester of the study to determine the purpose. It is better to do this immediately before the team works on the wrong objective. The verbal interaction necessary to draft the purpose statement helps bring focus to the study and quickly gets team members working together.

Two basic questions must be considered when writing a purpose statement: (1) what are we trying to do for our customer and (2) what are we trying to do for ourselves (the company)? The answers to either of these questions cannot come at the sacrifice or expense of the other. Discussion of these two questions brings focus to the purpose of what specifically the team (Project) is trying to achieve. The VOC/QFD team has a task to accomplish. This task is usually to improve some product/service that meets customer and manufacturing needs and that provides some competitive advantage over a specific period of time. A purpose statement should be a short, broad definition of what is to be accomplished by the team and the project and why. It essentially creates a target or goal for the team. Sample purpose statements might be "manufacture component x for $1.00 for delivery by 20xx; reduce the total elapsed time required to implement a design change." A purpose statement more than two sentences is generally too long and starts to introduce CYA content.

Question 2. Completion Date for VOC/QFD Process

1. When must the VOC/QFD project be completed?
    - ◼ When will the team present recommendations to the decision maker and other management?

Establishing an end date for the VOC/QFD project brings focus for completion. This, in turn, helps establish how often and for how long the team should meet.

Question 3. Alignment

1. Who is the decision maker?
   - Who is the person who will approve or disapprove team recommendations?
   - Who pays the implementation cost?
   - Who is it that the team will present an offer they can't refuse?
   - Who is the study sponsor? Who pays for the VOC study? This person may be different from those people in (1) and (2) above.

It is surprising how often teams have a difficult time answering these kinds of questions. It is not always clear who the decision maker is. The decision maker must be identified, otherwise, the team can do an outstanding job on the project only to make recommendations that the decision maker never wanted. A decision maker in the context of the VOC/QFD process is the person(s) to whom recommendations will be given, and who can approve or disapprove them. The decision maker may or may not pay for implementation of the recommendation. Sometimes there is a chain of decision makers. In this case, the first person in the decision chain that can say no is considered the decision maker and the person whom the team must keep informed.

The decision maker should be periodically informed of team progress and direction. In this respect, the decision maker should be used as a resource to the team. Through the interaction of the update sessions, the decision maker builds ownership in the team project. This, in turn, builds alignment so that the team and decision maker are congruent in their content, direction, and expectation. Alignment increases the chance of acceptance of team recommendations and their subsequent implementation, and reduces the chances of the team performing an academic exercise.

Experience shows that decision makers don't like surprises. Surprises generally are threatening to a decision maker and increase the chance of a veto. This can happen when team recommendations are radically different from status quo or when they make historical decisions made by the decision maker look bad. Therefore, identifying the decision maker and starting, to build ownership and alignment should be done as soon as possible. The quickest way to get started in stake building is to review the team-generated purpose statement with the decision maker. The more decision makers are consulted or interact with the team, the more

"Black Box" Transformation Model

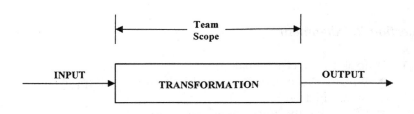

Figure 2.2 Black box transformational model. (From Shillito, M. L., *Advanced QFD Linking Technology to Market and Company Needs,* John Wiley & Sons, New York, 1994. With permission.)

ownership they will feel in the team project. By the time the team is ready to make its recommendations, the decision maker already knows what to expect. There are no surprises. There is a feeling of ownership. It is an offer that is difficult to refuse and the likelihood of approval is very high.

Question 4. Scope

1. What is included in the study?
2. What is not included in the study?
3. What is/is not the team able to control/change?
4. What are the boundaries within which the team operates?

It is important to bound the study so that it will be a manageable unit. The amount of time the team spends on scoping should not be jeopardized by frustration to prematurely start the VOC/QFD process. The danger of improper scoping is that the team may perform an excellent job and develop an excellent design for the wrong thing! Proper scoping increases the chances of the team doing the right things right. One model used in scoping is the black box input-output transformation model (see Figure 2.2). The black box is where some transformation or action takes place. It is the area of team responsibility. The inputs to the box are outside the scope of the team to influence.

The inputs are given and are characterized by certain parameters. Coming out of the black box is some output produced by the transformation. Once this output leaves the boundary of the black box, it is no longer in the team's sphere of control. So, the scope of the team's project is everything within the boundaries of the black box.

For more complex studies it may be necessary to conduct a preliminary evaluation of the scope itself and to modify the original to develop a better understanding of what is really wanted. Sometimes money or time constraints influence the scope and restrict the boundaries of the VOC/QFD project. Reviewing the scope with the decision maker early in the project, is time well spent.

Question 5. Time Horizon (Consumer-Type Products)

1. What is the introduction or implementation year (date) for the product under study?
2. Will there be more than one model (design)?
   - Will the models be time-phased for introduction?
3. Which model (design) does this current VOC/QFD study consider?

Too often, teams get frustrated because there are so many models to work on. Many models or design variations are dependent upon when they will be used or introduced. Input from upper management is necessary to establish model type and introduction dates. That is, management should select the product and introduction dates while the team selects the functions and features to be studied. It is obviously necessary to have proper product/model/date selected before beginning the VOC/QFD process.

Question 6. Product

1. What product? Model 1 or Model 2? Upgrade? Revolutionary? Too many times the product under study is taken for granted. More times than not product is poorly defined. This prolongs team time and is confusing. Sometimes we work on the wrong product!

Question 7. Market (for Consumer-Type Products)

1. What country? Domestic only?
2. What market?
3. What segment?
4. Who is the customer?
5. Who is the user?
6. Who is the chief buying influence?
7. What product?

Answers to these questions will shape the outcome of the entire VOC/QFD study. Product features and their importance will vary greatly across market segments. Segment also determines what products (both our company and other manufacturers) are considered. This can be a time-consuming and sometimes difficult task. A popular way to start the process of defining market segment is to establish a distribution of sales volumes by product line and market segment. When doing so, it is best to use unit volumes instead of sales dollars. There are various ways to correlate volumes such as percentage units sold versus market segment, percent units sold versus product line, product line volume versus market segment, and so on. Signals to watch for are things like 80% of total volume coming from one segment or 80% of total volume coming from one or two product lines. The team and project time should be spent on the vital few versus the trivial many. The team must determine whether volume is the correct indicator to establish which market segment to work on. Should the team be working on the high-volume areas to design or redesign a product to maintain market share? Should the team be working in low-volume areas to design a product to capture more market? There are many approaches to determine which product to work on. The final approach will depend upon product, market, management, and the line of business strategic plan. Sometimes market or segment is dictated by upper management.

For consumer-type products it is, many times, not as simple as it may appear to define market segment, customer, user and, chief buying influence.[1] It is important to define who these people are because they can each have their own set of needs. Tom Cook, president of Thomas Cook Associates, offers a good example:[1]

> "Consider a baby food product. The baby would be the user. The mother or father would be the purchaser or customer. However, the chief buying influence may be none of these, but would instead be the pediatrician...."

So, for whom are we designing the product? The resolution of customer, user and chief buying influence must be established before developing design parameters.

Daetz, Barnard, and Norman[2] have identified several ways to segment the market, such as by geographics, task (all people doing similar functions), perceived benefit of the product (how people group themselves according to how they perceive the benefits of the product), and profit segmentation (which markets offer the best possibility for making profit and which ones will require investment to gain profit).

Question 8. Study Team Members

1. Based on the answers to the preceding seven questions, are the right people on the core team?
2. Will ad-hoc members be needed on the team at certain times in addition to the core members?

When a core team is assembled, the members will remain on this team until the project is completed. Generally the core team consists of a minimum of the chief designer, the project leader, a process facilitator, and the VOC/QFD team leader. Experience shows that the proper number of members for the core teams is 6 ± 2. On numerous occasions, study teams discovered that certain key people are not represented on the core team. The missing representatives are discovered only after the teams have discussed the previous seven questions. Usually the proper people are already on the core team, but additional ad-hoc members may have to participate for a limited duration at appropriate times in the future. These people will have specialized knowledge for certain areas of the project. Making them a permanent member of the core team would not be practical.

Team members must represent both the customer (user) and the producer. This would suggest the following types of disciplines: design, manufacturing, operations, marketing, customer service, user/equipment operators, manufacturing engineering, product planning, and so on. When choosing team members, you should focus on a person's expertise and not on his or her position in the organization.

It has been my experience that the most successful teams were those that

1. Had clear goals
2. Freedom to work on their own
3. Free access to needed data
4. Full responsibility for the deliverable
5. Self-empowered to make decisions.

Question 9. Assumptions

1. What are the initial assumptions?
   - The study will proceed based on these.
   - As assumptions change or become fact, the study content and direction will be altered to reflect the changes.

All projects begin with a basic set of assumptions. Too often these assumptions are not documented or visible. Many times they are taken for granted. Forcing documentation of assumptions in the beginning of the project enhances communications and highlights gaps in information. It can also assist as a double check on the purpose statement. Assumptions are things like "the building will be occupied by the shops division; the building will have two floors; we will have in-line testing; we will use the current power source; branch offices will be located in areas x and y." For electronics products: orange book media compatible; minimum of 10k units per month; 5 1/4 half-height; SCSI interface, etc.

To keep assumptions visible and up-to-date, it is good practice to write them on a chart pad. This pad is then posted on the wall in every meeting. As new assumptions arise, they are added to the list. As current assumptions are confirmed, they are so noted. This on-going list is commonly referred to as a parking lot. Parking lots are also used for other subjects as well, such as premature ideas, questions and action items.

Question 10. Company Business Plan

It is surprising how often teams design products without knowing the business plan or the strategic intent of the company or line of business. Too often design teams never think to ask for this information. The worst cases are those where the company business plan is not allowed to be seen by the lower ranking individuals. The team is directed to design a product and upper management will decide whether or not the team's recommendations fit the need of the company. With poor communication, the study will surely be short-lived and company resources will be needlessly wasted. This is the price companies pay when individuals guard information and consider it power.

In hopes of averting such a situation, the following questions should be answered:

1. Does the team have a copy of or have access to the company business plan?
2. Do the answers to the previous nine questions fit or reflect the company business plan?
3. Does a business plan exist?

If a business plan does not exist, I tell the team that we will write the business plan. It may only fit on one piece of paper. We will then carry this business plan up the management chain for input, action and course correction. One thing is certain, it will surely get attention.

Question 11. Purchasing Drivers

What motivates a customer to purchase our products above all others? This is the realm of the value proposition and the value delivery system. Is it productivity? Reliability? Access time? Compatibility? One personal purchasing driver for a particular camera manufacturer is the fact that every time they come out with a new series of lenses they will fit all cameras to date. One does not have to purchase a new camera or a new system, unless he wants to take full advantage of auto-focus and other lens functions. With other camera manufactures one must purchase the entire system as the new are not compatible with the old. If one purchases a new copier or a minilab, productivity and reliability will be the major drivers, probably even more important than price. If we conduct a transaction at an ATM, access time is important especially if we are in a less than desirable location. How long we wait in line may dictate which bank or restaurant we choose. Purchasing drivers are important because they lead to choice-based decisions. Choice criteria are what a customer uses to choose our product over someone else's. They are important VOC. Purchasing drivers at this stage of the project will be macro in scope. Fine tuning will come later.

Question 12. Task/Functions/Deliverable

These topics were discussed earlier in Chapter 1. The task is what the customer wants to do. It is the reason for buying our product. Many times we take the task for granted and miss the customer's main intentions. The basic function is the reason for existence of our product. It is what allows the customer to complete the task. The customer is really not buying product, they are buying the functions that the product provides them. The deliverable is the output of the product. For example, a black and white copy, a photograph, an electronic image, an interactive game, etc. It is important to define the deliverable because assumptions and design options will be based on the definition of the deliverables. The deliverable is the net end result benefit derived from the product. The better we understand the task and the product functions the more focus we will have to prepare for VOC, collection and its subsequent deployment into product.

WHAT BUSINESS ARE WE IN? THE VALUE PROPOSITION

A complement to the 12 Questions is the questioning logic of the value proposition model.[3] The theory of the value delivery proposition has been around for about 20 years and was pioneered at Proctor and Gamble.

Lanning, Phillips, and Associates have further refined this model and it is the basis of their "Building Market-Focused Organizations"[4] process.

Using the Lanning and Phillips model, the generic definition of the value proposition is, "A simple clear internal statement of the target segment customer we will serve, and, for each segment chosen, the key benefits (desirable end results) we offer them, at the price we ask on the promised date to be delivered." This simple statement can be customized by substituting the company customer segment, the key benefits offered, the price and delivery date.

A check on the completeness of the value proposition is to ask, "What is the net end result benefit the customer receives by buying our product above all others?" This will focus on the business and help define strategy.

A value delivery system is the sum of all the functions a company performs to deliver the product (value proposition) to the customer, i.e., design, manufacture, delivery, marketing, sales, etc. This may also be termed the value chain. The value proposition is based on the strong points in the value chain. Benchmarking is also based on the strong points. The 12 Questions and the Value Proposition are two complementary approaches for defining the business. If they both produce the same answers we should have a reasonable definition of the business.

Another approach to defining the business is to describe it in two words. For example, Hewlett Packard is in the business of "Electronic solutions." Kodak might be in the business of "preserving memories." Xerox might be in the business of "handling data." Federal Express "delivers parcels;" a bank "completes transactions." Try to get to the bare essence of what you do.

We have to define our business because that will determine our markets, segmentation, and customers. Too often, the business is not well defined and a VOC team does an excellent job collecting VOC on the wrong customer. This, in turn, leads to an excellent design on a wrong product or one that does not meet customers needs, or, in the worst case, to a product no one ever wanted. Too often, VOC or design teams do not have this focused information or in some cases it has never been done. If so, the team must define the business as best they can and then run it up the management decision chain for course corrections.

CUSTOMER CHAINS

A deceivingly simple question is, "Who is the customer?" This question is difficult to answer without a good description of the business and the value proposition. Many design and commercialization teams have ago-nized over the answer to this question. We want to describe the person who is going to use our product.

Customer Chain for Copier

Manufacturer	Service/Business	End User
Color Copier	*Copy Center*	*Customer*
Product Functions	Features	Needs
Scan source	Productivity	Fast turnaround
Read signal	Consistent scan	Good color
Modify signal	Consistent exposure	Sharp edges
Expose medium	No artifacts	Deliver on stated date
Fuse toner, etc.		

Figure 2.3 Customer chain for a copier.

So, before we attempt to collect the VOC, we must first establish who the customer is. Many times this is not an easy task. The difficulty arises from the fact that there is usually a chain of customers. These customers can be internal and external. Each one in the chain has his own set of needs (VOCs). So, for whom are we designing the product? Who is affected by our product? Is it the final user? The purchaser? A person who recommends? All of the above? One might argue that we design for everyone in the customer chain, but doing so increases the chances for an over-designed, overpriced product. Here is where the marketing department must be consulted because it usually sets the target, in conjunction with the business plan, for country, market segment, and user. This is another example why it is necessary to use a cross-functional team. Marketing and/or business research must be participating members of the VOC/QFD team! A simple customer (VOC) chain for a color copier manufacturer might look like Figure 2.3. The basic question to define a chain is, "Who affects your system and who is affected by it?"

Internal to the manufacturer, there are numerous internal customers each with a need (VOC) such as product design, part manufacture, scale-up, assembly, distribution, marketing, and/or sales. Notice each function has its own customer and VOC. To avoid confusion, internal customers should be defined as "clients."

The middle customer, in this example, is the copy center or quick copy business who purchases the copier and, in turn, serves their customer, the ultimate end user. The copy center has needs and requirements which are served through the features of the product. The final customer also has a set of needs. So, who is the customer? Look at it from this perspective.

Customer Chain with Value Added Reseller (VAR)

Manufacture	VAR	Service/Business	End User
Product	Product	Product	Product
Scanner	Copier	Copies	
Functions	Features	Features	Needs
Scan source	Basic engine	Productivity	Fast turnaround
Store signal	Compatibility	Consistent scan	Good color
	Interchangeability	Consistent exposure	Sharp edges
		No artifacts	Deliver on stated date

Figure 2.4 Customer chain with value-added reseller (VAR).

The end user is the one who pumps money back up through the customer chain. Without an end user, there is no copy center. Without a copy center, you lose your market to sell copiers. Although the manufacturer sells to the copy centers, it must build and sell a copier that sustains the copy center business. The manufacturer's job is to sustain the copy center's business through the value proposition for building copiers. The copiers must satisfy the copy center's customers.

Figure 2.4 is a more complex customer chain. Here the manufacturer sells peripherals, such as a scanner, to a value added reseller (VAR) who integrates numerous pieces of equipment from various manufacturers into his product. The VAR, in turn, sells their equipment (a copier) to their customer, such as a copy center, who, in turn, services their end users. So, again, who is the customer? This can only be decided on a case–by–case basis. Sooner or later the manufacturer should understand the customer's "customer."

This may be a delicate situation because your customer is reluctant to let you interview his customer directly. Experience shows that communication to your customer's "customer" through your customer is just not efficient.

USEFUL TOOLS

The Customer Morphology[6]

What is it? — A morphological process to give focus to the world in which the product will be used.

Objective: — The objective is to develop a series of cascading Pareto distributions around where, why, who, what, when, and how the product is used. A Pareto is a maldistribution where 80% of the value of a group of items is contained in 20% of the items (the famous 80-20 rule).

Purpose: — The purpose is to document customer and product focus.
Instructions: — See example in Figure 2.5 and Appendix D.3.

1. Decide on the basic questions used to form the matrix. The most common are
   ■ Where is the product used?
   ■ Who uses the product?
   ■ Who makes the buy decision?
   ■ What method is used?
   ■ What are the SW interfaces?
   ■ What are the HW interfaces?
   ■ Whose product is currently being used?
   ■ Who are the chief buying influences?
   (Questions are written down the left column. Answers are expanded to the right. There are no columns in the matrix, only rows of answers.)
2. For each question determine the percentage activity for each item listed. These percentages must sum horizontally to 100.
3. Using the percentages, circle those items in each row that comprise 80% or more of the total activity.
4. Draw a boundary around the top Pareto 20% vital few and discuss whether or not this boundary makes sense and whether it reflects the target area for the product or service. If not, rearrange until the team agrees on a boundary.
5. It is helpful to list as many answers as possible to each question. It may even be helpful to list areas where product is not currently being used, or people who are not currently using product, etc. to indicate areas of potential market opportunity.
6. This is a living document and must be kept up to date.

The matrix may now be used to plan VOC collection. That is, who, where, what do we talk to, to get input on customer needs? For all of the options under each question above, it is revealing to list the number of units sold and convert units to a percentage. Likewise, list dollar volume plus dollar volume percentage. For other questions like who uses the product, who makes the buy decision, what method is used, what brand is used, an estimate of the percent occurrence for each item is entered. All percentage figures by question must sum horizontally to 100% as in the example.

Now that we have labels and percent occurrence of items for each question we can search for patterns. We can develop Pareto distributions. For example, we could circle all of the highest percentages and this would give us a vivid picture of where the activity is. Likewise, we could draw

Customer Morphology

Where is the Product Used?	Large Hospitals	Co-Op Buying Groups	Reg. Hospitals	Image Clinics	Gov't	Other	
	a units % units $K %$	b units % units $K %$	c units % units $K %$	d units % units $K %$	e units % units $K %$	f units % units $K %$	= 100% units = 100% $
Who Uses Product?	Radiologist	**Chief Tech.**	X-Ray Tech.	Dealer			
	%	%	%	%			= 100%
Who Makes Buy Decision?	**Material Mgr.**	Hospital Admin.	Dealer	Chief X-Ray Tech.			
	%	%	%	%			= 100%
What Method is Used?	Auto Cassette Handling %	**Auto Film Handling** %	Manual Cassette %				= 100%
Whose Product is Being Used?	% ABC Co. % DEF Co. % GHI Co.	**% ABC Co.** **% JKL Co.** **% XYZ Co.**	% ABC Co. % DEF Co. % GHI Co. % JKL Co. % XYZ Co.				
	100	100	100				

Boundary represents the playing field and the players we wish to engage in competition.

Figure 2.5 Customer morphology. (From Shillito, M. L., *Advanced QFD Linking Technology to Market and Company Needs,* John Wiley & Sons, New York, 1994. With permission.)

a corral around the lower percentages which would represent possible areas for market opportunity and market development. The corral drawn in our example (Figure 2.5) indicates where sales are coming from, who is the most active user, who generally makes the buy decision, the predominant method of handling the product, and which manufacturers have the largest volume according to method.

We now have an educated boundary around who the customer is. Attempts at documenting the VOC are best started after the customer or customer chain has been documented. Not documenting the customer results in repeated false starts and lost time defining the VOC on the wrong customer.

The morphology is a series of cascading Paretos. The visualization cascade should not be defined by using products. Products cannot be defined until the morphology is constructed and the 12 Questions are answered.

Advantages

1. The process forces the VOC team to focus on the customer and the company early in the product life cycle and the commercialization process.
2. It provides focus as to where and with whom VOC–collecting begins. It is a template for designing VOC acquisition.
3. It is an excellent fuzzy front end dialoguing tool.

Disadvantages

1. It is a living document that teams too often neglect to keep up to date.

Segmentation

Akin to the morphology, Elmer Magaziner[2,5] has developed a customer segmentation template consisting of eight generic categories of customers whose needs must be considered when designing a product. These categories are:[5]

Planner: Determines consistency of the product with organizational policy.

Funder: Pays for the product, its installation, maintenance, and operation.

Auditor: Prevents misuse of the product.

Installer: Integrates the product into its environment.

Maintainer: Repairs the product.

Operator: Provides resources and supplies to the product.

User 1: Directly benefits from using the product but is not the final user (e.g., distributor).

User 2: Directly benefits from using the product.

This is yet another interesting perspective of the customer definition. Both the morphology and the Magaziner categories emphasize the complexity of customer definition and segmentation. They also provide a cascade visualization to structure the complexity and allow us to look at the pieces one at a time or in clusters. Visualizing patterns and commonality allows us to launch an assault on this complexity through a structured process.

Customer Profile[6]

What is it? — Process to define a macro customer profile that can be defined early in the commercialization process.

Objective — Develop the operational elements of potential users of the product. Also considered are the basic technical requirements.

Input — 12 Questions data
         Customer morphology data

Output — Documented
         Customer operating requirements
         Macro technical requirements
         Customer families

Instructions (See Figure 2.6 and Appendix D.4)

1. Write the name of the customer/user type.
2. List elements of the customer's profile. Keep at a macro level. At this point we don't want an essay on the customer.
3. Based on the profile in (2), list major technical requirements. Do not list how to do it at this point.
4. Record the projected time horizon for the product for this customer.

Advantages

1. It forces the VOC team to dialogue about the customer and to assemble some description.
2. It will provide up front focus for VOC acquisitions.

Disadvantages

1. It is too often not kept current by the team.

The entire profile is written based on the current product description that exists at this point in the commercialization cycle. This is generally found in the business case or the technology strategy. Figure 2.6 is an example of a customer profile. Notice in the profile there is a description of the operation environment as well as the type of operators (employees) and skill level. The requirements section includes some of the basic elements

CUSTOMER PROFILE PRODUCT: XXX

Customer:
 Copy Center
Profile:
 Dedicated operator
 Low Skill level and high turnover
 Low volume per site
 May consolidate volume from other locations
 Wide range of computer literacy within company; but operators tend
   to be computer illiterate
 May participate in medium volume publishing houses
Requirements:
 Make Master files
 Upgradable from current system
 Able to use hardware for other products
 Low price
 Medium productivity
 Scan from hardcopy, nagatives and slides
 Keep simple to use
 Connectivity to consumer operated media
 Direct input from electronic media
Timing:
 20xx

Figure 2.6 Customer profile.

required for product design. Notice there is no technological "how-to" but
only a focus for operation technology.

Customer Needs Matrix[6]

What is it? — A matrix arraying macro level customer requirements
against a series of potential customers/users.
Objective — Construct a profile across several customers.
Purpose — To look for

1. common requirements across several customers.
2. clusters of requirements.
3. clusters of requirements by customer groupings.

Input — 12 Questions data
        Customer morphology data
        Customer profile data

Output — A set of what requirements are important to whom.

Instructions (See Figure 2.7 and Appendix D.5)

1. List macro level requirements from customer morphology and customer profiles down the left side.
2. Matrix these against the different types of customers/users in those cases where we have more than one customer.
3. Check off which requirements are important to which customers.
   a. Numbers indicating strength of importance may also be used.
4. Having completed the matrix, look for requirements that are important to all customers. These become basic requirements for a core design. Look also for requirements that are common to certain groups of customers. This can help in segmenting customers to build upon the core requirements above and for possible future positioning of the product. This can be a useful exercise for communication with marketing and possible helpful input to get them started on their research mechanisms.

Advantages

1. The matrix may be used to plan for VOC collection, that is, who to talk to, what to ask, etc.
2. It may be used early in product conceptualization in the front end of the commercialization process to design "plain vanilla" models, or basic engines, or core technology that can apply across various customers, customer groupings, and applications.
3. It is an excellent dialoguing process.

Disadvantages

1. The matrix is too often not kept current.

The matrix is used to determine which requirements are important to which customer. This may provide additional design of experiments type input to designing and balancing better VOC collection.

Product Profile — Macro Level[6]

Believe it or not, if we do a respectable job on the Twelve Questions, The Customer Morphology, Customer Profile, Customer Needs Matrix, the value proposition, customer chains, customer morphology and segmentation and have access to the business plan, we can start to piece together a macro level product profile. For evolutionary products there is usually

Customer Requirements Matrix

CUSTOMERS FOR PRODUCT XXXX

Requirements	Copy Center	Lab	Commercial	Institution	Quick Printer	Other
Master File	✔					
Master Hardcopy to file	✔		✔	✔	✔	
Print to file		✔				
Film to file		✔				
Negative to file		✔				
Electronics to file		✔	✔	✔	✔	
Professional Layout						
a.			✔	✔		
b.			✔	✔		
Portfolio			✔	✔		
Catalog			✔	✔		
Org. Chart				✔		
Miniaturization		✔	✔	✔		
Auto Mode	✔	✔	✔	✔		
Batch Mode	✔	✔			✔	
Upgradability						
a.	✔	✔	✔	✔		
b.						

Figure 2.7 Customer-requirements matrix.

enough existing VOC data to get a rough idea of major customer needs. Product features satisfy the customer needs but there is a range of how well each need is fulfilled.

What is it? — A macro level product profile based on fulfillment of basic customer needs (features). This method is also known as a Scoring Model discussed in Chapter 6.

Objective — To trace current and/or future product features at a macro level through a continuum of feature levels to develop a window of product options over time.

Input — Voice of the customer
    Marketing data
    Technical options
    Product features

Output — Quantified product features
    Product families
    VOC fulfillment levels

Tools — Product profile matrix.

Product Profile 3-Hole Punch

	Barely Acceptable	Tablestakes	Fully Satisfied		WOW!
VOC	1	2	3	4	5
Punch multiple sheets	1 sheet		≤5 sheets Δo		>10 sheets x
Will not jam	Often o		Some Δ	x	Never
Easy to align punch assembly	Difficult to see scale Δo				Easy visual Finger tight x
Punch assembly always stays in place	Comes loose after 100 punch; screwdriver to set o	Finger tight	Loose after 2000 punches; finger tight Δ		Never comes lose; finger tight x
Can pierce transparency mtl w/o jamming	0 sheets	1 sheet; some jam Δo	≥2 sheets; no jam x		>5 sheets no jam
Holes will not fall out	Holes fall out when used in hand; fall out when remove	Holes won't fall out when used in hand	Holes won't fall out while removing o	Δ	Holes won't fall out when dropped or when removing x
Etc.	Etc.	Etc.	Etc.	Etc.	Etc.

Current product   = o   x = 2.3   Less than satisfied
Competition product   = Δ   x = 2.8   Satisfied
Target product   = x   x = 4.5   More than satisfied

Figure 2.8 Product profile for 3-hole punch.

Instructions (See Figure 2.8) —

1. List important customer needs
    ■ From VOC
    ■ From customer morphology
    ■ From customer profile analysis
2. Develop a glossary for all needs
3. Using a 5-point scale, establish a continuum for each customer need. Develop short descriptors for at least three anchor points in the scale. That is, define in words (and/or numbers) what a 1, 3, or 5 means. Descriptors may be written for all 5 values if need be. Teams often use a score of 3 to use as a benchmark on "today." All other numbers would be better than or worse than "today." Sometimes "today" may be a 2 or a 4. When working with current/upgraded products, actual numbers may be used for things like reliability, maintenance, service calls, etc.
4. Once the matrix is established, various paths are plotted through the matrix by selecting one cell in each row. Each path represents a different configuration. Paths may be time sequenced. For example,

a path for 6 months, 18 months, and 30 months from present could be plotted. This would show product progression. A path may also be plotted for competitors for both today and best guess for future.

Advantages

1. It is possible to describe a product early in the fuzzy front end that relates to macro level VOCs.
2. It allows a product design team to establish the range of fulfillment around each VOC.
3. The matrix may be used to develop product design windows based on VOC ranges. The windows may be based on time frames or competitive benchmarks.
4. It is an excellent dialogue process.

A sample product profile for a 3-hole punch is shown in Figure 2.8. Current product as well as expected future product features can be traced through this profile. These various paths represent different options (offerings) for various uses within specific segments. The profile serves as a window within which we may expect to operate in the future. This window can be used as input to the various managers in the decision chain to reflect on the strategic and tactical parameters for business focus, that is, additional input for VOCo and VOM.

The business planner and the design team can construct various paths representing the minimum to enter the business or upgrade the product, the path for our current product, and the preferred path, sometimes called the people's choice path, for the future. It is possible to benchmark competitors by plotting their product through the various descriptors.

Once the paths have been selected a score may be computed by averaging the cell scores. In our example, our current product scored 2.3 or less than fully satisfied; the competitor (2.8) was satisfactory and our target path (4.5) would be more than satisfactory. An immediate basic question would be, is our target product overdesigned? Would a score of 3.5 to 4.0 be good enough? What would be the street price of a target path of 4.5? 4.0? 3.5? How volume sensitive is the unit manufacturing cost?

Even though this product profile is at a macro level and is early in the commercialization cycle it is good enough to start asking some critical questions that maybe would not have been asked otherwise.

Product Profile — Base Case Model

What is it? — A graphic device showing a step-wise progression of product feature buildup and associated approximate macro level cost.

Objective — To trace product feature and cost buildup from a basic line bare minimum entry level configuration.

Input — Customer Requirements Matrix (CRM)

Product Profile

Output — A step-wise set of product configurations from entry level to maximum number of features.

Instructions (See Figure 2.9)

1. Using input from the CRM and Product Profile construct the elements of an entry level "plain vanilla" model. List the features, the customers, and a best guess macro level cost.
   - The features would be those that are common to all customers as indicated in the CRM.
   - Information from the Product Profile may also be helpful here.
2. Building from this baseline, add additional features that are common to a cluster of customers as indicated in the CRM. Estimate a macro cost for this new set. If the base cost is $X, then step 1 costs $X + $Y.
3. Repeat step (2) for an appropriate number of iterations for the product project. The next cost buildup would be $X + $Y + $Z and so on until the highest step is reached which is probably a fully configured product for the highest end user. Such a configuration usually ends up being "one size fits all" and is over-designed and overpriced.

Advantages

1. The step-wise progression of product configurations very effectively shows the cost buildup due to segmentation, specialization, and "one size fits all."
2. Shows the baseline minimum just to enter the game.
3. Excellent early dialogue with marketing and may help them in beginning their research.

Disadvantages

1. It may be used too early in the product development process for some people to feel comfortable. It can erroneously be viewed as an early design "lock-in."
2. May be uncomfortable or intimidating to marketing or business research.

	Step		Cost ($)

| | Base + 1and 2
Customers
A, B, C, D, E | 1. Feature 8
2. Feature 9
3. Etc. | 2 | 900 |

$X + $Y +$Z — Base + 1and 2 / Customers A, B, C, D, E — 1. Feature 8 / 2. Feature 9 / 3. Etc. — 2 — 900

$X + $Y — Base + 1 / Customers A, B — 1. Feature 5 3. Feature 7 / 2. Feature 6 4. Etc. — 1 — 250

$X — Base Case — 1. Feature 1 / 2. Feature 2 / 3. Feature 3 4. Feature 4 / 5. Etc. — 0 — 100

Product Profile Base Case Model

Figure 2.9 Product profile, base case model.

The Business Case/Plan — Is There One?

It is not uncommon for commercialization teams to start and proceed with no business plan. In fact, a team may not have access to a business plan for several phases of the commercialization process. If this situation exists, design teams are encouraged to write a business plan at a macro level of detail. The team plan is then moved up the decision chain to get approval or course correction. This team activity begins to get some attention because they are saying that, without any input from upper management, this is the direction in which they are headed.

The tools just discussed can be very helpful in putting a business plan together. What is needed is an outline to help the team write a plan. Listed below are the macro level items of a generic business plan. (Figure 2.10) The team probably cannot provide text and information for each element of the plan. However, except for business strategy, marketing plans, and regional plans, the team should be able to provide detail for the remaining elements.

The format of the plan should be in outline/bullet form and should not be longer than two pages, preferably, one page. The more detailed and prose-like the plan is, the more permanent it appears. This makes it easier for someone to pick it apart, devote too little attention to it, or quickly discard it. Remember, at this point in the project all you want to

Business Plan — Generic

Executive summary	Manufacturing/sourcing plan
Business/technical strategy	Service/warranty plan
Product offering and requirements	Environmental plan
Marketing plan	Financial plan
Regional plans	Risks and issues
Development plan	Implementation

Figure 2.10 Generic business plan.

do is get management's attention and course correction. You are not doing the manager's job!

SUMMARY

In this chapter I have described the importance of setting the stage for defining VOC. That is, before we attempt to collect VOC, we must first define our business and our customers. Various tools are available to do this such as the 12 Questions, Customer Chains, Value Proposition, Customer Morphology, and Customer Profiles. It is not necessary to use all of the tools but rather the combination of tools that fits your particular needs. The point is that if all the tools that are used all cascade or point in the same direction, they all can't be wrong! Our company and customer focus should lie somewhere within the boundaries established by these tools. These boundaries can also help us write a macro level business plan if one does not exist.

ACKNOWLEDGMENT

This chapter was reprinted with permission from Shillito, M.L., *Advanced QFD, Linking Technology to Market and Company Needs,* John Wiley & Sons, New York, 1994.

REFERENCES

1. Cook, T. F., Determine value mismatch by measuring user/customer attitudes, in *Proc. Soc. Am. Value Engineers*, 21, May, 1986, 145-156.
2. Daetz, D., Barnard, W., and Norman, R., *Customer Integration, the Quality Function Deployment (QFD) Reader's Guide for Decision Making*, Oliver Wight Publications, Essex Junction, VT, 1995.
3. Barnard, W. and Wallace, T. F., *The Innovation Edge,* Oliver Wight Publications, Essex Junction, VT, 1994.
4. Lanning, M. J. and Phillips, L. W., *Building Market-Focused Organizations,* unpublished manuscript, Lanning-Phillips and Associates, Atlanta, GA, 1994.

5. Magaziner, E., *Very High Quality Customer Requirements*, Project Linguistics International, Sedona, AZ, internal seminar with the author.
6. Shillito, M. L., Customer and product profiling in the fuzzy front end, *Trans. 8th Symp. Qual. Function Deployment*, Novi, MI, 1996, 221-230.

3

COLLECTING VOC

BACKGROUND

There are numerous collection schemes available to capture VOC. Which tool or combination of tools to use depends on each situation. There is no one precise template that guarantees total accurate VOC capture. Primary before any VOC collection is to be sure that the customer is correctly identified as discussed in the previous chapter. The type of data (qualitative or quantitative) is just as important as knowing which collection method use. According to Barnard,[1] it is important to distinguish between market research and customer research. Market research has been around for a long time. Its tools are based on applied math and statistics. That is, the world of statistical acceptance sampling, statistical validity, confidence intervals, regression analyses, design of experiments, and other high powered mathematical and statistical models. Customer research, on the other hand, is visiting the user of your product, observing them, talking to them, asking questions about how they perceive the value of purchasing your product. They are close personal visits in the context of their world where your product must fit. Business research is based on customer satisfaction decisions, whereas customer research is based on choice–based decisions. It is important to know how satisfied a customer is with your product. It is probably more important to know what goes through a customer's head when he made the choice decision to buy your product in the first place. Satisfaction and choice may not be correlated.

The world of VOC is based on choice decisions and customer research.[1]

QUALITATIVE AND QUANTITATIVE VOC

There are two types of VOC data, qualitative and quantitative, or linguistic and numerical. The qualitative VOC data is in the form of labels. It is subjective and exploratory and tends to be open-ended. It can be both divergent and convergent. It provides structure and surfaces relationships and is a database for further focus.

Quantitative VOC, on the other hand, is numbers–oriented and tends to be more objective and specific. The numbers show magnitude and assist us in our dialogue in being more convergent. They provide metrics for focus within a qualitative database. This type of data is more business research oriented. Numbers show the importance and strength of qualitative relationships.

Which of the two types do you use and when? First, it is important to establish a database using qualitative VOC. Data must be labeled before it can be measured. Figure 3.1 depicts the shifting balance between qualitative and quantitative VOC data over the product life cycle from vision to sales.

The slope of the line between qualitative and quantitative VOC is determined by how well we understand the VOC. That is, the more we understand the VOC, the faster we change the balance between qualitative and quantitative VOC over time. This is more commonly known as experience and learning. Like other things, the VOC also has a learning curve.

Next we apply the most basic numerical measures (subjective estimates) to determine the hierarchy of importance across the labels of the qualitative database. The combined qualitative and quantitative data will highlight what we know and what we don't know about the VOC. At this point it is equivalent to completing the rows of the House of Quality (HOQ) or the left side of a Customer Oriented Product Concepting (COPC) matrix. Those items where we are uncertain either about the label or its numerical measure, or both, are highlighted by a yellow marker. Once the VOC database is finished, the entire matrix can be easily and quickly scanned for unknown and missing VOC data. It is this highlighted questionable VOC data that becomes the input to do a more organized, specific and focused inquiry. At this point it is helpful to call in business research and/or marketing for help in designing surveys and focus groups. The activity now reflects that which is used more in traditional market research. We now have a firm foundation from which to build better research.

When Do You Start?

The majority of QFD teams believe that in order to do QFD, surveys, focus groups, interviews, etc., must first be held to collect the VOC before doing the HOQ. My question at this point is, how do you know this early in the project what questions to ask? Sometimes market, segment, and user have not been well defined. There is a risk at this point that such VOC collection can be a shot in the dark. It too easily can produce a

Ratio of Qualitative and Quantitative VOC

VOC

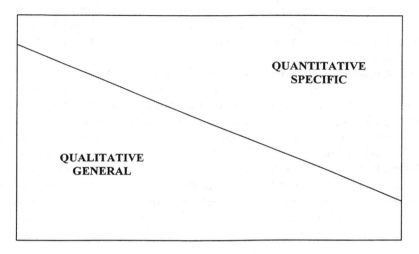

Product Life Cycle
(Time)

Figure 3.1 Ratio of qualitative and quantitative VOC. (From Shillito, M. L., *Advanced QFD Linking Technology to Market and Company Needs,* John Wiley & Sons, New York, 1994. With permission.)

database biased by strong-willed individuals covering up what they don't know.

One suggestion and mode of operation is to take all existing internal VOC data and, using affinity and tree diagrams, construct the rows of the HOQ first! Rate the customer verbatims for importance, do a competitive analysis, and rate market leverage. This will give order and structure to what information is already present. It will show what is known and what is not known, as discussed in the previous section. Knowing and structuring what is not known now puts us in a position to formulate more and better questions to design focus groups, interviews, and other VOC data collection methods. New data would be entered into the blank spaces and replace questionable labels and numbers in the preliminary HOQ.

Remember the HOQ, in particular the VOC data, is a living document that should continually be updated. Therefore, we should be obtaining VOC all the time from trade shows, sales calls, customer service, and so on.

Customers — How Many to Talk to?

How many customers should we talk to? When is enough enough? What is the curve of diminishing returns? Griffen and Hauser[2] have shown in their research that 90 to 95% of customer needs are obtained after 20 to 30 interviews and that 80% of the needs are acquired after approximately 10 to 12 site visits. They assumed all interviews were one-on-one and that each customer interview was independent of all the others, two major assumptions.

They made no mention about variation across categories of customers, geography, or various customer sites. Will this necessitate more visits? Due to time and budget constraints of most companies, perhaps we can learn from their experience. If customer categories and geography are factors, then perhaps 10 to 12 different sites are visited and five to six people are interviewed at each site. Of these five or six, each should represent a different function within the site. For example, a manager, an equipment operator, a clerk, a maintenance person, etc., could all be interviewed. Remember, we are collecting the labels on those things a customer wants (qualitative data) and this type of data collection does not require statistically significant samples and data points.

Customer Selection

Once market and segment(s) are defined, it is necessary to select potential customers for data collection. A customer selection matrix is useful.[3] This matrix arranges the traditional customer segmentation (e.g. lead users, early adopters, laggards, etc.) with the non-traditional, such as the names of the customer types within each segment.

Customer Selection Matrix

What is it? — A matrix of product user types versus actual customer names/locations.
Objective — Develop a list of potential interviewees for VOC collection.
Purpose — A design of experiments approach to developing a balanced list of customers to interview; to be sure a broad range of users is covered and reduce sampling bias; to develop geographic clusters to develop interview trips and assign teams.
Instructions (See Figure 3.2 and Appendix D.8)

1. Create/develop user/stakeholder categories. In the photographic business, example categories have been:
   - Type of print (e.g., kiosk, portrait, event, schools, specialty)
   - Digital vs. film

CUSTOMER SELECTION MATRIX
3-HOLE PUNCH

		CUSTOMERS AND CATEGORIES							
CUSTOMER	FUNCTION	Demanding Customer	Satisfied Customer	Unhappy Customer	Lost Customers	New Customers	Paper Only?	Trans. Mat'l.	Geography NE,SE,C, SW, NW
School	Secretary Teacher Pupil Admin.								
Office	Secretary Manager Executive								
Industrial	Secretary Engineer Supervisor								
Home	Parent Child, K-6 Child, HS								

Figure 3.2   Customer selection matrix, 3-hole punch.

- Lead user vs. average user
- Source of input (e.g. digital camera, silver halide, negative, slide, CD, etc.)
- Large company, small independent
- Environment (e.g., humidity, dust, temp, etc.)
- Mobility (e.g., static, portable, transportable)
- Current supplier
- Happy vs. unhappy
- Location (geographics)
- Usage (personal, business)
- Durable print needed? (Yes/No?)
- Channel (direct, indirect)

2. Categories should be as mutually exclusive as possible.
3. List actual customer names/locations down the left side of the matrix.
4. For each customer row, check off those stakeholder categories that pertain to each customer.
   - Can one customer be in multiple categories? The goal is to get the smallest number of customers to receive the largest cross section.
5. Within each customer, list the various functions/people to visit. Examples of functions are:

- Printer operator
- Owner/boss
- Service/Maintenance
- Technical support
- QA
- Business planner
- Purchasing

6. There should be enough customer rows to be sure we have a total of five different customers for each stakeholder category column.

Figure 3.2 is a customer selection matrix for different categories of users of a 3-hole punch. The customers listed are schools, office, industrial, and home. Within each segment users have been further identified by function area, such as teachers, students, secretaries, parents, engineers, etc.

These, in turn, are further categorized by demanding, satisfied, unhappy, lost, and new customers, as well as whether they punch paper only and/or punch overhead transparency material. Specific names of schools, offices, industry or families are written in the rows of the matrix. Names of individual users (teachers, engineers, students, etc.) may be written in the individual cells. The completed matrix is to be used as a guide to a balance of potential interviewers by category. It is equivalent to a design of experiments to balance customer input.

The customer selection matrix is the natural next step after defining answers to the 12 Questions and the customer profile process discussed in Chapter 2. Each tool provides additional focus and naturally cascades one into the other.

Daetz, Barnard, and Norman, as part of their customer integrated decision making (CIDM) process, have devised what they call the customer dimensions matrix. Their approach is based on the fact that "the amount of information you require from each category of customers depends on their involvement with your product."[1] They categorize the customers into three dimensions, none of which are mutually exclusive. The categorizes are

1. Customers that you sell to have to believe that your product has the ability to fulfill all requirements.
2. Customers that you must understand who influence those that use the product, but their job may be affected by the product.
3. Customers that you must understand who usually don't directly use the product.

Daetz, Barnard, Norman Grid (BDN)[1]

PRODUCT X

	Segment 1	Segment 2
Planner		
Funder	Sell to	
Auditor	Influence	
Installer	Understand	
Maintainer	etc.	
Operator	etc.	
User 1		
User 2		

Sell to   =   "Customers must believe that your product has the ability to fulfill all requirements."

Influence   =   "Customers we must understand who influence those who use the product but their job may not be affected by the product."

Understand =   "Customers we must understand who usually don't directly use the product."

Figure 3.3 Daetz, Barnard, Norman (DBN) grid.

They use these categorizes in conjunction with Magaziner's[4,5] eight customers to determine who you must sell to, influence, or understand for each of the selected segments (Figure 3.3). An example of this Daetz, Barnard, Norman (DBN) grid applied to customers for a 3-hole punch is shown in Figure 3.4. All of these approaches can help us better define our customer and their needs which, in turn, gives us more structure to prepare for the collection of VOC.

DBN Grid For 3-Hole Punch

Product: 3-Hole Punch
Market: Commercial

Viewpoint	Segment 1: Office	Segment 2: School
Distribution Channel Buyer (User 1)	Sell to	Sell to
Secretary/Teacher (User 2)	Understand	Understand
Materials Mgr./Buyer (Funder)	Sell to	Sell to
Stock Clerk (Installer)	Influence	Influence

Figure 3.4 DBN grid for 3-hole punch.

VOC COLLECTION TECHNIQUES — WHICH? WHEN? HOW?

Deciding how and when to collect the VOC is half the effort. Many times this can be decided by comparing the different collection techniques. It is wise to work closely with the business research department or equivalent of your company. After all, this is their line of work. It is important to remember, don't do it alone! The most common collection methodologies are

- Surveys, mail, phone, comment cards
- Interviews, group or individual, phone
- Focus groups
- Location studies (like industrial engineering surveys)
- Direct observation: visitation to site of usage
- Internal brainstorming
- Commercially prepared stock reports
- Panels
- Electronic databases and searches
- Service calls
- 1-800-hotlines
- In-context customer visits
- Internet

Sources of VOC Data	Type
1. Internal (marketing, sales, customer service)	Recorded
2. Customer direct	Observational
3. Trade shows	Observational

4. Sales calls	Observational
5. Service/repair calls	Observational/recorded
6. Literature (trade and consumer)	Recorded
7. Complaints/warranty records	Recorded
8. Visitations	Observational (subjective)
9. Electronic data bases and searches	Recorded

Answers to the following set of questions can help you determine the appropriate collection technique for you and your project.

1. What is the collection technology? How does it work?
2. When is the best time to use it?
3. How long will it take?
4. What will it cost?
5. What are the advantages?
6. What are the disadvantages?
7. What level of detail do you get? System, subsystem, piece/part, etc.?
8. What are the prerequisites for using?
9. What are the assumptions?
10. What is the output? What do you get? A report? A computer disk full of numbers?
11. What is the lapse time to output?
12. What is the format of the output? Labels only? Numbers? Levels? All the above?
13. Do you know what questions you want to ask? How were they derived? Did you use the customer selection QFD Matrix to assist in generating the questions?

There is no one VOC collection technique that will give you everything you need. Use several techniques in concert to help you cover all the bases you wish to cover. Also, different VOC techniques support each other. If several different collection techniques come up with the same answer or point in the same direction it lends more credibility to the study. It is highly unlikely that they are all wrong.

Surveys

Surveys take many forms. Their basis is a questionnaire that may be used by mail, used over the telephone or provided as comment cards like at restaurants or theme parks. The major assumption is the you have identified the correct respondents and designed the correct questions because those are the only answers you will get. Remember, all surveys are perfectly designed to produce the answers you get. Response rate to surveys is generally very low, around 30%. People, if in a hurry or inconvenienced, may even whitewash answers to get it over with, like shoppers at a mall. The main problem with surveys is control. Once the questionnaire is in the mail, you are at the mercy of the respondents. Likewise, the telephone is impersonal and many times it is hard to keep the person on the line. How many of you have been called by a computer at meal time?

Surveys are good if you want to ask convergent questions to obtain specific answers. This also assumes that you have identified specific customer needs that require more detailed clarification. Cost is low if you use methods like comment cards. Using the mail and the telephone will start to increase cost. Many companies prefer to use outside market research firms that drive cost to a higher plateau.

Some pitfalls and disadvantages are (1) mail response rate can be low, (2) during face-to-face surveys people may get impatient and tend to whitewash answers to get it over with, (3) many times telephone survey respondents easily hang up, (4) incorrectly selecting the appropriate respondents and calculating correct sample size, (5) wording questions that invite ambiguity, (6) you do not have direct contact with respondents to observe body language and to ask probing questions about their answers, and (7) the amount of time it takes to analyze and summarize the data.

Interviews

Interviews may be done face-to-face or over the telephone. Eye contact is best as there is more control and hard copy illustrations may be used. Single individuals or groups may be interviewed. Groups are good as long as there is no peer pressure and everyone is at ease. Group interaction and synergy can produce more information, although there are some who argue that individual interviews are best. Preparing for the interview is extremely critical and can be time consuming.

Focus Groups

Focus groups are conducted with six or more people who are familiar with the topic. It is run by a moderator using a moderator's guide prepared by the team. The session is video and audio taped for later transcription. A special room is used behind which there is an observation room screened by one-way glass. Focus groups are generally conducted by research firms who specialize in the process and who own or have access to the specially designed facilities. They can be very expensive but also very effective. They are usually conducted after working hours in the evening with a meal provided. The actual product is often present at the focus group for customer reference and interaction. The video and audio tapes are usually transcribed for hard copy distribution for the team and other appropriate distribution. The assumption is that you have enough knowledge about the customer needs to allow you to design the right focused questions to derive the specific answers you need. Focus groups are totally dependent on the fact that the correct questions are being used with the correct customers.

The benefits of focus groups are (1) the video and audio tape to preserve the session as well as analyze after the session; (2) you have direct observation of real customer's response and interaction to your questions and/or sample products, mockups, or generic models or service elements and activities; (3) you can add/modify questions during the session; (4) the focus group sponsor is anonymous; (5) each member can hear and respond to other group member's comments; (6) hitch hiking — one member's comment may prompt another group member to discuss a topic not thought of before; and (7) cost/efficiency — several customers are interviewed in the approximate time it would take to interview one customer.

There also are some pitfalls and disadvantages, such as (1) dominant individuals may command the majority of airtime and bias the session if the facilitator is weak or ill-prepared; (2) people can choose to participate just for the money and a free meal, and give poor, unrepresentative answers just to get it over with; and (3) the amount of time it takes to transcribe and analyze the tapes.

Location Studies

Location studies are direct visits allowing direct observation of operations, and, in some cases, direct interaction with operators or the process. For example, some larger companies will send a team of industrial engineers to study operations. The intent is to improve the customers' operations and save them money and maintain the client account. Since they study the operation in detail, they learn how their product is used and discover areas for improvements. They learn what is important to the customer and about gaps in our product delivery. They are another pair of eyes to observe VOC.

Internal Brainstorming — Caution!

Product development teams may also brainstorm customer needs. This must be done with an interdisciplinary team consisting of no less than marketing, customer service, product design (hardware and software), and research and development (for new technology). Such sessions generate an interesting list but one never knows how valid all the items on the list are. Some items may be a team's or company's personal wishes, about which the customer may care less. Such brainstorm lists should be verified with the customer by other means. To this end, VOC brainstorming can be very useful in designing other inquiry mechanisms for completeness such as focus group questionnaires, etc. This method is used quite often and caution should be exercised in its use. It is too easy to incorporate entrenched company paradigms that may easily be accepted as real VOC. More than enough design and VOC teams have been burned by this method. Be careful! It is, however, a good focusing mechanism to take stock of what we think we know or don't know.

Customer Panels/Councils

This device can be very effective. Groups of customers are invited, usually quarterly, to the company to interact with the design team. They sign a confidentiality agreement and use the product in its latest version and make comments and suggestions for improvement. The design team installs the changes and repeatedly brings the panel members back until a final design is derived. Care must be taken that there is no conflict of interest among panel members. In some cases, customers/users are paid to be actual members of the design team. They may participate in meetings one to five days a week, and, in some cases, have their own office right inside the manufacturer's plant!

Service Calls

Service calls are another excellent source of information. It is a first hand direct observation to see how the product performs and how the customer uses and interfaces with the product. If the product is continually abused or breaking down there may be an unmet customer need or problem that needs further inquiry. Similar information may be obtained from warranty work and 1-800-HELP lines.

Contextual Inquiry

This is one VOC collection technique that is attracting some attention. It is called contextual inquiry or in-context customer visits. The process involves a visit to the customer in the context of their real work environment. That is, you sit beside an operator or user and observe what is happening and ask questions. This may last anywhere from four to eight hours. The process provides an opportunity to intervene when the customer is having a problem. It places the observer in the context of the customer's actual work and allows observation of unavoidable distractions or out–of–the–ordinary special activities or operations. It permits the observing engineer/designer to imagine and invent (real time) possible solutions and design changes or upgrades based on the observed activity. During the in-context visit there is an opportunity to ask many open-ended, probing, content–extracting questions. To help give focus to the process, the interview team should treat the customer visit as if it were making a video, "A Day In The Life of the Customer." The interview team must recognize that it is not looking for solutions that day. Contextual inquiring implies a partnership of sharing information versus an interview which is an I ask-you answer situation.

The purpose of the visit is to observe and participate in the customer's experience on their turf as it relates to our product and service. Often it is best to begin the inquiry process by having the customer give you a tour of the facility and/or trace his activity or process in order of execution. From this you can construct a process flow chart (discussed later) to show exactly where and how your product fits into his business.

Although contextual visits and inquiry are not an interview per se, an interview guide can be useful for collecting information and checking to see that the appropriate topics are covered. A useful opening question is, "What do you need to be successful in your job or business?" Encourage the customer to give many examples or "war stories." It is helpful not to encourage the customer to talk so much about the product of their dreams but rather about the job of their dreams. Doing so will evoke images that lead to revolutionary hows and exciters rather than simple evolutionary and fire-fighting improvements.

When talking to customers who integrate your product into a larger system or service, you want to learn how and where your product fits. By learning their entire system you may discover other areas of opportunity for your product which can lead to new products or expanded designs.

The following is a typical "day in the life of a VOC interview trip."

1. Travel in pairs, three is even better if budgets permit.
   - Team assigns each person the job of (1) interviewer, (2) note taker, and (3) observer. The roles are switched for the next interview.
2. Travel to the site.
3. Explain to interviewee(s) the background and reason for being here.
4. Interview the first person.
   - Tape record session (permissions only).
   - The interviewer or moderator.
     – Asks questions.
     – Keeps the momentum of interview going.

       – Does not take notes.

       – Probes between questions.

   ■ The note taker:

       – Takes notes, all words as best as possible.

       – Observes.

   ■ The observer:

       – Also takes notes.

       – Records images.

       – Assists the interviewer/moderator.

5. The interview team does NOT sell and does NOT defend the company's current problems or the way certain things may have occurred.
6. Interview all remaining persons.
7. Return to hotel and debrief notes and transcribe the tape recordings.
   - ■ Extract customer verbatims (needs, wants).
   - ■ Type data into laptop computer if available.
   - ■ Code verbatims by customer, location, interviewee, interviewer(s), interviewee's, function, etc.
8. Proceed to next site.
   - ■ Guidelines are one interview site per day with approximately one to three interviews per site. The rest of the day is spent transcribing notes and tapes.
9. After the trip, send notes electronically to common collection point which is generally an intranet home page.

Interview Tips

Do:

1. Take copious notes.
2. Probe deeply; use the Sony 5-why's. (Sony claims that you cannot get to a customer's root need unless you ask the question "why" five times and get an answer.)
3. Let the interviewee vent frustrations and gripes.
4. Ask interviewee to give examples.
5. Write down any observations/descriptions of the site/location.
6. Develop empathy.
7. Probe for examples, motivation, problems of the product/site/location.

Do Not:

1. Get into problem solving.
2. Defend or make excuses for current situations.
3. Make negative comments about others or competitors.
4. Do not sell.
5. Do not tell the customer he is wrong.

Words that invite probes:

1. Good.
2. Bad.
3. Like.
4. Dislike.
5. Numbers (i.e., machine speed, gas mileage, etc.).
6. Percentages (i.e., 10% improvement).

Internet

The age of electronic information and communication is here. Access to and use of the Internet is increasing exponentially. Everyone is surfing for and interacting with correspondents. Internet may also be a source of collecting and listening to VOC. It has the potential for being a vehicle to use other inquiry mechanism like surveys, panels, and interviews. The use of electronic ordering over the Internet is starting to produce customized customer profiles.

Process Flow Mapping

When observing and dialoguing with the customer it is helpful to construct a process flow diagram of the customer's operation(s). When confirmed by the customer, the flow diagram can be used to show exactly where your product fits into the customer's operations and the general scheme of things. They are useful to reveal interactions, bottlenecks, inputs, outputs, and transformations which involve the use of your product. Figure 3.5 is an example of a process flow map for a copy center for making black and white copies from walk–up counter orders. Many new questions regarding copier design and features may arise from looking at this flow. For example, should interleaving be a new feature on a copier? Should billing software and printout be an option in the copier?

Process Flow Diagram Copy Center

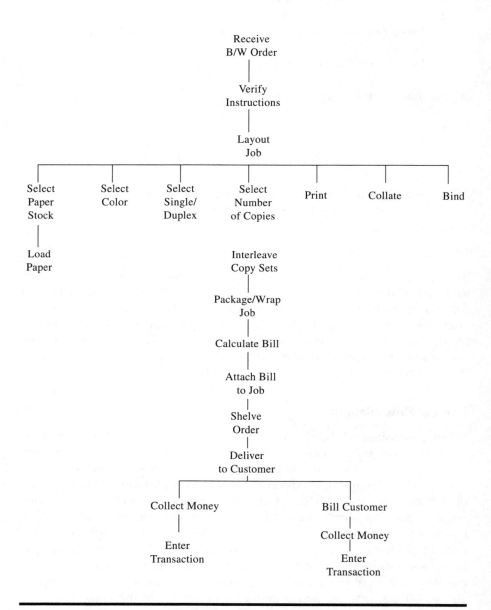

Figure 3.5 Process flow diagram for copy center.

Customer Visits — General

Probably the most definitive source on customer visits is that by Edward McQuarrie in his book, *Customer Visits*.[6] A very important part of customer visits is the preparation of the interview guide. The guide is not a script to be read to the customer but rather a guide, a practice tool to increase the interviewer's chances of asking the right questions in the right way to get the customer information needed. The objective is to create an atmosphere where the customer speaks candidly and freely about the answers to open-ended questions. The interview is a conversation not an interrogation.[7] The guide is to help the interview team create a comfortable dialogue.

The structure of the visit generally has three parts, the opening, the dialogue, and the closing. The opening consists of the background and the reason for the visit. It is the interview team's chance to establish rapport to seek the kind of information they are after. The middle portion or dialogue is where open-ended questions are asked to get an under-standing of the customer's needs. The initial questions are general in nature, such as, "What results do you expect from our product or service?" Once dialogue is opened up, more specific, open-ended, probing questions are used to cover areas not covered by the interviewee. For example, "What problems do you experience when using our product; how do you use our product for other than what it was designed to do?" The closing is where responses are clarified, and the interview team is given a last chance to cover any remaining questions. Most importantly, it leaves the door open for any follow-up that may be necessary.

The Interview Guide — Generating and Selecting Questions

What is the determination and selection process for the questions included in the interview guide? Once the 12 Questions have been answered and a customer and product profile has been established (discussed in Chapter 2), the VOC team can brainstorm questions to ask. All questions are written on sticky pads (one per pad). The team then constructs an affinity diagram (Chapter 5) of questions. The label of each cluster of questions generally become the primary or main questions. The questions within the cluster become the backup probes.

If the interview team feels that the necessary topics of interest are not being covered using the primary questions or backup probes, an additional inquiry method is to use "buzz" words. These are single words that relate to specific topics, such as productivity, reliability, waste, service time, down time, etc. Buzz words are used in the following manner. The interviewer instructs the interviewee: "I am going to mention some single words and I want you to tell me the first thoughts, visions, or reflections that come to your mind." Usually the words prompt a response, sometimes they don't. Buzz words are usually used as a last resort to obtain information.

NGT (Nominal Group Technique)

Another method to generate questions is to use nominal group technique (NGT). With this method each member of the VOC team is given a pack of sticky pads and a wide felt-tipped pen. The process facilitator instructs the team to start writing questions on the pads, one question per pad. However, with this process, the entire question generation portion is done in complete silence. When the facilitator feels or asks the team if they are finished writing questions, the questions will then be recorded on a wall, or 5 to 10 flip charts taped together in one long wall chart so it can be rolled up and carried to another location. Recording of questions is also done in silence. The facilitator instructs the team members to read aloud one of their sticky pad questions. The pad is then given to the facilitator to post on the wall chart. The same procedure is repeated by going round-robin around the table until all team members have exhausted all of their questions. If, during the listing, a team member hears a question that they believe is identical to one of theirs, they discard that sticky pad. On the other hand, if they hear a question that triggers a new question in their mind, they generate a new sticky pad question. This is commonly known as hitch hiking. After all questions have been posted, the team goes through the questions for any redundancy that may have unknowingly been generated as well as any clarification that may be needed on particular questions. At this point the team constructs the affinity diagram mentioned above (see Chapter 5).

To derive some idea of the relative importance of the questions, team members are each given five colored sticky dots, usually red. They are then asked to post the dots on the five questions that they believe to be the most critical for deriving the information for the project. Only one dot may be placed per individual per sticky pad question. The distribution of these "energy dots" gives some indication of the hierarchy of importance across all of the questions. This dot distribution further helps in defining the right questions for the interviews.

The Interview Guide

Opening

Thank you for volunteering your time to talk to us today. As we discussed earlier, we want to talk to you about your wants and needs concerning _____. Your data, along with interview information from other users of our product, will be used to improve our product in order that we can better meet your needs.

In order to help us we ask that you be as candid as possible. Please be assured that the contents of this session will be kept confidential and will be used only by our design team.

Main Questions

1. What are problems you face when using a _____?
2. What are issues you deal w/today in using a _____?
3. What is the net end result benefit you would like to receive when you purchase a _____?

Backup Probes

1. What problems do you face when _____?
2. What other problems do you face when _____?
3. Are there any other needs you may have for a _____?
4. What comes to mind when you think about purchasing your next _____?
5. What features do you think of when selecting a _____?
6. What new features might address your future needs?

Closing

1. Are there any topics we should have discussed?
2. We will most likely contact you again regarding clarification of things we discussed today.
   a. When is the best time to call?
   b. What number is best to reach you?
3. We will be contacting you regarding the importance of needs and features that evolve from these interviews.

The Interview Team

Interview teams consist of two or three people, and roles should be assigned to each member. This should never be attempted by one individual alone. One person should be a moderator or interviewer to ask questions, follow-up with probes, and keep the interview moving. The second person is the listener who takes detailed notes and operates the tape recorder. If a third person is used, he is the observer to listen and to take notes on the image and atmosphere of the customer's work area.

He can also construct a process flow map of the operation. This can be important later if the image and demeanor of the work area is not in sync with the interviewee's answers or descriptions. Using more than three people has an appearance and feeling of being overwhelming and may make the interviewee uncomfortable. A tape recorder should always be used if cleared by the interviewee. It is impossible to take notes and not miss some important points. When transcribing the tape it is always amazing to find something you missed or misinterpreted.

What Questions to Ask

One thing is for sure. Closed ended questions that require yes/no or multiple choice answers should not be used. All you get is a simple answer to your question, which also assumes that you asked the right question. It is important to let the customer do the talking. This requires the use of open-ended questions. One such set of questions comes from the Lanning and Phillips value proposition model[7] as follows:

1. What is the net end result benefit you expect to receive from buying our product?
   ■ What are the issues that are complicating your ability to provide the result required from your work (business)?
   ■ What is your problem? What keeps you up at night?
   ■ What end results will you pay for? Why?
   ■ What other results will you trade for? Why?

Shiba et al.[3] also have a set of open-ended questions that they recommend. They are

1. What images come to mind when you visualize this product or service?
2. From your experience, what complaints, problems, or weaknesses would you like to mention about the product or services?
3. What features do you think of when selecting the product or service?
4. What new features might address your future needs?

Notice that the above questions basically pertain to a leveraged or upgraded product from one that already exists. What questions do you ask for non-existing products that your company has never made before? This is the time to use in-context questions that are derived from various situations or usage. You can't ask questions about the product because the customer never had or used yours. Instead, the team develops all kinds of situations and circumstances in which the product will be used. At the same time we direct our question around the functions that must be performed rather than the product and its attributes and features.

Let's pretend that our company is going to design and build a dishwasher. This is our first entry into the dishwasher market. We could ask, "What is the value of doing dishes?" "Are dishes hard to do?" We could even invite the customers (invitation only) to a day long workshop. We could let the customer be a co-designer and also make a presentation at the end of the day. During the day we would ask questions around the functions of doing the dishes. That is, washing, drying, removing them, stacking them back in the cupboard. We could ask questions about dysfunctions such as heat radiated into the room, noise level, leaks, plumbing, etc. Next we can ask questions around tradeoffs ("It's noisy, but I like the way it scrubs!"). In general we would ask positive and negative open-ended questions around the task of washing dishes.

We could also develop questions around situations or contexts such as:

- Learning to use the product
- Trouble shooting
- Installation
- Service
- The buying decision
- Hardest thing to do
- When you are in a hurry
- Leaving the machine running when you are away from home
- The most peaceful moment
- When you have company, guests at home
- When you were definitely glad you had the dishwasher
- Your most uncomfortable moment

Again, the above contexts would be used to generate open-ended questions. For example, "What images or feelings come to mind when you think about using the dishwasher when you have company?" "What mental picture do you have of your most frustrating (or most satisfying) moment?"

Probing

Probing questions are the most important questions you will ask. It allows you to "peel back the layers of the onion." The answer to the open-ended questions discussed earlier merely give the outer layer of the onion. Probing is necessary for further clarification and understanding, that is, to get to root cause. They should be neutral and nondirective. The following are typical response probes; use them liberally:

1. Tell me more about that.
2. Why is _____ important to you?
3. Why did you mention _____?
4. What does _____ mean?
5. Why is that important to you?
6. Why is that not important to you?
7. How did you feel when that happened?
8. What would you have done differently?
9. If you were able to do that, what would you be doing differently today? How would it affect your operation/business?
10. Who else or what else is/was involved when that happens?
11. Why?

The probes that work the best are those that lead to examples rather than generalizations. Also refrain from asking second party questions. For example, don't ask the "boss" about his peoples' problems and concerns but rather ask him about his concerns. First person questions work the best.

Scheduling Interview Visits

Probably one of the most difficult tasks of the collection phase is scheduling the interview trips and visits. It really comes down to time, location, number of sites, number of interviewees, budgets, and deadlines. It is always best to work and schedule the visits in conjunction with the sales representative or technical representative for a particular customer. There is nothing more aggravating than scheduling interviews in a salesman's territory and customer without his knowledge. This can cause the team problems and political upheaval quick time! Let the sales person pave they way for you. Some will merely give you names and numbers to call and leave the team on its own for scheduling. Other sales people want to attend the interviews. Be very careful in this situation. Sometimes sales people who are not in good standing with the customer use the interviews to patch up problems, and, in the worst case, take over the interview and the team leaves with nothing accomplished. (I know, I've been there.) The customer selection matrix discussed earlier will be one of the most important tools to use in scheduling interviews and trips. Customer site geographic locations should be selected to get the smallest number of customer locations to get the largest cross section while minimizing travel distance and cost. Scheduling interviews should be initiated by a phone call and followed up with a letter confirming date, time, and, in some cases, the functional type of interviewees you wish to talk to.

It has been my experience that questions sent out ahead of the interview add little value. If an interviewee has more time to reflect on the questions, the more likely it is that they will censor their final answers. Consequently, you will receive more surgically clean and sterile responses. The interviewee will try hard to help you and try to develop the answers he thinks you want to hear. Conversely, the more spontaneous the answers, the more chance that the interviewee will make a spontaneous comment that will be a distinct signal to an open invitation to prompt us to ask many probing questions; ones that most likely we may not have asked and that will get us farther underneath the iceberg where the root needs reside. We are not trying to catch the interviewee off guard per se, but rather we are trying to understand the interviewees, their motivations, their desires, their problems; what they like or dislike about the way they do things today so we can design a product or service they will enjoy tomorrow.

The problem underlying this paradox is that the customer talks in terms of features and solutions but we want the customer's root needs. Root needs, which are practically invisible to the customer, lead to more exciting and creative ideas for the design team to discover leap changes that lead to tomorrow's dominant product. Solutions and features lead to today's dominant product and more of the "same old stuff" which is short-lived and must be continually updated to stay in the game. This frequent updating drives up product cost, increases price, and reduces margin. We want to derive the delightful aspects of functionality which, in my opinion, come from spontaneous incontext face-to-face interviewing. I also have found that many interviewees do not read the preinterview questionnaire until a few minutes, if at all, before the arrival of the interview team.

Should you conduct individual or group interviews? There are advantages and disadvantages to both. In my experience, individual interviews seem to work best. There is no peer pressure and more creativity in the answers. I have also had successful group interviews where the interviewees could hitch hike on other individual's answers. It is best if all members in the group get along with each other and peer pressure is absent. However, if peer pressure is present, you will probably get fewer answers and more bias in favor of the strongest personality in the group.

Recording Observations

"A picture is worth a thousand words." Observations can be just as information-rich as a picture, especially if they are recorded or documented. They should be obtained in addition to the interview activity. As you will experience, interviews do not always extract all the needed information. Interviewees do not always respond well to questions based on their own experience and interaction with the interviewers. The interview itself can be intimidating and interviewees may sometimes be less than truthful.

The classic observation method is to ask for a plant tour or a demonstration. This is especially helpful if done prior to the interview. Things to observe are

1. The process flow or sequence of operations.
2. Bottlenecks, pinch points, problems, frustrations.
3. Time sinks.
4. Redundancy, repetition.
5. Product features that were positive or negative.
6. Interaction of user and product.
7. Display of emotion, frustrations, excitement, boredom.

Observations backup and help to verify the interview, which, in turn, can lead to further probes. For example, a customer says he doesn't like our scanner or copier because it creates spots as artifacts that are not in the original image. During our plant tour we observe that the image scanner is located in a very undesirable area and has not been cleaned or dusted in three weeks, we have a conflict that may require further probing.

Debriefing the Visit

It is important to debrief the interview as soon as possible after the session while things are still fresh in your mind. This is especially important if numerous people have been interviewed. Things can get confusing very quickly. Each team member may bring a different point of view which they can carry forward to their respective functions. The debriefing promotes consistency among team members and any resulting communications. If there is time, the tape recording should be transcribed. Outside services are generally available to do this.

As customer verbatims are extracted from the interview notes and tapes they should be coded so that each verbatim can be traced back to the source. These will be helpful later if clarification is necessary. Some teams also code the verbatims by interviewee type, for example, secretary, machine operator, clerk, supervisor, manager, etc. Additional coding can be used to distinguish whether the verbatim is a need, solution, problem, feature, etc. This information can then be put in a computer data bank and sorted in many different ways to look for signals and trends. Coding and interpretation will be covered in the next chapter. In addition to a computer list, verbatims can also be written on cards (one item per card) which, in turn, are used for structuring the data as discussed in Chapter 5.

VOC Collection Verbatim Classification

Product: 3-Hole Punch; Model 2.0

Item	Use	User	Interviewer	Customer	Interviewee Verbatims
1	01	01	01, 03	01	Easy to insert paper
2	01	01	01, 03	01	Easy to insert multiple sheets
3	01	01	01, 03	01	Can pierce multiple sheets
4	03	03	03, 04	02	Easy access to punch assembly
5	03	03	03, 04	02	Punch always stays in place
6	02	02	Etc.	Etc.	Etc.
7					
8					
9					
10					

Product: 3-Hole Punch Model 2.0

Customer	Interviewer(s)	Use Category	User Type
01-Customer A	01	01 Office	01 Secretary
02-Customer B	02	02 School	02 Teacher
	03	03 Exec. off.	03 Executive
	04		

Figure 3.6 Verbatim classification data bank.

Verbatim Classification Data Bank

The individual verbatims should be entered and stored in a data bank as soon as possible after the visit and debriefing. Each verbatim is given a unique identification number along with a set of classification codes. The most frequently used codes are customer name, interviewer(s), use categories, and use type. These roughly correspond to some of the data in the customer morphology (Figure 2.5). This data bank is extremely valuable for doing cuts and sorts, as well as word or combination word search in the text of the interviewee verbatims. Figure 3.6 is an example page of one such data bank.

One needs some way to sort through this "pile" of interview verbatims. For example, what if a manager asked you the questions, "What were all of the comments about printer productivity in walkup kiosk copy locations?" or, "What comments were made concerning printer reliability in high volume printer locations?" or, "What did customers say about response time regarding mortgage transactions?" How would you respond to this manager's request? Would you have to flip through hundreds of pages of messy interview notes to find the answers? Coding verbatims into a database for electronic search is much faster and easier. Such searches sometimes reveal signals, trends, or needs that may have otherwise been missed.

There are spreadsheets available that are nicely suited for this task. In addition, some of them allow key word searches within the text itself.

Function Trees

In Chapter 1 we discussed the function-feature system (Figures 1.1. and 1.2). A function tree is a useful device for describing a product. It is also useful for cataloging product features and customer verbatims. As such, it can be useful for checking the completeness of topics and questions to be covered during VOC collection. Function trees can highlight gaps in information.

What is it? — A function tree is a diagram depicting the interrelationship of functions in a hierarchical order. It orders two-word definitions based on cause and consequence, and is verified through a how-why logic.

Objective — To map or describe a "product" based on function. To depict what a "product" must do to accomplish its overall basic function and allow the customer/user to accomplish his intended task.

Purpose — To provide another mechanism for generating additional questions to ask during VOC collection.

Input — Functions and customer task.

Output — A function map (tree) of the product verified by how-why logic.

Use — Function trees are very useful for searching for missing elements of the voice of the customer (VOC). They can be used to generate additional questions to collect VOC from the customer.

Instructions (See Figures 3.7 and 3.8)

1. Use the rule for describing functions: one verb and one noun.
2. Determine the customer task. What is the task users want to accomplish when they buy and use your product?
3. Based on customer task, establish the overall basic function of the product. Why does the product exist? The customer task must flow directly to the basic function.
4. Expand the tree from left to right asking "how." Verify functions right to left by asking "why." The logic must fit in both directions. The answer must be with the immediate adjacent function(s). Branching may quickly occur.

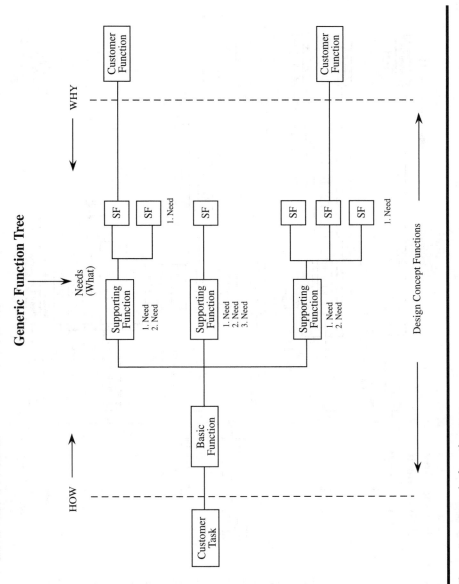

Figure 3.7 Generic function tree.

5. Draw two scope lines: one between the customer task and the product basic function, the other at the far end of the diagram. Functions inside the scope lines are performed by the product and are design related. Functions outside the scope lines are performed by the user and are called user input functions.

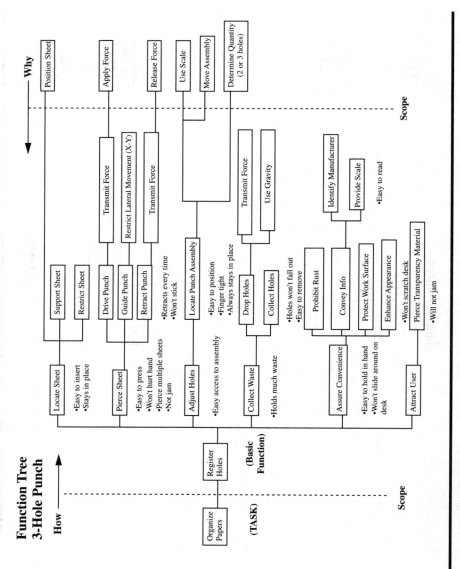

Figure 3.8 Function tree, 3-hole punch.

6. For each function, ask "what" in the vertical direction. This leads to customer requirements which may be written underneath the function.

Advantages

1. Provides another perspective on customer and product.
2. Can be used to generate additional VOC questions.

Disadvantages

1. Can be time consuming to generate.

Once the functions are established, many customer-oriented questions may be asked regarding them. Designing questions around the functions brings to the surface many VOC questions that may not have been asked before. For instance, from our punch example in Figure 3.8, we may want to ask additional questions regarding waste collection, rust, appearance, printed information, punch retraction, transmission force, locating material in the punch, ease to adjust punch assembly, case to remove waste, etc.

Company Intranet Homepage

For those companies that have an intranet system it is very useful to establish a homepage for all of this data as well as the data generated in the upcoming chapters. Only the team members and all other people associated with the project would/should have access to the homepage. Doing so should reduce the number of people giving excuses for not having access to pertinent project data. I have used the project homepage system several times. The result is that information transfer among members increased many-fold.

Transcribing Interview Tape Recordings

If budgets allow it and the service is available, it is very useful to have all of the interview tapes transcribed so it is possible to generate both electronic and hardcopy data. Hardcopy makes it easier to extract customer need verbatims. A disk allows all of the interview data to be sent to the intranet homepage discussed earlier. The typical transcript page is equal to approximately 250 words. Typical interviews last 45 to 90 minutes or as long as four to five hours or more. A 45 to 90 minute interview produces transcripts of 3000 to 6000 words. Viewed from another perspective, a person records less than 2500 to 3000 words per interview and is totally exhausted at the end. However, a tape recorder typically captures 10,000 words. So, a transcription is more information rich. Reading the hardcopy transcription will produce many customer needs that may normally be passed over even during review back at the motel after the interviews. Another method for getting an interview transcription is to hire a court stenographer. Unfortunately, stenographers are extremely expensive, but you do get the notes the same day plus an electronic file to download.

SUMMARY

In this chapter, the important elements in the large task of collecting VOC were discussed. First, collecting VOC involves customer research to ultimately determine what is important when making a choice decision to buy something. This is different from market research which is used to determine customer satisfaction. Customer selection is important to be sure we interview the right people with the right balance of backgrounds.

There are two types of data, qualitative and quantitative. VOC involves both types. Initially, mostly qualitative VOC is obtained. Quantitative VOC is developed after VOC is structured.

Many collection techniques are available but the final method chosen depends on budget, time, schedule, location, and subject. In-context customer visits are an excellent method to obtain VOC. The visits are further enhanced by developing an interview guide, selecting the right people for the interview team, and assigning responsibilities for moderator, note taker, and observer.

Designing the right questions is very important. Open-ended questions should be used to let the interviewee do all the talking. Specific open-ended probes can be used to get more specific information. For non-existing products, questions can be asked around the functions of the product as well as different situations or usage scenarios.

Finally, there is the task of debriefing the visit. This should be done as soon as possible after the interview while memories are still fresh. Coding verbatims will be helpful later if further inquiry is necessary from customers as well as structuring the data.

We must remember that we are in the business of solution delivery. It is a solution, not just the product, that the customer is after. A solution is an answer to a need or unsolved problem. The person who uses your product is the originator of the need. It is this need that has to be documented and quantified. Since customers usually cannot tell you directly what their needs are, we must do in-context interviewing and observation.

My close friend, Glenn Mazur,[8] President of Japan Business Consultants, uses the following comments to help in determining customer needs and formulating questions:

1. "Only the questions we ask get answered."
2. "Only the customers we survey get questioned."
3. "Only what the customer wants us to know gets indicated."

4. "It is what the customer does, not what he says, that counts."
5. "Only by direct personal observation of the customer at work using your products/services in actual conditions can the true needs be ascertained."

BIBLIOGRAPHY

Clausing, D., *Total Quality Development*, ASME Press, New York, 1994.

Cohen, L., *Quality Function Deployment: How To Make QFD Work For You*, Addison-Wesley Publishing, Reading, MA, 1995.

GOAL/QPC, *Voice of the Customer*, Methuen, MA, 1995.

Woodruff, R. B. and Gordial, S. F., *Know Your Customer: New Approaches to Understanding Customer Value and Satisfaction*, Blackwell Publishers, Cambridge, MA, 1996.

REFERENCES

1. Daetz, D., Barnard, W., and Norman, R., *Customer Integration, the Quality Function Deployment (QFD) Leader's Guide for Decision Making*, Oliver Wight Publications, Essex Junction, VT, 1995.
2. Griffen, A. and Hauser, J. R., "The voice of the customer," *Mark. Sci.*, 12, 1, 1-27, 1993.
3. Shiba, S., Graham, A., and Walden, D., *A New American TQM, Four Practical Revolutions for Management*, Productivity Press, Portland, OR, 1993.
4. Magaziner, E., *Very High Quality Customer Requirements*, Project Linguistics International, Sedona, AZ, internal seminar with the author.
5. Magaziner, E., "What Has Happened to the Voice of the Customer?", *The Journal*, Quality Assurance Institute, Orlando, FL.
6. McQuarrie, E. F., "Customer Visits," *Building A Better Customer Focus*, Sage Publications, Newbury Park, CA, 1993.
7. Lanning, M. J. and Phillips, L. W., "Building Market Focused Organizations," unpublished manuscript, Lanning-Phillips and Associates, Atlanta, GA, 1994.
8. Mazur, G., communications with the author.

4

INTERPRETATION AND TRANSLATION OF VOC

PREPARATION FOR TRANSLATION

Customer needs and wants are recorded verbatim. The verbatims must be translated into terms that the design/commercialization team can understand. That is, we go from the emotional, subjective information of the customer ("I hate operating this machine!"), to a more rational or objective language that is used to convey information that can be measured or validated ("the control lever is on the right side and I am left handed").

We can prepare for this later translation during the actual data collection by continually asking, why? Sony uses the "5-whys" process. They believe that root cause or customer need cannot be surfaced unless you ask this question five times. This will be especially important during indepth interviewing on incontext visits. As an example, let us assume we are in the business of making candles. During an interview with one of our customers, a reseller or dealer, the interviewer said that he would like to have more stearic acid in the wax formulation. Why #1: Why more acid? Answer: Because it controls the rate of burn. Why #2: Why is this important? Answer: We want the candles we sell to be longer burning. Why #3: Why is this important? Answer: Because your candles are better than others in most attributes when benchmarked with other manufacturers, but they don't last very long and our customers want longer burning candles. In our example we got to root cause (longer burning) using three "why" questions. Many times it is not this simple. Notice, also, that the answer to the first why is stated in terms of a solution. We had to proceed further to find the need (or problem).

Needs, Features, Solutions, Etc.

It is important to understand the following terms described in the glossary in Chapter 1:

Need: Long term oriented; what a customer wants; future–oriented; lead to *tomorrow's* dominant product. Cannot always be recognized or described by the customer.

Want: Short term oriented; temporary or quick fix; something a person believes will fill a need; can quickly change with time.

Solutions: The answer to a customer problem or a need; may be short-term or long-term.

Feature: Physical fulfillment (solution) of a customer need or problem; generally short-term and lead to today's dominant product. This is a short-term solution to a long-term need.

Problem: Wants and needs expressed in negative terms.

When collecting and interpreting VOC, the above terms become very important because they will influence how you interpret what you have collected.

Customers generally cannot express their true needs because their thinking is short-term oriented and they are used to fighting fires. Customers live and react day-to-day. Consequently, customers like to talk in terms of features and solutions. The burden is on the interviewer, note taker, and interpreter to properly probe for information leading to hidden (longer-term) needs. Customers talk in features and solutions because they are trying to be helpful. They want to help you solve the problem. Remember, we, our company, are in the business of solution delivery.

Let us look at some examples of needs vs. feature/solutions for an attaché case.

Customer Needs	Features/Solutions
Easy to carry	Padded handle
Won't scuff	Has metal corner guards
Scratch resistant	Vinyl (not leather)
Secure contents	Combination locks
Large capacity when I need it	Expandable
Tamper proof	Alarm system

Customer needs are the "what's" of the function–features system. The features (solutions) represent the "hows." When asking a customer what he would like to have in an attaché case, he will usually answer with features. He is trying to solve some of his concerns by suggesting features. The customer should be the expert on needs, while the company should be the expert on solutions. Tony Ulwick[1] uses another analogy from the world of mathematics to describe this situation. The mathematical domain consists of constants and variables. Customer needs are akin to constants, and features and solutions are represented by variables. The two cannot be combined because doing so will not allow the equation to be properly solved and will produce sub-optimal results.

Product designers/developers must be able to detect the customer's true needs, often buried under customer responses in the form of technical solutions. Technical features and solutions represent the tip of the iceberg, whereas the needs reside underneath the water in the bottom of the iceberg.

What To Do With Things Like Regulations

The question of what to do with things like government regulations/standards, international standards, and other regulatory requirements arises quite often. These standards are more than customer wants. They are givens and absolutes, and cannot be overlooked. To always keep them visible, they can be added as a grouping in a separate row at the bottom of the list of customer functions and needs. The functional equivalent can be labeled as "satisfy regulations." There is no compromise with regulatory requirements. They are not brainstormed or tested, but they need to be satisfied.

Regulations are equivalent to musts. They are either satisfied or they aren't. To be sure, they may be considered needs to the customer but it is assumed that the manufacturer will comply with these musts. Sometimes these musts don't surface until we talk to the customer because there may be local codes or musts about which we are not aware.

Listen Carefully! Translating the VOC

One has to listen carefully when talking to the customer about what he wants in your product. This is also true when compiling survey comments. Many times customers will offer solutions to some of their unsolved problems. Sometimes they may even state their needs in terms of problems. Obviously these problems have been around for some time and our product has not eliminated them. The customer in many of the cases is aggravated and has decided to come up with his own solution to pass on to you because he figures you cannot solve his problem. Consequently we are given solutions disguised as needs!

In these cases, further, more penetrating questions must be asked to seek and clarify the real need. Questions can be asked for clarification such as:

1. What is the unmet need that this solution is satisfying?
2. What is the unsolved problem this solution is satisfying?
3. Why is this a problem?

Let me illustrate with an example. I purchased a minivan and a company representative is interviewing me about my experience and needs for the car:

QFD Interviewer: *What would you like to have in future minivans?*
Customer: *I want splash guards as standard equipment on my van!*
QFD Interviewer: *What is the need that this solution would satisfy?*
Customer: *Splash guards will prevent stone chipping and sand blasting behind the fender wells and rocker panels.*
QFD Interviewer: *Why is this a problem?*
Customer: *Chips in the paint in and around these areas can quickly turn to rust, especially here in my home town where we use lots of salt on the streets in the winter.*

What is the real customer need? Based on the above dialogue and appropriate questions from the interviewer, we can quickly see that the real need is to prevent rust around fender wells. Splash guards are just one of many ways to alleviate this occurrence but will not necessarily eliminate the problem. The customer, with an extra $20, decided to address the problem himself. We can also see that rusty fender wells would also make an excellent QFD project.

Now let's take another example. Let us assume we are in the business of designing and manufacturing printers. We are now interviewing the customer:

QFD Interviewer: *What would you like to have in a future printer?*
Customer: *I need a printer that will print at 750 dots-per-inch (dpi).*
QFD Interviewer: *Why do you need 750 dpi?*
Customer: *Because I do high-quality printing for very demanding customers like colleges and universities. Therefore, it is essential that I have very sharp edges on the fonts in the text. Our text and fonts must be as sharp and crisp as possible. I am having problems meeting these demands today.*

Now let us assume that the QFD interviewer did not probe further on this subject. Our research people back at the company know for a fact that 500 dpi will more than give the customer what he needs. If we incorporate the customer's recommendation (solution) of 750 dpi we will in fact over-design the printer. When we over-design, our manufacturing costs go up which, in turn, will drive up the selling price. Therefore, we must be careful of incorporating the customer's solution in product design.

Always remember this, the customer is the expert in the "what" and the producer or service provider is the expert in the "how"!

AT THE INTERVIEW

Be careful of your own interpretation of customer statements during customer dialogue. Always ask for further clarification when things are not clear. Ask the customer to give many examples. Follow up leads with responses like, "describe...", "give me examples of..." or "give me a war story...." Don't always assume you are interpreting customer responses correctly. We all have our filters and biases. Semantics and jargon many times lead interviewers astray. A classic goof for me was the customer mentioned that he would like to be able to purchase "shipping cartons" for our product. I erroneously interpreted this to mean he would like to buy extra cartons in which the product was originally packaged so he could use them to further ship product within his company locations. No! He was really suggesting a brand new product line for our company. That is we would build rubber-lined "tank proof" shipping containers and he would happily purchase them from us to transship his product. Fortunately the co-interviewer caught this misinterpretation.

Even clearly stated needs can be explored further with the right questions. The following questions would take a customer well beyond his original comments:

1. Why is this a benefit?
2. You want _____ so you can _____? Why?
3. Why do you want that?
4. What do you really want?

Such questions may uncover new hidden needs the customer didn't think about. Sometimes stated needs can be the object of unfulfilled fantasies.

Product developers must determine why the customer is asking for a technical solution. By asking the generic question, "what do you want in a _____?" you encourage the customer to answer in terms of technical solutions. The follow up question to such an answer is, "why do you want _____?" Unfortunately product designers are not used to or skilled in this kind of inquiry.

Glossary of Terms

It is best to record the features in the customer's own words when possible. If customer quotes are used, it is also recommended that a glossary of terms be established that includes precise translations of the features into terms that are more meaningful to the team and technical community. For example, regarding a television set, customers might say they "want a sharp image." This is important to know, but the technical community needs to know how sharp is sharp. The descriptor would be recorded in the glossary of terms along with a descriptive translation. The feature as translated in the glossary might read: "The image on the TV screen should have clear definition around the edges. Perception of sharpness may be influenced by contrast." The glossary is especially useful if there is turnover in team members or if there are ad–hoc members. It helps get members up to speed. Be careful in translation. It is important to be able to always track the team translation back to the original words of the customer.

A glossary of terms for customer verbatims is very helpful and can save the team a considerable amount of time over the life of the QFD team. Many hours of communication can be lost because team members had their own interpretation of a customer need. Building a glossary at the outset improves communication among team members. The dialogue that must take place to build the glossary is also an education process where team members learn things they never knew before. A good set of terms is needed both for the VOC as well as the product technical requirements in the HOQ.

Remember, the glossary is the team's interpretation of what they think the customer verbatim means. Sometimes this must be clarified with the customer.

VOICE OF THE CUSTOMER TABLE

Another useful tool to expand VOC is the Voice of the Customer Table (VOCT) developed by GOAL/QPC.[2] VOCT is a method to gain more in-depth understanding of needs by expanding current needs through the use of the "who, what, where, when, why, and how" questions. Expansion would not be performed on all of the VOC verbatims. Generally the most important ones are selected for further study. GOAL/QPC uses the VOCT before doing an affinity diagram and the HOQ. The VOCT is a tool to further explore customer needs into the future to derive more needs of the exciting quality variety. The VOCT can be used internally within the QFD team and may or may not be used directly with the customer.

A variation of the VOCT is shown in Figure 4.1. The customer's statements go into the first column exactly as heard. No editing is done. This will be our VOC audit trail later on. The second column is where the reworded verbatims are recorded. This is where compound statements are broken into single thoughts. For instance, in Figure 4.2 we see an example VOCT for a 3-hole punch. One verbatim is "easy to adjust locate

Voice of the Customer Table

Interviewee: _____
Interviewer(s): _____

Market Segment(s): _____
User(s): _____
Product: _____

Customer Verbatim	Re-worded Data	I/E	Need	Solution	Feature	Other ---->

Figure 4.1 Modified VOC table.

sheet and punch at the same time." This breaks into two separate verbatims, "easy to hold sheet in place with one hand" and "punch/paper won't move during down stroke with other hand." In order to track statements that may be used in other documents, we label them as internally or externally generated. Obviously the original verbatims are external and

Voice of the Customer Table

Customer Verbatim	Reworded Data	I/E	Need	Solution	Feature	Other →
1. Easy to insert paper	1. OK	E	X			
5. Easy to locate sheet and punch at same time		E	X			
	5a. Easy to hold sheet in place with one hand	I		X		
	5b. Punch/paper won't move during down stroke with other hand	I		X	X	
11. Takes less than 10 lbs. force to activate		E		X		
	11a. Easy to activate assy. Force TBD	I		X		

Voice of the Customer Table

Customer Verbatim	Reworded Data	I/E	Need	Solution	Feature	Other
12. Punch shaft should be stainless steel		E		X	X	
	12a. Punch shaft retains sharpness	I	X			
	12b. Shaft will not corrode	I	X			
13. Padded punch cover so won't hurt hand		E		X		
	13a. Too much force to activate punch; improve leverage	I			X	
	13b. Punch spring too stiff				X	
19. Holes will not fall out when handling and when unloading		E	X			

P. 2

Voice of the Customer Table

Customer Verbatim	Reworded Data	I/E	Need	Solution	Feature	Other →
	19a. Holes will not fall out when handling	I	X			
	19b. Holes will not fall out when emptying	I	X			

P. 3

any company/team interpretations are labeled internal. These are coded in column three. Next is the more difficult part, documenting whether or not the team judges the internal/external statements to be a real need, a solution or a feature. Checkmarks are placed in the proper column to signify the interpretation. The last column, "other" is used for non-need items like cost, specific technologies, regulations. Regulations are not needs they are givens, absolutes or musts. They are either satisfied or they aren't. Some excellent variations and enhancements to the VOCT can be found in Mazur[3] and Rings et al.[4]

KANO COLLECTION AND INTERPRETATION METHOD

Noriaki Kano of Tokyo University has developed another process to determine customer needs which he defines as "must be," "one-dimensional" and "exciting" quality. This method is described in detail in Appendix B. His method is used as a supplement to the current tools for interpreting VOC.

Shiba, et al.[5] have also put together a set of seven translation guidelines for converting verbatims into processed customer needs. They are

1. Avoid statements in a negative form. For example, "the punch will not jam when punching 15 sheets." This can be reworded to, "can punch multiple sheets."
2. Avoid two-valued concepts.
3. Avoid abstract words. For example, reliable, provides, minimum, maximum. These words are ambiguous and some connote goals. Use words specific to the product.
4. Avoid statements of solution. An example might be, "punch must be made from stainless steel." This may be translated as, "punch retains sharpness."
5. Avoid premature detail. Example, cassette is "3 inches by 4 inches." It is presumptuous to attach dimensions this early in the life cycle.
6. Avoid the auxiliary words should or must. Such words imply foregone conclusions. Instead use present tense verbs like "is" or "are."
7. Avoid intangible concepts. Example, "the shirt feels comfortable." This may mean the shirt is cool, the shirt lets the air flow through, the fit is good, the sleeves/armpits are comfortable, etc.

SUMMARY

Interpreting or processing VOC can be a delicate operation. It is too easy to misinterpret what the customer says. But, it is necessary to translate customer verbatims into the language of the company so they can be deployed into the product and the commercialization process.

There are various tools to assist in interpretation. Some can be used during the actual data collection such as the Sony "5 whys." That is, we can actually plan for our subsequent translation.

To best understand the translation it is necessary to recognize and understand the difference between a customer need or want, a solution, a feature, and a problem. Customers generally talk in terms of features whereas the company communicates in terms of solutions. Since features are short-term solutions to customers wants and needs, the VOC team must be able to penetrate the customer's unconscious to discover root cause. Customers also talk in compound statements which further complicates translation. A very useful processing tool to help in all of these concerns is the VOCT. It is used to condition customer data for later deployment into the commercialization process.

REFERENCES

1. Ulwick, T., "What Do Your Customers Value Most? Who Should Your Customers Be?," Keynote address, *Proc. 1st Pacific Rim Symp. on Qual. Deployment*, Macquarie University Graduate School of Management, Sydney, Australia, 1995, 258-261.
2. Marsh, S., Moran, J. W., Nakui, S., and Hoffherr, G., *Facilitating and Training in Quality Function Deployment*, GOAL/QPC, Methuen, MA, 1991.
3. Mazur, G., "Voice of the Customer Analysis: A Modern System of Front-End QFD Tools with Case Studies," *AQL*, American Society of Quality Control, Milwaukee, WI, 1997.
4. Rings, C. M., Barton, B. W., and Mazur, G. H., "Consumer Encounters of the Third Kind: Improving Idea Development and Concept Optimization," *Proc. 10th Symp. of Qual. Function Deployment*, Novi, MI, 1998, pp. 89-99.
5. Shiba, S., Graham, A., and Walden, D., *A New American TQM, Four Practical Revolutions In Management,* Productivity Press, Portland, OR, 1993.

5

STRUCTURING CUSTOMER DATA

DATA REDUCTION

Before structuring VOC it is necessary to reduce the huge amount of data that will be accumulated from the interviews. To begin, we have to get all of the customer verbatims extracted from interview recorder's notes and the tape recordings. This is where hard copy transcriptions, discussed in Chapter 3, are extremely useful. The extracted verbatims are typed on peel-off labels that are affixed to three–by–five index cards. The cards should be coded (discussed later) to represent team, customer type, interviewee function types, customer name, customer location, etc. Obviously, we now have a large number of index cards. To reduce the data (cards), we will use the the Multi Pickup Method (MPM).[1]

MPM is a methodology for narrowing down the number of cards (verbatims) to a manageable number. The principle for eliminating the number of cards is to focus on the importance of the verbatim in relation to the project/product purpose and theme.

The first step is to have a warm-up session by discussing the project/product purpose. The verbatim cards are all laid in an orderly fashion on a large table. The team members slowly walk around the table to read all of the verbatims to calibrate their thinking for later culling of cards.

Step two now involves unconstrained pickup where the team members dot those cards with a red felt-tip marker that they consider likely candidates for final consideration for carrying forward to the structuring process. The unconstrained pickup is repeated for several rounds. During each round the team members, using a different color for each round, continue to mark those cards that are considered important. At the end of each round unmarked statements are removed for consideration. At no time are any unmarked cards permanently discarded. What develops is a pile of culled cards that may or may not be brought back in for re-consideration. If this is the first time team members have done such a data reduction, there is natural anxiety about removing cards for consideration. All verbatims are important or they would not have been written in the first place. What we want the team to do is reduce the number of verbatims to those Pareto critical few from the trivial many.

During the third and final stage, focused pickup, the team members are given a limited number of choices, say five to ten depending on the number of cards remaining on the table, to designate the final candidates for structuring. The method is to use Pareto Voting discussed in the next chapter. This method involves giving each team member a limited number of yellow sticky dots to post to those cards they believe to be the most critical and final candidates. This process produces a Pareto distribution number of candidates to carry forward to the structuring process.

It is important to note that MPM is a value screening and data reduction process and should not be construed as a voting process where a majority can shut out a minority view.

STRUCTURING TOOLS

After translating VOC, it is necessary to structure it in order to see relationships among the verbatims as well as the hierarchy of importance across them. That is, having a random pile of perfectly translated customer verbatims will not do us much good unless we understand the interaction and relationship among them.

In keeping with my assumption, stated in the preface, that the reader is already familiar with QFD, I do not consider the following structuring tools as part of QFD. They are part of the VOC process which is the precursor and driver to start the QFD process, particularly the House of Quality (HOQ).

Why Structure?

We structure VOC verbatims so we can eventually plan and design products and services around the needs of the customer. An obstacle to planning is conventional wisdom and past success and failure. We often assume the past will shape the future. Continuous improvement demands that old logic patterns be circumvented and that new ones be explored. The structuring techniques allow people to react to issues from creative gut feel and intuition rather than from traditional logic approaches to creative response.

Candle User Needs (Random Generation)

Be Visually Attractive	Be Fragrant	Be Dripless
Have a Large Flame	Be Smokeless	Burn a Long Time

Figure 5.1 Candle user needs (random generation). (From Shillito, M. L., *Advanced QFD Linking Technology to Market and Company Needs,* John Wiley & Sons, New York, 1994. With permission.)

The structuring tools to be described allow us to see relationships and interconnections between the verbatims. These relationships can reveal patterns that elicit responses to the verbatims. Patterns and hierarchies can also help us economize and be more focused in our responses to the verbatims. That is, rather than respond to and try to satisfy 200 verbatims, we may be able to be just as effective by responding to the "Pareto vital few." The structuring tools and the later quantification methods (Chapter 6) can direct us to those critical elements that will lead us to better product and service design.

Affinity Diagram[2,4,5]

What is it? — A bottom-up clustering technique to group large amounts of language or qualitative data, such as VOC verbatims, based on the natural relationship or likeness between items.

Objective — To organize a large group of items into natural sets to look for relationships to elevate the individual items to a higher level of indenture for further observation and analysis.

Purpose — To develop a hierarchical structure of verbatims to allow for a more creative response with regard to meeting customer needs.

Instructions — (See Figure 5.1 and Appendix D.19)

1. Write each item (verbatim) on a sticky pad or index card (one item per card).
2. Display all sticky pads or cards on a table or wall.
3. In silence, the team arranges the cards into clusters that intuitively group together.
   ■ Some cards may fall in more than one cluster.

4. Edit the items.
   - Eliminate redundancy. Be careful, however, one item may fall in more than one category.
   - Look for compound statements that should be broken into single unique items.
   - Reduce overly verbose statements to as short a phrase as possible.
   - Be careful of generic or higher level items that may pertain to many items. These may be at too high a level of abstraction to be useful.
   - Be careful that clusters do not become too big, otherwise, you may go full circle with too few clusters.
5. Develop a title for each grouping
   - Look for a card in each grouping that best captures the essence of the group. Place this card at the top of the grouping. Highlight it with a red frame.
   - If no such card exists, create one using a simple concise statement.
6. Repeat steps (3) through (5) by sorting the groupings into clusters of groupings using the header or title card.
   - The process is repeated until there are three levels of groupings. Level 3, the initial set may contain 50 to 250 items; Level 2, the first sort may have 15 to 30 groupings and Level 1, the second sort, may have 8 to 12 groupings.
   - When using sticky pads, to sort groupings, stick all pads together under the header card and move the entire pack as one unit for sorting. When using cards, rubber bands or paper clips may be used for the same purposes.

Advantages

1. A fast effective way to bring order out of chaos.
2. A graphic way to see patterns and relationships.
3. The bottom-up clustering approach uses a "clean slate" approach to creatively observe and respond to customer verbatims by circumventing presumptions.
4. Working with the higher levels (primary or secondary) can help reduce the number of verbatims to work with or carry forward into deployment.

Disadvantages

1. The many cards and table and/or wall space that are sometimes needed.
2. Transcription time to reduce the diagram to notebook size format.

To illustrate the affinity diagram we will apply the process to the customer needs of a candle. Based on market surveys, interviews, and/or internal brainstorming, individual customer needs are generated by team members and written on cards (Figure 5.1). The number of items is considerably reduced for this example. Normally there may be 20 to 80 items. Cards are then rearranged by team members (Figure 5.2). For example, the team decided that "be visually attractive" and "be fragrant" were related to a general theme of aesthetics. In like manner, the other four customers needs were grouped. Note that the team did not develop categories first and then assign the items to the categories. It is more creative and more information-rich to cluster items first and then assign a heading to the cluster. This is usually done by taking a verbatim label from the cluster that best represents all items in the groupings. The affinity diagram forces organization, fosters a general level of understanding, and surfaces hidden relationships.

Another tool, the *Interrelationship Diagraph* (ID) is also useful to depict the interrelationship between the clusters.

Affinity Diagram Of Customer Needs

Aesthetics	Lighting
• Be visually attractive • Be fragrant	• Have a large flame

Convenience	Efficiency
• Be smokeless • Be dripless	• Burn a long time

Figure 5.2 Affinity diagram of customer verbatims. (From Shillito, M. L., *Advanced QFD Linking Technology to Market and Company Needs*, John Wiley & Sons, New York, 1994. With permission.)

Tree Diagram of Customer Verbatims

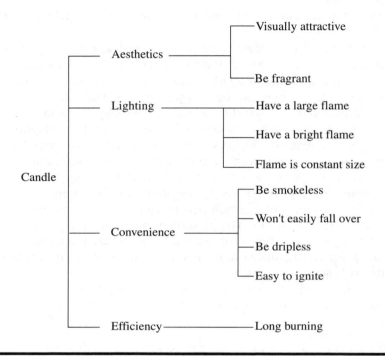

Figure 5.3 Tree diagram of customer verbatims. (From Shillito, M. L., *Advanced QFD Linking Technology to Market and Company Needs*, John Wiley & Sons, New York, 1994. With permission.)

Interrelationship Digraph[4,5]

What is it? — A digraph that maps out the logical or sequential links among related items.

Objective — A companion process to the Affinity Diagram to trace logic patterns through the clusters.

Purpose — To draw the logical connections between the groupings of the Affinity Diagram. The Affinity Diagram allows initial creative patterns to emerge but the ID lets logical patterns to become apparent.

Instructions — (See Figure 5.4 and Appendix D.20)

1. Beginning at the primary or secondary level of the Affinity Diagram, draw causal arrows that indicate what leads to what. That is, connect the header labels.

2. Observe and analyze the connections
   - Look for those header cards that have many arrows emanating from the label. This signifies that that label is a key factor or influencer.
   - Look for labels that have many arrows coming into it. This item obviously is heavily influenced by many external factors. It may also indicate a bottleneck, or, in the positive sense, an opportunity.
3. The key connection question to ask is, "Does this item cause something else to happen?"

Advantages

1. Shows connections between items to reveal causes and effects.
2. Allows for multi-dimensional thinking.
3. It is both logical and creative.
4. A companion to the Affinity Diagram to look for logical linkages.

For example, in Figure 5.4 we see that efficiency (burn rate) can have some affect on convenience. Convenience, in turn, may have a constraining affect on lighting. Lighting (flame size) contributes to aesthetics. We see a sort of system where altering one attribute may have a positive or negative affect on others. These are commonly known as tradeoffs. It may not be possible for a cradle to have a large flame and be dripless and smokeless.

The clusters of items from the Affinity Diagram can then be arranged horizontally into a second tool called a Tree Diagram (Figure 5.3). That is, the Affinity Diagram, which is based on intuition and gut feeling, is used to construct a Tree Diagram based more on logic and analytical skills.

Tree Diagram[3,4,5]

What is it? — A logic based, top-down hierarchical branching tool to structure language data into sequential dendritic logic paths.

Objective — To organize a large group of items into a logic flow based on stimulus and response.

Purpose — To provide a check on the Affinity Diagram. A companion process to the Affinity Diagram to enhance the completeness of the VOC database and structure.

Instructions (See Figure 5.3, D.19)

1. Start with the elements (sticky pad) and structure from the Affinity Diagram.

Interrelationship Diagraph

Aesthetics	Lighting
• Be visually attractive • Be fragrant	• Have a large flame

Convenience	Efficiency
• Be smokeless • Be dripless	• Burn a long time

Figure 5.4 Interrelationship digraph.

- Start at the most abstract level, for example, the primary level of the Affinity Diagram.
2. Analyze the elements at that level for completeness and correctness. Further analyze by branching to the secondary level.

    If incomplete, brainstorm, or develop the missing pieces. Affinity Diagrams are not always complete because the customer may respond in a stream-of-consciousness manner or our VOC collection techniques resulted in gaps in information.
    - The basic expansion questions are:
        - "What needs to be addressed in order to _____?"
        - "What needs to happen or exist if _____ is going to occur?"
        - These questions are used to expand each item for completeness.
3. Continue to expand to the third level, again, looking for completeness.

Advantages

1. Where the Affinity Diagram is a convergent process built from the bottom-up, the Tree Diagram is a divergent process built from the top down and is used to check the completeness of the Affinity Diagram and expand the VOC structure.
2. New branches and groupings are discovered.
3. The tree provides the structure for the rows of the HOQ.

4. The tree can be used to reduce the member of verbatims to work with or carry forward to the HOQ. That is, if the third level is too detailed, one can work at the secondary level.
5. One can trace various paths through the tree from level one to level three. Each path can be used as a creativity process to brainstorm responses to the path.
6. It provides a double check on the Affinity Diagram.

Disadvantages

1. Too many teams do not want to use the tree. For example, in our Tree Diagram in Figure 5.3 we discover two additional elements, "have a bright flame" and "flame is constant size," that are missing on the Affinity Diagram (Figure 5.2). These evolved by expanding the element "lighting." Likewise, "convenience" was expanded, and "won't easily fall over" and "easy to ignite" surfaced. The Tree Diagram, then, helped us increase the completeness of the Affinity Diagram through the use of logic. These newly found elements did not surface in the original contextual interviewing.

Another useful structuring tool is a *function tree* as seen in Figure 1.1 and 1.2 and discussed in Chapter 3 (Figure 3.7 and 3.8). As you recall, the customer interacts with our product through a set of product functions. A customer does not buy a product, he purchases the functions that our product performs. Related to each function is a set of customer needs which are satisfied by product features. The function tree may be used to check on the completeness of the VOC as well as the structure and completeness of the Affinity Diagram and Tree Diagram. The function tree begins with the customer task and progresses from the top down similar to the tree diagram above and was discussed in Chapter 3.

SUMMARY

Data structuring is necessary in order to understand the verbatims and their relationship to each other as well as the system. We cannot randomly deploy customer needs into the product and commercialization process for the same reason we cannot effectively and efficiently drive on a vacation from point A to point B unless we have a map with route numbers, scale, and distance. The structuring tools provide the map and routes. Scale and distance are provided by quantification (value measurement) tools discussed in the next chapter.

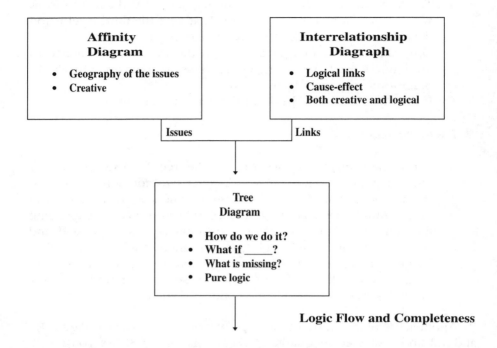

Figure 5.5 Structuring system.

The qualitative tools show connections. The Affinity Diagram is an intuitive process based on gut feel. This, in turn, increases the chances of discovering unexpected relationships which can foster breakthrough thinking. The Tree Diagram coupled with the Affinity Diagram brings completeness to VOC data. However, caution must be exercised when using the Tree Diagram in respect to the original customer verbatims. It can be easy for a team to brainstorm new customer needs that sound good but may not really exist.

How do the structuring tools work together? (See Figure 5.5) The Affinity Diagram is a purely creative process to map the geography of the issues. The ID is used after the Affinity Diagram to map the logical links and the cause–and–effect relationships. It is both creative and logic–based. Once focus is obtained using the Affinity Diagram and the ID, the Tree Diagram is used to expand the issues for completeness using pure logic in a "How to do it" mode. All of the tools should be used in combination. They are used to map VOC and to increase the possibility of our ability to garner a more creative response to customer needs through better product design.

Not all of the structuring tools have to be used all of the time. The team should choose the combination of tools that works best for them and brings focus and attention on the right elements to carry forward to deployment.

BIBLIOGRAPHY

Bossert, J., *QFD: A Practitioner's Approach*, Quality Press, Milwaukee, WI, 1992.

Cohen, L., *Quality Function Deployment: How To Make QFD Work For You*, Addison-Wesley Publishing Company, Reading, MA, 1995.

Marsh, S., Moran, J. W., Nakui, S., and Hoffherr, G., *Facilitating and Training in Quality Function Deployment*, GOAL/QPC, Methuen, MA, 1991.

Shiba, S., Graham, A., and Walden, D., *A New American TQM, Four Practical Revolutions In Management*, Productivity Press, Portland, OR, 1993.

REFERENCES

1. Shiba, S., Graham, A., and Walden, D. M., *A New American TQM. Four Practical Revolutions in Management*, Productivity Press, Portland, OR, 1993.
2. *The Language Processing Method*, Document ML0060, Center for Quality Management, Cambridge, MA, 02140, 1995.
3. *Tree Diagrams*, Document ML0070, Center for Quality Management, Cambridge, MA, 1995.
4. King, B., *Better Designs in Half the Time*, GOAL/QPC, Methuen, MA, 1987.
5. Mizuno, S., *Management For Quality Improvement: The Seven New QC Tools*, Productivity Press, Cambridge, MA, 1988.

6

QUANTIFYING STRUCTURED
VOC (VALUE MEASUREMENT
TECHNIQUES)

QUANTIFY CUSTOMER NEEDS FOR IMPORTANCE

It is now necessary to determine how important each feature is to the customer. After all of the processed features for all functions are listed, they are quantified for perceived importance to the customer. This chapter is not a treatise on measurement, scaling, or psycho-physics. It is a description of value measurement techniques that have been successfully used in many and varied applications. It is a "how to" document based on experience. I do not present the mathematical or statistical foundation for the techniques described. The mathematical and psycho-physical basis for these techniques should be obtained from the references provided as appropriate. The chapter is a learning guide for quick access to needed measurement techniques for quantifying customer verbatims. A variety of value measurement and value screening techniques are described. Obviously, some techniques lend themselves better to certain situations than others.

The techniques have been divided into two sections, value measurement and value screening techniques. Value measurement techniques are used to evaluate items or attributes of items where a numerical measure is needed to indicate the relative strength of a respondent's perception of the item(s). For example, the importance of a customer verbatim.

On the other hand, value screening techniques are more qualitatively oriented and are generally used to reduce a large list of items to manageable size. They are not necessarily used to quantify the attributes of items where numbers and scales indicate some measure of importance.

Value screening techniques are generally used to reduce a large list of items so that further attention and analysis can be focused on the vital few rather than the trivial many. The more discriminating value measurement techniques are generally applied to those items that survive the value screening process.

Numbers, as they are used in the value measurement and screening techniques discussed in this chapter, are used as a numerical language to aid communication. The numbers themselves will not provide a decision. They will, however, enhance communications which will allow groups and individuals to make more informed decisions. People can debate numbers and the reasoning behind their choice. The debates encourage multiple viewpoints among participants to challenge the reasoning needed for decisions.

The techniques may be used for measurement in general and are not limited to customer verbatims.

VALUE MEASUREMENT TECHNIQUES

Simple Ranking

Description

This is one of the most common methods of determining the relative merit of a series of items. Once the items are ranked, numerical values can be assigned.

Method

Rank a list of items, 1st, 2nd, 3rd, etc. in order of importance. Reverse numbering can also be used where the highest number equals the best so that reverse ranks can also be used as scores.

Advantages

1. Simple, easy, intuitively appealing.
2. Allows one to put a number on things.
3. Process is fast and draws out information from a group.
4. Process also draws out differences of opinion. It makes differences of opinion visible; one can then re-rank after group/team discussion of those differences, if so desired.
5. Participants don't need knowledge of math or detailed instructions on how to use it.
6. Can be used without a group leader.

Disadvantages

1. The process assumes linearity. It is easy to pick out the "extremes" (low and high ranks) but there is much noise in the middle of the distribution of items.
2. Linearity also gives no real picture of "spread" or separation between judgments of different items. The interval or distance between ranks is constant. This uniformity of equidistance between ranks distorts reality. There is no way to determine how much more, or less important one item is from another along the continuum of attributes being ranked. No one really knows whether a scale has been established.
3. Participants become impatient and rush the process. The easiest way to get started is to identify the most important and least important items and then distribute the remaining items between these extremes.

Discussion — General

1. The technique is okay if one doesn't need ultimate accuracy or spread of the relative magnitude difference between items. It does have error.
2. The process should be used with less than 15 items, otherwise, the process becomes exhausting and more noise develops "in the middle" of the distribution of ranks.

Alternative Ranking

Description

Alternative ranking is a method for developing a list of factors of any kind, weighted to indicate relative importance. It can be used with groups of most any size, but six to nine people seems to be preferable. Larger groups can be used by dividing them into groups of this size.

Method

1. The facilitator asks each person to write the items to be ranked on 3x5 cards. The cards are then placed face up in front of the participant.
2. The facilitator asks, "If you had to throw away (n-1) of the items, which one would you keep?" (n being the number of items being

considered). The participant marks this card with the number n, and removes it from the rest and places it aside.

3. For the remaining items, the question asked is, "If you could only keep (n-2) of these items, which one would you throw away?" The participants are then asked to mark this card with a 1 and remove it from the rest. The questioning process is repeated, changing the numbers to reflect the number of cards that remain, until all cards are placed aside. As an example, assume there are 5 items to rank. First question is: "If you had to throw away four of the items, which one would you keep?" Label this card "5" and set it aside. Next question: Of the four remaining items, if you had to throw one away, which one would it be? Label the card "1" and set it aside. Next question, "Of the remaining three items, if you had to throw two items away, which one would you keep?" Label this card 4 and set it aside. "Of the remaining two items, if you had to throw one away which one would it be?" Mark this card "2" and set it aside. The remaining card mark "3."

4. A tally is taken by asking each member to read off the number they have written for each item. The rank numbers are summed for each item, providing a total rank vote. The votes are discussed and, if necessary, the process is repeated until the vote reflects the true opinions of the majority of the group.

Advantages/Disadvantages

1. This method is quick and simple to use. It is an easy way of discriminating between a relatively large number of items.
2. The process needs a "leader" to lead the group through the process, as compared to regular ranking where people can be left alone to do it.
3. The process is good for establishing anchor points, that is, tails of the distribution.
4. It is easier to work through all the "noise" in the center of a group of items. The zigzag approach forces a decision.
5. This process discriminates more easily between a larger group of items than regular ranking.
6. In addition to the rank total for each item, one also has the distribution of ranks for each item. This shows the spread of opinion across the group.

Pair Comparison

Description

Pair comparison is a highly discriminatory rating-ranking technique used to set a priority order and a relative magnitude to a number of related items. The method presents items to be judged in all possible pairs and then asks for judgment about each pair. A scale is created as each item is weighted against every other item and a relative zero point results. The list of items will be ranked in order of merit. Pair comparison provides a method of more accurately setting a priority order and relative magnitude of a number of related factors than arbitrary ranking. The process can be used to rate both positive criteria, like importance, quality, reliability, etc., and negative criteria like cost, maintenance, downtime, etc.

Method

1. Generate a list of the items to be ranked and establish a framework for the comparisons to be made.
2. Prepare a matrix or graph to accommodate all of the entries being considered. Items to be evaluated are arrayed against themselves in a triangular matrix (Figure 6.1).

Technique 1 — Regular Pair Comparison

1. Compare items in pairs working across the rows until each item has been compared with every other item. The rater must decide for each pair which item is more important (assuming importance is being rated). The code letter of the more important item is entered in the appropriate matrix cell representing the intersection of the two items.
2. Total the responses for each row. The item with the highest total frequency represents the concern with the overall greatest importance and so forth.

Technique 2 — Scaled Pair Comparison

1. Design a set of preference weightings to reflect different degrees of importance.
2. Compare items in pairs until each item is compared with all other items. In each comparison, the rater must decide which of the two items is more important. The appropriate letter signifying the more

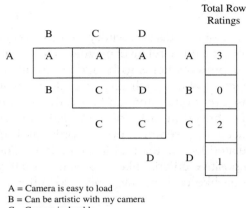

A = Camera is easy to load
B = Can be artistic with my camera
C = Camera is durable
D = Can tell all adjustments are correct

Figure 6.1 Regular pair comparison.

important items is recorded in the cell representing the intersection of the two items. In addition, a numerical weight chosen from the rating scale is also entered along with the letter. See Figure 6.2.

3. Total the numerical scores for each concern. The item with the highest total score represents the concern with the overall greatest importance.

To express each component as a percentage of importance of all of the items, sum the totals for each component row and divide this sum into each individual component score. An average value of component importance for a group of raters is obtained by averaging the value of all of the individual component ratings.

In Figure 6.2, as well as Figure 6.1, a zero occurs for item "B." Many times people and computers have difficulty working with zero. This can easily be eliminated by adding 1 to each row total score for each item and summing the new totals. Likewise, a new percent importance is calculated based on these new totals. This conversion could also have been used in Figure 6.1.

Usage

1. The process is useful in those applications where a high degree of subjectivity is present but where a need for one-to-one pair-wise comparison is essential.

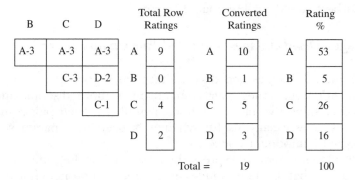

B	C	D		Total Row Ratings		Converted Ratings		Rating %
A-3	A-3	A-3	A	9	A	10	A	53
	C-3	D-2	B	0	B	1	B	5
		C-1	C	4	C	5	C	26
			D	2	D	3	D	16
					Total =	19		100

Preference Ratings
1 - Slightly more important
2 - Reasonably more important
3 - Much more important

A = Camera is easy to load
B = Can be artistic with my camera
C = Camera is durable
D = Can tell all adjustments are correct

Figure 6.2 Scaled pair comparison.

2. It is useful for prioritizing items that are extremely close in importance and therefore difficult to separate and rank.
3. A zero score should not be included in the rating scale. It makes it too easy to avoid making a decision and cheat to get the process finished faster.

Advantages — Regular Pair Comparison

1. Highly discriminating prioritizing technique.
2. Forces the participant to make a choice — there can be no ties.
3. Very thorough and methodical.
4. Forces pair-wise evaluation between every combination of pairs of items to be evaluated.
5. Popular among those people who like a methodical approach.

Disadvantages — Regular Pair Comparison

1. Very time consuming, especially if there are eight or more items to evaluate. For example, with 8 items there are 28 comparisons; with 12 items, there are 66 comparisons and with 36 items there are 360 comparisons! The formula to calculate the number of combinations is

$$C = \frac{n(n-1)}{2}, \text{ where } n \text{ equals the number of items evaluated.}$$

2. Due to the number of comparisons and time consumption, its use is best suited for less than 10 items.

Advantages/Disadvantages — Scaled Pair Comparison

1. Same advantages and disadvantages as regular pair comparison.
2. In addition, scaled pair comparison is more discriminating than other subjective rating methods including regular pair comparison. This is especially useful when it is used to separate seemingly equally important concerns.
3. It allows voters to express their "spread" in importance between pairs. That is, how much more important one choice is over another. Overall, there is a better indication of the magnitude difference between items. This can be seen by comparing the row totals of Figure 6.2 with Figure 6.1. Weighting factors or scales tend to amplify the extremes of the selections and, unfortunately again, leaves some noise in the middle of the distribution of scores. However, using the scale to express the magnitude of the difference between items is more discriminatory even though much of the information is contained in the initial choice.
4. Scaled pair comparison is more time consuming than regular pair comparison.
5. Total scores, as seen in both examples, can be normalized. These percent scores can then be used as weighting factors in other measurement techniques like criteria analysis discussed later.

Direct Magnitude Estimation

Description

Direct Magnitude Estimation (DME) is a method that enables participants to assign numerical indicators as a function of relative merit to a list of proposed items, usually generated from previous discussions. The objective is to obtain ratings from a group. The ratings are then averaged and normalized.

Method

1. Each person randomly assigns any positive number to the first item in a list.
2. A number is assigned to each succeeding item in proportion to the number given the item proceeding it.
3. Calculate the geometric mean:

Where:

$$\text{GM Item } 1 = n\sqrt{R_1 \text{ Item } 1 * \ldots R_2 \text{ Item } 1 * \ldots R_n \text{ Item } 1} \qquad (6.1)$$

R_1 Item 1 is the rating given to Item 1 by the first person.
R_2 Item 1 is the rating given to Item 1 by the second person.
R_n Item 1 is the rating given to Item 1 by the last person.

4. Normalize the geometric means so that their total adds to 100%.

Where:

$$\text{GM\% Item } 1 = \frac{\text{GM Item } 1 * 100}{\text{GM Item } 1 + \text{GM Item } 2 + \ldots \text{GM Item } M} \qquad (6.2)$$

M = the number of items rated.

5. Steps 3 and 4 are best done by a computer.

Advantages

1. DME can be applied to any list of items requiring individual attention by a group.
2. It establishes group preference.
3. Can be used to graphically illustrate group consensus and dissension.
4. Simple and easy to use.
5. Excellent way to show the magnitude of difference between items.
6. Effective way to quantify the intangible positive and negative aspects of something.
7. Effective vehicle for dialogue; good communications device.
8. Can be used with any number of items; preferably less than 30.
9. DME provides a simple way to quantify importance.
10. DME leads to rapid definition of poor value areas.

Disadvantages

1. The necessary calculations can be cumbersome without a computer.

2. Requires a computer computation program to compute geometric means.
3. Waiting for computer output delays feedback unless an on-line or interactive program is used.
4. The open-ended (psycho-physical) scaling process tends to confuse people at the outset. Some people have difficulty with all the freedom of expression.

Discussion

1. How does one compare ratings between different people if each person uses a different scale? Normalize all ratings to a % (percentage sign). With DME, every participant can use his own number scale. In order to compare ratings between different participants, it is necessary to normalize each participant's ratings to a percentage and compare the normalized ratings.
2. Psycho-physics shows that people think in ratios which implies a log-normal scale. Therefore, a geometric mean is used as opposed to an arithmetic mean.
3. The geometric mean also minimizes the effect of extreme ratings, which, if using an arithmetic mean would considerably skew the results.
4. Randomization. If computer generated rating sheets are used, the items can be listed in random order. This may be necessary to minimize order effects or dependencies or subsets. Interaction of items, however, is most prevalent in a list generated by a brainstorming session where there is considerable hitch-hiking of ideas.

Category Scaling

Description

Where DME uses an open-ended scale to allow people to assign numbers to express their perception of merit of ideas or other items, category scaling employs a closed, finite scale with category descriptors.

Background

With DME, each rater uses his own scale which means that each person has their own reference set. Consequently, consistency in rating and perception across raters is weakened and is not fully compensated by normalizing a respondent's ratings. Having everyone use the same close-ended category scale (developed by the group) alleviates this inconsistency by providing a common reference set.

Method

1. Each person assigns numbers to items using a group-derived category scale with rating descriptors to represent their perception of the importance of the item.
2. Calculate the arithmetic means across all raters for each item rated.
   - In this case, an arithmetic mean is used because a close-ended scale with boundaries (e.g., 1 to 100) is used. Intervals between scales are preset and are presumed to be equal and linear.
3. Arithmetic averages can then be normalized across items to derive percent merit on a relative basis.

Advantages

1. Category scaling has the same advantages as DME.
2. Category scaling has more advantages than DME:
   - It is easier and less confusing to use than an open-ended scale. It requires less explanation.
   - Category descriptors are more meaningful.
   - A category scale is more convenient.
   - A category scale promotes greater consistency among raters in terms of their interpretation, perception and quantification. Everyone uses the same reference set.

Discussion — Scaling

If a scale is used, descriptors should be written by the team for at least three or four anchor points in the scale (e.g., 1, 5, 10). The descriptors should be stated in the words of the customer as best as possible. Such a rating scale might be as follows:

Rating		Descriptor
Scale1	Scale2	
10	5	I must have this _____. I expect it and would definitely switch brands and pay more to get it.
8		I would like to have it: all else being equal, I would probably change brands or pay more to get it.
5	3	It would be nice to have; it would make me happy, but I wouldn't go out of my way to get it. I might switch brands to get it but would not pay more to get it.

1   1   I am apathetic about this _____; it really doesn't influence my buying decision.

Descriptors written by the team members are used in order to promote consistency across raters. For example, without scale descriptors, what one person rates an 8, another person may rate a 10, and so on. Developing the descriptors encourages a dialogue among team members that results not only in more consistent ratings, but a sharing of viewpoints that might not otherwise have surfaced. In turn, this dialogue leads to better understanding. Caution must be observed, because there is a tendency when establishing rating descriptors to state them more in marketing terms like "must have this in the product to have a superior competitive advantage." This is a producer-oriented phrase. The actual user of the product probably does not care whether or not the company's product has a competitive advantage to the producer. The user is concerned about his own competitive advantage. Rating scale descriptors must be tailor-made by the team for each project/product. There is *no* universal rating scale!

The actual rating should be discussed verbally as a group. Numerical flash cards or an electronic voting system can be used to get discussion started. The full-scale range of rating numbers (1,2,3,4,…,10) is used for rating. It is advisable to have a team recorder/secretary record pertinent comments resulting from team discussions that lead to the final team rating. For example, it is not uncommon to have a bimodal or even a rectangular distribution of ratings. When this happens, the facilitator asks those who had high ratings to share their viewpoints leading to their ratings. Likewise, those who had low scores share their views. After the ratings discussion, the team is usually asked to vote again. The discussions and feedback generally lead to a convergence of votes in the second round. There is considerable information generated during these rating discussions that can be valuable later on. Such notes document the rationale behind a rating. This is especially important months after the team sessions when memories begin to fade.

What happens if the study team wants to list more than one customer for determining importance of customer verbatims? Will all customers have the same verbatims? Will each customer have his own measure of importance for each verbatim? Our experience shows that the labels on the customer verbatims generally do not change across customers. What does change across customers is the importance of those verbatims. One way to capture all of this is to have an importance column for each customer. A separate importance rating would be given to each. In addition, weighting factors could be assigned to each customer according to their importance, volume of business, and so on. To do this, 100 points would be allocated across the customers instead of using a rating scale. The weighting factors would then be multiplied with the importance ratings. The products would be summed for each customer verbatims row. The final sum of products would then represent an overall weighted importance across all customer columns. It is then possible to interpret the customer matrix to better understand the weighted importance scores. Caution is advised if you include a large number of customers, say more than 10. Including every possible customer can dilute the overall weighted importance score so that it can be almost meaningless.

It is obvious that marketing, customer representatives, or service and repair people should participate in rating the verbatims for importance. The ideal state for determining customer importance would be to interview real customers or have them participate in the team exercise. This could prove difficult depending upon confidentiality and product disclosure.

Having the right people participate in this exercise will also enhance the credibility of the project. Another advantage resulting from customer feature identification and quantification is that gaps or missing information readily surface. If answers are missing, question marks are inserted, and the topic is addressed later. The gaps in information can be very useful input for designing surveys or focus groups to obtain the needed information. Therefore, identified missing information can be just as useful and important as known information. Information gaps that surface highlight the fact "we didn't know the information was missing."

Nested Hierarchy Process (NHP)[1]

Discussion

Experience in some cases shows that when rating customer features for importance the team discovers that the features are not at the same level for analysis. There is a hierarchy of importance. This happens when functions or components differ in their level of indenture or when some features cluster as subsets under another feature. Consider an automobile, for example. A feature such as "withstand force" most likely would get a high rating, say a 10, regardless of the function or component to which it pertains. However, a score of 10 for the feature pertaining to the bumper or seat-belt system is considerably different than a score of 10 for the same feature pertaining to the arm rest on the door. When this situation occurs, and it often does, the analytical hierarchy method,[1] also known as the *nested hierarchy process*, of scoring should be used to mathematically convert all feature importance ratings to the same equivalent level of indenture. This produces a tree-like hierarchy whose number of levels of features may vary from two to four, similar to an Affinity Tree discussed in Chapter 5.

(Level 1)		(Level 2)		Weighted Importance Score			
Score	%	Score	%	%L1		%L2	x100
		10	50	0.32	x	0.50 =	16.0
8	32	5	25	0.32	x	0.25 =	8.0
		5	25	0.32	x	0.25 =	8.0
		Sum 20	Sum 100				
		8	80	0.40	x	0.80 =	32.0
10	40						
		2	20	0.40	x	0.20 =	8.0
		Sum 10	Sum 100				
2	8	Sum 8	Sum 100	0.08	x	1.00 =	8.0
		5	18	0.20	x	0.18 =	3.6
5	20	5	18	0.20	x	0.18 =	3.6
		10	36	0.20	x	0.36 =	7.2
		8	29	0.20	x	0.29 =	5.8
Sum 25	Sum 100	Sum 28	Sum 100				

Figure 6.3 Nested hierarchy of feature importance ratings (two-level tree). (From Shillito, M. L., *Advanced QFD Linking Technology to Market and Company Needs,* John Wiley & Sons, New York, 1994. With permission.)

Figure 6.3 has two levels from an Affinity Tree. It may happen that the first–level verbatims vary in their relative importance. All of these verbatims are important. However, some of the verbatims, relative to one another, are more important than others. When this happens, the second–level items relating to the more important first–level items also take on a more important significance than those second–level items belonging to the lesser important first–level items. So, even though some items may have the same second level rating, they may not in actuality be of equal final importance. The final importance rating is dependently factored by the relative importance of the higher level verbatim to which it pertains.

Method

The following procedure (a two-level tree) is used to rate and stratify two levels of verbatims (see Figure 6.3).

1. Rate the highest level verbatims for relative importance using a rating scale established by the team, as discussed earlier.
2. Normalize these ratings so that the normalized ratings total 100. To do this, sum up the individual rating scores from Step 1 and divide this sum total into each individual verbatim rating. The result is original rating scores converted to a percentage that sums to unity.
3. Repeat Step 1 by rating the second level point scores within each first level verbatim.
4. Normalize the second–level point scores within each first level verbatim such that the normalized second-level ratings total 100 for each first level item.
5. To obtain the final feature importance score, multiply the normalized second–level scores within that first level verbatim by the corresponding normalized first–level cluster score. The resulting product is the weighted score for each verbatim. By weighting the individual normalized second–level score by the normalized first–level score, we have now brought the final second–level scores to the same level of comparison. Figure 6.3 illustrates the two-level nested hierarchy computation. The final scores are multiplied by 100 to make the final numbers more convenient.

Sometimes situations require a three- or four-level tree. This usually happens when some features are subsets of other features. A three-level tree involves the following steps (see Figure 6.4):

1. Rate and normalize Level 1 items.
2. Rate and normalize Level 2 items.
3. Rate and normalize Level 3 items.
4. Compute the final Level 3 importance score by multiplying the normalized score for Level 1 by the normalized feature score for Level 2, times the normalized score for Level 3. The final products of the three normalized scores is the final importance score calibrated to the equivalent level for analysis. Figure 6.4 depicts a three-level nested hierarchy tree. Likewise, as with the two-level tree, the final factored items (verbatims) importance scores are posted to the House of Quality or COPC matrix in place of the original non-factored scores. In both cases, the hierarchy trees and calculations are retained for reference in case questions arise concerning their derivation. Figure D.23 depicts yet another NHP application for a 3-Hole Punch.

(Level 1)		(Level 2)		(Level 3)		Weighted Importance Score
Score	%	Score	%	Score	%	%L1 x %L2 x %L3 = 100
				10	40	0.32 x 0.50 x 0.40 = 6.4
		10	50	10	40	0.32 x 0.50 x 0.40 = 6.4
				5	20	0.32 x 0.50 x 0.20 = 3.2
				Sum 25	100	
				9	60	0.32 x 0.25 x 0.60 = 4.8
8	32	5	25	6	40	0.32 x 0.25 x 0.40 = 3.2
				Sum 15	100	
				10	59	0.32 x 0.25 x 0.59 = 4.7
		5	25	2	12	0.32 x 0.25 x 0.12 = 1.0
				5	29	0.32 x 0.25 x 0.29 = 2.3
		Sum 20	Sum 100	Sum 17	Sum 100	
				9	60	0.40 x 0.80 x 0.60 = 19.2
		8	80			
10	40			6	40	0.40 x 0.80 x 0.40 = 12.8
				Sum 15	100	
		2	20	10	100	0.40 x 0.20 x 1.00 = 8.0
		Sum 10	Sum 100	Sum 10	Sum 100	
2	8	(...)		(...)		(...)
5	20	(...)		(...)		(...)
Sum 25	Sum 100					

Figure 6.4 Nested hierarchy of feature importance ratings (three-level tree). (From Shillito, M. L., *Advanced QFD Linking Technology to Market and Company Needs*, John Wiley & Sons, New York, 1994. With permission.)

Scoring Models

Description

Scoring models are similar to category scaling. The difference is that a performance measurement scale is established for each criteria. Alternatives are scored against the established performance measurement scale instead of the category scale as discussed under Category Scaling.

Method

1. List the criteria. Criteria may be selected VOC verbatims. For scoring models the criteria descriptors should not contain measurement words. These will be provided in the performance measurement scale.

2. For each criterion construct a semantic differential scale (See Figure 2.8 and D.25).
   - A unique scale is developed for each individual criterion based upon its characteristics.
   - A "1 to 5" scale is often used.
   - A scale descriptor is established for each measurement unit and may be based on objective or subjective data. The purpose of the scale descriptor is to convert each measurement space into comparable units to permit comparison across equivalent criterion scale descriptors.
   - In all cases "5" is "good" and "1" is "poor."
   - It is necessary that the same number of categories be specified for each criterion and that the same numerical scale (i.e., 1-5) be utilized.
3. Evaluate each alternative against the criteria. This is done by reading the 1-5 scale and selecting the performance measurement scale descriptor that best fits the characteristics of the alternative.

Advantages

Because ratings are calibrated across the criteria, ratings on one criteria are equivalent to ratings on all the others. Thus a score of "2" on one criterion is equal to a score of "2" on another.

Discussion

1. One underlying assumption is that there are relatively few criteria needed to discriminate across alternatives.
2. The Product Profile discussed in Chapter 2 (Figure 2.8) is an example application of a scoring model and a scoring model performance measuring scale.

Constant Sum

Description

Constant sum is the allocation of weights to a set of items such that their sum equals unity or 100. Weights may be changed but the sum must always equal 100.

Method

1. Provide the list of items to be evaluated.
2. Discuss items (verbatims) for clarification. Use or develop a glossary if necessary.

3. Instruct everyone to individually allocate 100 points across the list of items such that the distribution of points always totals 100.
4. On a chart pad, tally everyone's ratings and discuss the distribution of individual ratings for each item related. Individuals may change ratings based on the discussion.
5. Take the average across all individual ratings for each item.
6. Discuss the final distribution across all items. Adjust if necessary.

Advantages / Disadvantages

1. Constant sum is a more accurate method to determine the relative importance of each item relative to all others because the individual or the team must consider the tradeoffs and interrelationships when distributing the points. The individuals have only a finite amount of importance to allocate, so what is awarded to one item must be taken away from another and so on.
2. The process can be cumbersome and the numbers may become too small if there are more than 10 items. The process should be restricted to less than 15 items.
3. The process may also be done verbally as a team as opposed to silently by individual. This can promote more interaction and discussion, but takes longer to do.

VALUE SCREENING TECHNIQUES

Pareto Voting

Description

Pareto voting is a formalized, preliminary screening to reduce a list of alternatives to a more manageable size. The principle behind the technique is based on Pareto's law of maldistribution which, when applied to importance, states that 80% of the importance is invested in 20% of the items. Using this principle, it is possible to narrow down a list of times in order to extract those that possess the greatest amount of importance. Once the list has been reduced by pareto voting, the critical few items can be further evaluated by more powerful discriminating value measurement techniques described earlier.

Method

1. All items on the list are numbered so that each item has its own unique identification number. This will ease group communication

List of Eight Items Voted on by Eight Participants

Item	Total Group Votes
Camera is easy to load	6
Camera is comfortable in my hands	4
Camera is durable	3
I can tell all camera adjustments are correct	2
Camera is secure in my hands	1
Can be artistic with my camera	0
Show my skills as a photographer	0
Makes me feel relaxed	0

Figure 6.5   List of eight items voted on by eight participants.

and comparison of items. The team edits the large list of items to eliminate redundancy and similar items. If there is not unanimous agreement on combining certain items, it is best to let the items remain separate as is. The editing promotes team interaction and clarification.

2. Participants vote on the list of items. The total number of votes allowed per person is restricted to 20% of the total number of items generated. Of the allowed number of votes, only one vote is permitted per selected item and the full allotment of votes must be used. Group members vote by secret ballot, recording the identification number of the items they have selected.

3. The team leader collects the ballots and tallies the votes before the group. The number of votes is recorded alongside the respective item on the original chart pad.

4. The entire list is typed and distributed to the team members. Those items receiving no votes are retained on the list for reference but are separated from the rest of the items and are excluded from further consideration. The items are typed in descending order of the number of votes each item received.

5. If the list needs to be further reduced, the procedure is repeated with the already shortened list (Refer to Figure 6.5. The total number of votes is 16 (20% × 8 = 2 × 8 people = 16 total votes).)

Usage

1. A quick priority setting method.

2. Reduce a very large list of items to a manageable size.
3. Isolate topics for further discussion/clarification.

Advantages

1. Fast, simple, immediate feedback.
2. Quick feedback allows momentum of meeting to be retained.
3. No forms are needed.
4. Minimizes conflict and bickering at meetings.

Disadvantages

1. Does not allow maximum discrimination between all items.
2. Does not produce a real scale.

Limitations

1. May not work with a small list of items (e.g., less than 10) that does not have a wide dispersion in votes.
2. Will not work if there are only a few raters (less than three or four).
3. May not be valid where items are not listed in random order such as a list generated from a brainstorm session where there is much overlap and hitch-hiking of ideas, and items are recorded in thought clusters.

Ranked Pareto Voting

Description

Ranked Pareto is performed in the same manner as regular Pareto except that after the participants have picked their 20% of the most important items, they are also asked to rank the chosen items where the highest rank number represents the best. Then, in addition to tallying votes, one tallies the ranks and sums the rank scores for an overall total score by item. See Figure 6.6. Alternate ranking is the preferred method to obtain the ranks.

Advantages

1. Using rank totals gives more separation between items. This can be important especially when several items receive the same frequency of votes. For example, items (5) and (8) both received five

votes, but, when viewing the rank totals, item (8) clearly is more important.
2. The distribution of ranks within each item shows the spread in participant perceptions, and gives a good picture of group consensus. The distribution of ranks can be used to trigger further dialogue.

Disadvantages

1. Same as regular Pareto.

Ranked Pareto Exercise

Total number of items = 15
Total participants = 5
Number of votes per participant = 3 (20%)
Total number of votes = 15
Rank scale = 3 (best), 2 (next best), 1 (least best)
Rank total = 30

Item	Distribution of Ranks by Participant	Vote Frequency	Rank Totals
1			
2	2,3	2	5
3			
4			
5	3,1,1,1,2	5	8
6			
7			
8	3,2,3,2,2	5	12
9			
10	1,1	2	2
11			
12	3	1	3
13			
14			
15			
		15	30

Figure 6.6 Ranked Pareto excerices. (From Shillito, M. L. and DeMarie, D. J., *Value its Measurement Design and Management*, John Wiley & Sons, New York, 1992. With permission.)

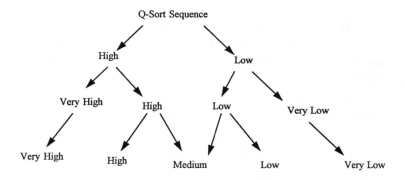

Figure 6.7 Q-Sort procedure. (From Shillito, M. L. and DeMarie, D. J., *Value its Measurement Design and Management,* John Wiley & Sons, New York, 1992. With permission.)

Limitations

1. Same as regular Pareto.

Q-Sort

Description

Q-Sort is a screening technique (Figure 6.7) which is very useful in determining qualitative differences in the values of a series of items. It can be useful as a starting point from which to assign quantitative values to the individual items. The result of a Q-Sort is a qualitative ranking of categories of items in which items of similar value are grouped together.

Method

1. Write the name of each item on a separate 3 × 5 card.
2. Separate the items into two piles, those of high importance and those of low importance.
3. Separate the "high" value items into "high" and "very high" piles. Separate the "low" value items into "low" and "very low" piles.
4. Separate the "high" items into "high" and "medium" and the "low" items into "low" and "medium", putting all the "mediums" into one pile. The result will be five distinct categories: very high, high, medium, low, and very low. See Example 6.7.
5. Examine each pile to make sure it contains only the items desired.

Advantages / Disadvantages

1. This method becomes very useful with a large number of items when only a qualitative ranking is desired. The categories, however, may not be equally spaced and only a hierarchy of categories is obtained, not a continuous scale of values.
2. Quick and "very dirty."
3. Good for grouping "like items" into sets for further analysis. For example, "let's work on all the 'L' items." Also those items in the "very high" group may be candidates for further, more discriminating value measurement techniques discussed earlier.
4. Q-Sort is very useful with a large number of items if only a qualitative ranking is desired.
5. Categories may not be equally spaced; only a hierarchy of categories is obtained.

Choice or Satisfaction

As mentioned in Chapter 3, there are two types of importance criteria. Choice criteria are those parameters that are used to make a choice, a buy decision. They are rated for importance in order to determine the hierarchy of importance across the criteria set. Satisfaction criteria, on the other hand, are the same set of labels as the choice criteria except they are rated as to how well they are currently being satisfied by the current product.

Just as we used scaling to rate importance, we can also derive a scale to rate current satisfaction for each customer verbatim (need). Such a scale may be as follows:

Rating	Description
5	Exceeds need; wow!
4	
3	Meets need.
2	
1	Barely meets need; may not meet need at all.

Each verbatim may be rated for both importance and satisfaction. Having done so, they may be plotted together on the same graph (Figure 6.8). The graph provides an effective visual representation to locate gaps in importance and satisfaction, such as items 1, 3, 4, 5 in Figure 6.8, as well as those verbatims that are on target, items 2 and 6. Another perspective are those items that exceed expectations on something that is of lower importance, as illustrated by item 7.

Importance/Satisfaction Graph

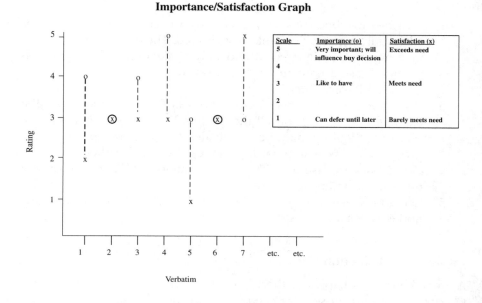

Figure 6.8 Importance/satisfaction graph.

A value graph may also be used to depict the same relationship. Verbatim importance can be plotted against verbatim satisfaction. See Figure 6.9. Verbatim number 5 in Figure 6.9 should command some attention as it ranks low in importance but the customer is satisfied. Does this make sense? Can this be an over-design problem? Verbatim number 7 should also be questioned. It is very important to the customer but ranks very low in satisfaction. The ideal area to be is the shaded area, north and east from coordinate 3,3. From here, importance and satisfaction are increasing from an already good score. Any plot outside this quadrant may require some attention.

Utility Curves

Another dialogue-rich and useful quantification method is utility curves. Utility curves are generally associated with conjoint analysis, which is a highly statistical business research technique. They apply to VOC as well. Utility curves used in VOC are certainly more subjective and are drawn free-hand based on more qualitative input which sometimes is an educated guess.

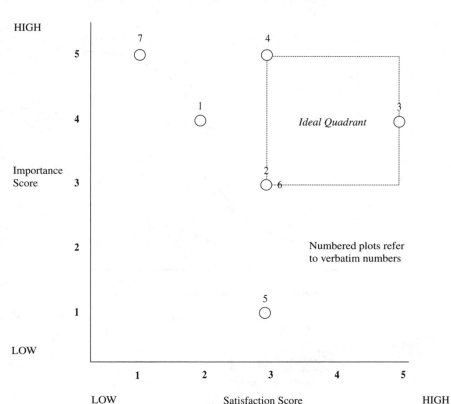

Figure 6.9 Value graph — verbatim importance vs. satisfaction.

A generic utility curve is shown in Figure 6.10. It arrays degrees of customer response against the metric for the particular verbatim. Two metric anchor points are identified, the "table stakes" or minimum entry to play the game, and the other the point beyond which "nobody would buy" no matter how great the metric at that level.

Once these beginning and end points are established by team dialogue, the curve shape is estimated and drawn free-hand between the two anchor points. Next a target metric is established somewhere along the curve continuum, which represents the team's best estimate of the launch metric level for that particular verbatim.

Competitor benchmarks may be plotted on the curve to serve as reference points. Discussion of the benchmarks also helps the team

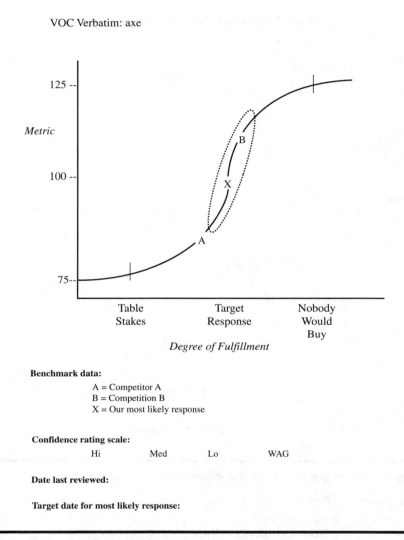

VOC Verbatim: axe

Figure 6.10 Utility curve (genetic).

establish the target value. If several benchmarks are plotted, they also help establish the target window.

The team may also want to rate their responses on a confidence rating scale. Hopefully, confidence will increase over time as new data is gleaned from experience and the field. This also emphasizes the fact that the curves are living documents and need to be updated over time. Drawing these curves also highlights gaps and things we don't know. Curve shapes may be linear, logarithmic, s-curves, step functions, etc. The important point is to force anchor points and curve shape to encourage team dialogue.

I have worked on projects where the team established utility curves for every VOC verbatim, sometimes 80 or 90 in all! Information transfer among team members skyrocketed. There were many arguments, but, in the end, all team members were focused in the same direction and many action items were created, many of which would never have surfaced without the utility curve exercise.

SUMMARY

It is necessary to quantify customer needs for importance in order to determine the needs hierarchy. When designing products it is impossible to design for everything, otherwise, the product will be overdesigned and overpriced. Consequently we must quantify the needs. A decision must be made as to which needs are quantified. Do we rate all needs for importance? Or, do we work from the Tree Diagram described in Chapter 5? If using a Tree Diagram, it is best to work from the primary level to the tertiary level, because the lower level may contain too many verbatims to deal with. Specific secondary levels may be expanded further to tertiary quantification. There are numerous value measurement techniques for quantifying verbatims. Some of the most common are discussed here.

ACKNOWLEDGMENT

This chapter was reprinted with permission from Shillito, M. L. and DeMarle, D. J., *Value, Its Measurement, Design, and Management,* John Wiley & Sons, New York, 1992.

BIBLIOGRAPHY

Delbecq, A. L., Van deVenn, A. H., and Gustafson, D. H., *Group Techniques for Program Planning, A Guide to the Nominal Group and Delphi Process,* Scott Foresman, Gleanview, IL, 1975.

Melin, A. F. and Souder, W. E., "Experimental Test of a Q-Sort Procedure for Prioritizing R&D Projects," *IEEE Trans. Eng. Man.,* EM-21, 4, 159-164, 1974.

Meyer, D. M., "Direct Magnitude Estimation, A Method for Quantifying the Value Index," *Proc. Soc. Am. Value Eng.,* 6, 293-298, May 1971.

Mudge, A. E., "Numerial Evaluation of Functional Relationships," *Proc. Soc. Am. Value Eng.,* 2, 111-123, 1967.

Shillito, M. L., "Pareto Voting," *Proc. Soc. Am. Value Eng.,* 8, 131-135, 1973.

Shillito, M. L. and DeMarle, D. L., *Value: Its Measurement, Design and Management,* John Wiley & Sons, New York, 1992.

Souder, W. E., "Field Studies with a Q-Sort/Nominal Group Process for Selecting R&D Projects," *Res. Policy*, 4, 172-188, 1975.

REFERENCES

1. Saaty, T.L., *Decision Making For Leaders*, RWS Publications, Pittsburgh, PA, 1988.

7

VOC INTEGRATION

HOW MANY VOCS?

In Chapter 1, four levels of vertical VOC within a company were discussed. These vertical VOCs are necessary to bring focus to the commercialization process. These VOC levels can be viewed from another perspective. They can be interpreted from the Voice of the Customer (VOC), the voice of the company (VOCo), voice of the engineer (VOE), voice of management (VOM), and finally, the collective voice (CV). All of these voices have needs and we cannot attempt to satisfy one voice at the sacrifice of any of the others. They all have to be considered. So, how do we integrate all four?

Remember, in Chapter 1, we discussed answering two basic starting questions. Those questions are, "What are we trying to do for the customer?" and, "What are we trying to do for the company (ourselves)?" The four voices are indentured under these two questions. The VOC obviously helps to answer the first question, what we are trying to do for the customer. The VOCo and VOE are directed toward answering the second question, what we are trying to do for the company. To reiterate, our attempt to answer and document one of the two questions cannot be at the sacrifice of sub-optimizing the other. There must be a good balance in satisfying needs between customer and company.

When we think about all these different voices it is hard to do so without implying some sort of stratification. All of these voices enter the product development process in different layers. These layers can represent the levels of perspective, (strategic, tactical, and operational), and sometimes levels within the company hierarchy. Figure 7.1 is an illustration of the stratification.

The top part of the triangle represents the strategic level and must reflect the Voice of Management (VOM). VOM is a cross-functional representation of the worldwide business. Its focus is on leveraging technical

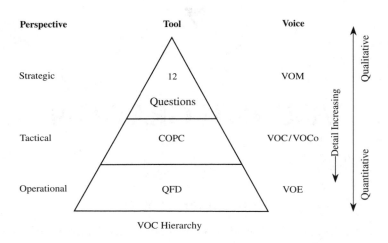

Figure 7.1 **VOC hierarchy.** (From Shillito, M. L., *Advanced QFD Linking Technology to Market and Company Needs*, John Wiley & Sons, New York, 1994. With permission.)

competency in most promising market segments. It sets strategic direction. The 12 Questions discussed in Chapter 2 are a useful mechanism to collect VOM. The middle portion represents the tactical level and integrates the VOC and the VOCo and, to some extent, the VOE. VOE is the technical community's interpretation and understanding of what they think the customer verbatims mean. Finally, the lower level involves the VOE at an operational perspective to complete a final product design to carry forward to the end. This operational level is where traditional QFD really begins to come into its own. It is the design and problem solving process to put together and drive design down to the shop floor and statistical process control. Answers to the engineer's or designer's VOE make this possible.

For the entire product development process to work, all of the voices from all levels must be compatible, synchronized and congruent. The chain of voices forms the communications link and becomes the spinal cord for the company product commercialization or TQM program. The various voices serve as disks in the spinal cord.

Finally, all of these voices must be integrated into a balanced scenario which I refer to as the collective voice (CV). The quality of this CV scenario is what can make the difference between a great product and an okay product, and, in the worst case, between winning and losing.

To illustrate the interconnectedness of all the elements, I developed a matrix, Figure 7.2. The column headings across the top represent the functional steps in the VOC process from the strategic level through the

VOC Process

FUNCTION	VOM	VOMKT	VOC/VOE					VOC
	Set Global Strategy	Frame Market	Collect VOC Data	Interpret VOC Data	Structure VOC Data	Quantity (Prioritize) Data	Deploy Processed VOC Understanding	Observe/ Feedback Product Performance
ACTIVITY	Define market Develop business plan/strategy Segment market Scout future Survey impacts	Develop product family Develop product strategy	Select targets Select data sources Select collection method Select personnel Collect data Process solutions and unknowns	Process customer solutions and unknowns Identify which items to carry forward Process compound statements	Show relationships Cluster similarities Plot	Select appropriate value measurement tool Quantify VOC/VOE verbatims for importance	Incorporate VOC into HOQ or COPC Deploy to subsequent QFD matrices as fit	Collect feedback data Structure feedback Send to management for update of VOM, VOMKT
TOOLS	Strategic planning Decision risk analysis Scenarios Trend analysis Impact analysis	Framing 12 Q's Is/is not Pareto distribution Customer morphology Customer profile Customer matrix Product profile	Personal customer contact Survey Interview Focus groups Direct observation Direct visit Customer panel Customer council Product mentors	VOC table 5-Whys	Tree diagram Affinity diagram Interrelationship diagraph	Value measurement Ranking Pair comparison Scaling Constant sum Scoring model	COPC QFD-HOQ QFD-higher matrices	1-800-HELP Industrial engr. studies Customer visits Tech. reps. Opinion survey
SOURCES	VOC Competitive intell. Business intell. Customer contact Managers	VOC Personal customer contact Business research	Direct customer contact Complaints Warranty 1-800 Publications Business research	Personal customer contact Collected verbatims	Processed VOC/ VOE verbatims	Personal customer contact VOC verbatims Marketing best guess	Processed VOM, VOMKT, VOC/VOE	Sales records Complaints Warranty Direct observation Tech. reps. Sales people Dealers Channel partners Repair centers
PRODUCT	Business plan Technology strategy	Product families Product family strategy	Unprocessed customer verbatims	Processed understanding of verbatims	Structured verbatims	Structured VOC/ VOE verbatims quantified for importance	HOQ COPC	Satisfaction report Other reports

Figure 7.2 VOC process guide. (From Shillito, M. L., *Advanced QFD Linking Technology to Market and Company Needs*, John Wiley & Sons, New York, 1994. With permission.)

operational level. Down the left-hand side, defining the matrix rows, are the activities/tools that can be used at each step of the process. This listing of tools is by no means complete. Row three represents the data sources and documents that are appropriate for each VOC process function. These sources are generic and each company will have its own data sources in addition to those listed here. Finally, the last row lists the products or output of each VOC function.

To simplify the matrix and the VOC process, I have used four VOCs. VOM represents the voice of company management, VOMKT represents the voice of marketing. VOC/VOE represents both the voice of the customer and the voice of the engineer, and VOC is the voice of the customer but in a product usage and feedback mode. These voices closely correspond to the levels illustrated in Figure 7.1.

Hopefully the matrix will illustrate the interaction and complexity of the VOC process. It also illustrates what must be in place in order to do a proper QFD or COPC. Too often the contents of Figure 7.2 are assumed and a QFD project gets into trouble quickly. When things don't work out well, QFD usually gets the blame!

PUTTING IT ALL TOGETHER

Figure 0.1 in the Introduction illustrates the VOC template and the accompanying tools at each phase. You will recall that each chapter discusses a separate phase of the VOC pathway. In this chapter the functions (phases) of the VOC pathway and the related activity will be discussed. Figure 7.3 illustrates the VOC Process Model where the functions are listed across the top and the corresponding activities are listed vertically underneath. It is a variation of Figure 7.2 which related tools, activities, and data sources to the type of VOC and process functions. Let us now look at the functions and activities in this living model.

Focus — Before any VOC project can begin, it is necessary to develop company and customer focus. This is the purpose of the 12 Questions discussed in Chapter 2. That is, the objectives of the VOC project must be clarified. For example, are we to collect VOC for upgrading an existing product, designing a new product, or merely updating our existing VOC database? Next we define the scope of the project. What is included and what is not included? The scope helps us to define our product/service target domain. For example, if we are in the printing/copying business we may choose to concentrate only on the printing/output side of the system as opposed to building hardware or software for the entire system. Or, if we are in the banking business we may elect to be a specialty bank compared to a general service bank. Within these product/service targets we must then define country, market, segment, and user. Defining the target domain and market is extremely difficult and is the most important part of the VOC process. Next we document our assumptions and select the customer targets. Exactly what customers are we going to talk to that best represent our product/service target domain and market?

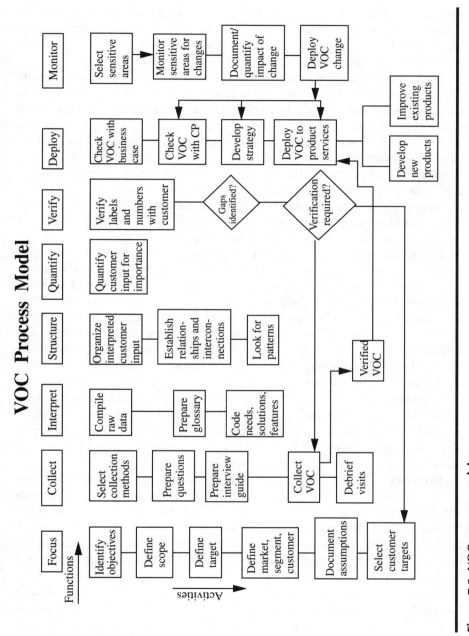

Figure 7.3 VOC process model.

Collection — Having identified our target customers we must now select our collection methods and data sources. Selection of collection methods will depend on our budget and time constraints and how many people are available to do the job if we choose to do the collection ourselves. Another option is to have it all done by an outside agency. Many outside firms are very good but very expensive. They can generally give fast turnaround.

Next, the team must prepare the questions and an interview guide. These may have to be customized depending on who the interviewee is; an owner, operator, clerk, salesperson, etc. The question must be tailored to the type of data and information you are seeking. The questions and backup probes must also be framed and based on your focus, that is, whether it is an upgraded product or a "leap" product. For example, if it is an upgraded product, you ask about the "product of your dreams." If it is a "leap" product you ask about the "job of your dreams."

Finally comes the logistics of collecting the data. First, who and how many different people go out to collect? How are geographic locations and sequences arranged to economize on travel expenses?

Once completed, interviews and data should be debriefed as soon as possible before memories fade. The ideal is to do it the same day at the motel. Note taking is furious and can be very shorthanded and sketchy. Memories fade quickly, especially on a multiple–interview trip. Tape recording is a must if permission is granted. The debriefing is to fill in gaps in the notes and recordings, identify quotes, label problems and solutions, and extract images and opportunities. A laptop computer is very helpful here to transcribe handwritten notes into electronic form. Once in electronic form, notes can be posted to a "home page" on the Internet or a company intranet with select password access for all people involved on the VOC project as well as people from marketing, business research, product development, research, development and management. Customer visit information should also be reviewed at team meetings on a regular basis so team members can learn from each other.

Interpret — In addition to electronic transcription, interview data may also be coded and entered into a classified retrieval system for future cuts and sorts. A glossary of customer verbatims which is the team's translation of the original customer quotes should be compiled. Many times these quotes must be translated into terms that the development community understands. It is the team's processed understanding of what they heard the customer say. Constructing the glossary often raises questions which necessitates going back to customers for clarification. What the customer means may not always be obvious. Verbatims should also be identified as a need, solution, or feature. Remember, needs are long–term and lead to the future. Solutions and features are short–term and are usually oriented to the present. The three closely reflect on the focus of the study (upgrade or "leap").

Structure — Having data banks of coded transcribed verbatims is very useful but is not sufficient to do the entire job of deploying VOC for designing products and services. The verbatims must be organized into a structure. The first organization is the clusters resulting from the Affinity Diagram. The most useful structure is the Tree Diagram, which is an extension of the Affinity Diagram. The reason for structure is to put verbatims in a form that allows the team to search for relationships, patterns, and interconnections. The geography of the issues puts the VOC and development team in a better position to develop more creative responses to customer's needs. Structuring also gives us the organization to begin developing product/service specifications to help meet those things the customer desires. The structuring process allows us to develop a taxonomy of customer verbatims similar to phyla and geneses of the plant and animal kingdom. Study and communication did not really evolve in the biological world until a structure laid the foundation.

Quantify — Structure is necessary in order to study relationships but it is also necessary to know the hierarchy of importance across those relationships. We cannot pursue and/or deploy every customer verbatim due to time and budget constraints resulting from information overload. Value measurement is used to help us direct our attention to the most critical areas of greatest potential return to both company and customer. Quantification helps direct our attention to the most important customer verbatims. It also is used as a weighting factor for factoring customer importance to product/service specifications and target values. Without a numerical hierarchy magnitude of importance is lost as well as the vectors to shape product/service design.

Quantification is very often performed by the VOC team after the structuring process. This certainly is one way to begin the process but caution is advised if the process stops there. The team may be wrong! They may not represent the customer properly due to bias and honest wrong beliefs. Verification with the customer is required.

During quantification several things may happen. The team may not feel comfortable with some of their numbers and require customer input. Or, there may be some verbatims that the team cannot possibly quantify for importance, more commonly referred to as gaps. Customer input is clearly indicated.

Verify — Customer verbatims, the team's processed understanding (glossary) of the verbatims, and the quantification should be verified with customers. The team must make a list of questions regarding verbatim labels, numerical importance, and gaps.

Once the verification list and questionnaire is established, a target set of customers must be established to talk to. The customer target list may be original customer contacts, new ones, or a combination of both. The collection process is repeated. Many times verification can be done by telephone.

Deploy — Verified VOC is now double–checked with the business case and commercialization process for any changes that may have occurred. If company strategy has not changed, VOC can now be deployed to product/services to develop new products or improve existing products. The usual deployment mechanisms are QFD or COPC (Appendix C).

Monitor — An on-going process conducted parallel with deployment is to monitor selected VOC for changes in the future. First it is necessary to select sensitive areas to monitor. Many times these are obvious. Many times, also, no one thinks to ask the question whether or not select VOC's should be monitored! Too often VOC teams think that when VOC is collected, processed and deployed, VOC activity is finished. This may not always be the case.

The monitoring process involves selecting sensitive areas to monitor using appropriate tracking techniques to detect changes. These changes should be documented and quantified for their impact on the company, business, or product if they occur. Once documented, the VOC change should be deployed into the company strategy and product/service.

Feedback — Once the product is in use in the field, feedback on performance and customer reaction begins to come in. This feedback should be collected and organized and deployed back into the product/service development process.

VERIFICATION

After VOC is interpreted, structured, and quantified, it should be verified with customer/issues. It is quick and easy to perform these operations internally. However, doing this without verification could get a team into trouble due to personal and company paradigms and biases.

The verification process starts by first identifying what needs to be verified. Regarding labels and numbers, it is usually the numbers indicating importance that must be verified. The most useful document to use for locating areas needing verification is the quantified affinity tree as seen in Appendix D, Figure D.23. This tree contains both labels and numbers. A colored highlighter marker is used to color code areas needing attention. For example, labels that need additional customer input or definition are colored in yellow. Numbers representing the importance of labels about which we are very uncertain are coded in pink. Those labels for which we do not have numbers for importance (gaps) are coded in blue and so on. A new collection process may now be organized to verify data and fill in gaps. The color coded affinity tree provides the road map for verification collection.

The next step is to identify which customers to talk to for verification. Some may be the original VOC interviewees or they may be completely new interviewees, or a combination of both. Once customers are identified, VOC verification collection is organized and conducted similar to the initial VOC activity. Many of the original collection techniques may also be used for verification. Customer visits are especially good and are preferred over telephone interviews where affordable. Customer panels have also been used with good success. With customer panels, customers are invited to the company on a periodic (say quarterly) basis to review project/product information with the team. Focus groups are also in vogue today — they are very good but very expensive. Information for the focus group questionnaire/discussion guide comes from the gaps and questions that surface from internally processed verbatims.

VOC data may be verified on a staggered basis. That is, you can verify labels and relationships, then come back and update the data. Then you can verify importances, and so on. On the other hand, you can assemble the semi-finished pack of VOC and verify it all at one time for labels, structure and importance. Some companies have customers as members of the design team making it possible to get concurrent verification.

Phone conversations and questionnaires do not work very well for verification because there is little control and interaction. Face-to-face communication is definitely the way to go.

SUMMARY

There are many voices that make up the VOC. All voices must be considered when developing the final collective voice. Each voice has associated with it certain activities to develop it, specific tools that are useful for structuring and quantification of importance as well as recognized data sources for its collection. A structured process flow of activities is needed to develop processed VOC. A template has been provided for this purpose.

BIBLIOGRAPHY

Shillito, M. L., *Advanced QFD, Linking Technology To Market and Company Needs*, John Wiley & Sons, Inc., New York, 1994.

8

DEPLOYING VOC

BACKGROUND

Once VOC has been collected and processed it must be deployed into the product and the commercialization process. The two most widely used deployment mechanisms are Quality Function Deployment (QFD) and Customer Oriented Product Concepting (COPC). Both are structured matrix processes that provide a translation template. Unless these or some equivalent process is used, deployment of VOC will be weak and random.

As mentioned in the Introduction, this chapter will not discuss in detail the QFD deployment process. It is my intention to discuss the preparation of VOC for deployment. The deployment mechanisms go well beyond VOC and into the details of product design, problem solving, specifications, manufacturing design, etc., which is outside the scope of this book.

However, to make the book complete, COPC, a hybrid QFD-type deployment mechanism integrating value engineering, is discussed in minute detail in Appendix C to introduce the reader to a new VOC deployment process.

PREPARING VOC FOR QUALITY FUNCTION DEPLOYMENT (QFD) AND CUSTOMER-ORIENTED PRODUCT CONCEPTING (COPC)

The time has finally come to deploy the VOC into the product and commercialization process. The two most widely used deployment mechanisms are QFD and COPC.[1] So far, from our previous chapters, we have a glossary defining each of our VOC verbatims, we have a structure (tree), and we have importance ratings on each verbatim. In the QFD and COPC processes we will go through the normal House of Quality (HOQ) type routine of benchmarking our product, determining scale-up and market leverage in order to complete an overall weighted average importance for each verbatim.

The real VOC deployment begins, however, when we translate the VOC verbatims into product technical requirements (PTR) also referred to as substitute quality characteristics (SQC) for QFD, or when we align VOC verbatims with product/service functions for COPC.

WHICH VOC VERBATIMS SHOULD BE CARRIED FORWARD?

First let us decide which of all our verbatims we wish to carry forward for deployment. Do we bring them all? Do we bring only the most important ones? Many times, if we bring them all, we risk the possibility of information overload and the VOC deployment may become overly complex. The best way to structure thinking on this matter is to go back to the tree diagram discussed in Chapter 5 and the Nested Hierarchy discussed in Chapter 6. If we have a three–level tree, it is not unusual to have several hundred verbatims at level three, 20 to 30 at level 2, and eight to ten at level 1. At what level should we proceed? Level three may be too much detail to deal with. If so, go up to level two and carry those forward. Another option at level 2 is to carry forward only the most important ones (the Pareto 20% vital few). Then, if you still need more level three detail, you can carry forward the level three verbatims just for those Pareto vital few from level two. Once the agreed upon verbatims are built into the HOQ, or the functions of COPC, they are used for the traditional HOQ and COPC planning operations.

Daetz, Barnard, and Norman[2] have a unique tool for locating the more important customer needs. They have developed the Voice of Value Table (VOVT) where all customers needs are listed. The team is then given $100 to distribute across the needs, similar to the constant sum method, but in this case they do not have to allocate points to every item. They actually use this tool to narrow down specific customer probing questions they want to concentrate on in the in-context visits. I believe VOVT can be used to narrow down which verbatims should be deployed to the QFD or COPC matrices.

TRANSLATING VOC TO PRODUCT TECHNICAL REQUIREMENTS

First of all, let us define customer requirements. The following terms are interchangeable: customer requirements, product technical requirements (PTR), substitute quality characteristics, the "hows," product features, engineering characteristics. There are probably a few others I have missed.

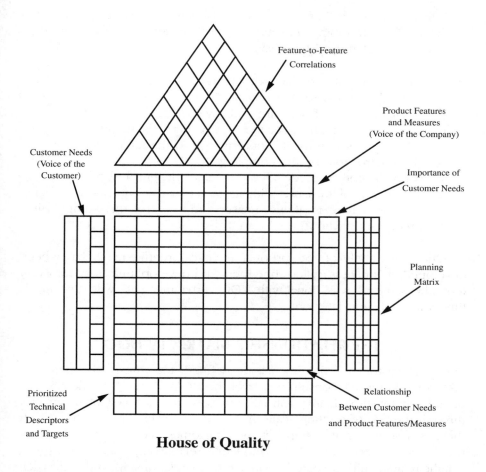

Feature-to-Feature
Correlations

Product Features
and Measures
(Voice of the Company)

Customer Needs
(Voice of the
Customer)

Importance of
Customer Needs

Planning
Matrix

Prioritized
Technical
Descriptors
and Targets

Relationship
Between Customer Needs
and Product Features/Measures

House of Quality

8.1 House of quality.

The objective is to translate the VOC into the voice of the engineer, designer, etc., that is, into terms they can understand. These usually turn out to be systems level facilities, processes, methods, functions, activities, etc. We brainstorm for answers to such questions as, "what are some of the ways we accomplish the list of customer needs verbatims?," or, "what will it take to satisfy the customer for this want or need?" Generally the process starts at the top, progresses down the list of needs, and continues writing the product technical requirements across the top columns of the matrix. See Figure 8.1. Note that there can be more than one technical requirement for each customer requirement. It is not necessary to have consensus at this point, just get the technical requirements list started — it will be edited by the team later on.

William Barnard of Barnard and Associates has developed some useful guidelines for developing substitute quality characteristics[3,4] as follows: The quality characteristic must:

1. "Be an attribute and/or a capability."
2. "Be value-added for the product."
3. "Include a unit of measure and a value."
4. "Not be a solution or related to a particular solution."
5. "Must be testable for its conformance to the target value."
6. "Be controllable by the company."
7. "Contain both a predictor of customer delight and/or satisfaction and a unit of measure with its target value. The question being addressed here is, If we measure and control this 'thing' will it predict satisfaction?"

Once the labels of the product technical requirements have been developed, it is necessary to refine them and develop a glossary for every term the same as was done with VOC verbatims. This will save much time and confusion later on.

THE RELATIONSHIP MATRIX IN HOQ

Once the customer requirements are defined, the true deployment will take place in the relationship matrix of the HOQ, Figure 8.1. The strength of the relationship, if any, will be described in each cell of the matrix through the use of a rating scale. A 1, 3 and 9 scale is generally used. If there is a strong relationship between customer need and the customer requirement use a score of 9; a moderate relationship is scored a three; a light relationship is scored a one. For no relationship, the cell is left empty (zero). The HOQ is finished in the traditional manner. The VOC, however, has now been deployed to product through the relationship matrix.

POSTING VERBATIMS TO THE COPC MATRIX

A complete description of the COPC process and its application is contained in Appendix C. COPC is based on the function approach to product design. All functions that a product must perform to accomplish its overall basic function are identified and listed in order of occurrence. VOC verbatims are posted to the respective functions to which they pertain. A verbatim may pertain to more than one function. The customer may not be aware of all the product features and functions. But, how well our product performs those functions will have a direct affect on those things that the customer will be aware of. Part one of the COPC process involves all of the operations in the columns of the traditional HOQ Planning matrix (i.e. company/competitor benchmarking, scale-up, sales point and normalized score). The difference is that the relationship matrix is replaced by product functions. Verbatims are used to develop and select technology or solutions for each product function as compared to product technical requirements in the HOQ.

VOC DEPLOYMENT — HOW DO YOU KNOW YOU'RE DOING IT RIGHT?

The following is a checklist of observed behavior when VOC is deployed properly:

1. VOC verbatims are in a retrievable format. A computer database is established as discussed in Chapter 3. This allows the team to cut and sort by category. It also allows for updating and editing as needed. It is a living interactive database. Even the basic database programs in some of the word processing and spreadsheet programs allow one to search on key words. It is yet another way to exercise an individual's or team's creativity and intuition to organize creative thoughts and responses with regard to product design and response to customer comments.
2. Glossary of Verbatims. The glossary, as discussed in Chapter 4, can save an inordinate amount of team time normally consumed by miscommunication. All team members are singing the same song from the same hymnal. There is consistency in interpretation and understanding of the verbatims. We maintain the original verbatim quotes in the database. This glossary is our processed understanding of those verbatims, generally in more technical terms that the product/service designers can understand. It is this processed understanding that can lead to better product technical requirements.
3. Structure (Affinity Diagrams, Interrelationship Diagraph, Tree Diagrams): Without structure we cannot relate and see connections. Without being able to see patterns and relationships we cannot develop creative responses for product design. Structuring allows us to carry forward the critical vital few which, in turn, allows us to economize on the size of the deployment matrices.
4. Quantified verbatims: Quantified verbatims, especially those calibrated to the same level of indenture by NHP, also allows us to quickly identify those items that most likely will have the most leverage for deployment into product design. It can also help us economize on deployment matrix size.

5. Audit trail: After verbatims have been labeled and quantified for importance, they need to be verified with real customers. This can be done through customer visits and interviews, customer panels, focus groups, etc. The point is, good deployment demands good verification and an audit trail. Internal brainstorming for labels and numbers without external verification is a sure path to trouble.

6. Input: Good deployment requires all around input from the company business unit planners, the project team, and external and internal customers. That is, it requires a balanced communication — both vertically and horizontally, and internally and externally. Without balance, designs are off course and cycle time expands.

7. Customer requirements document (CRD): The line of business management and marketing must produce a customer requirements document. The final document is not generally produced by the VOC team. However, the bulk of the data to produce it does come from a VOC team. The CRD must contain traceable evidence of processed VOC. Likewise, the CRD must be supported by the competitive assessment and the planning matrix from the HOQ and/or the COPC matrix. Disconnects between the CRD and the VOC data should quickly send out alert signals or a temporary halt or a course correction.

8. Clear relationship to the business plan: The early-on customer morphology, customer profile, and product profiles (all in Chapter 2) should be in sync with the business plan. If congruency is not there at the beginning, course corrections should be made or at least discussed before we steer too far off course, which can lead to misdirected VOC collection and improperly designed products, that is, poor VOC deployment. The concept path from the COPC Matrix (Appendix C) and the COPC Strategy Matrix must also be aligned with the business plan because at this stage we are already dealing with product concepts.

9. Team vision: Each multifunctional VOC and design team member thoroughly understands the customer as to who he is and what he wants. There is a customer intimacy, the company, and the team have a deep profound insight of the customer ("a day in the life of a customer").

10. Definitive process: The team consistently follows an effective structured process for assessing customer needs. A VOC process is in place with automatic use and updating.

11. Monitoring: A system has been set up to track and monitor certain selected sensitive or potentially sensitive verbatims into the future.

MIXING CUSTOMER SEGMENTS VOC

Do not mix VOC from different customer segments in the same deployment mechanism! Too many teams have combined all VOC verbatims across different segments into one deployment matrix. When this is done there is considerable confusion and incorrect conclusions begin to surface. What particular segment does this combined one-size-fits-all matrix represent? There must be a separate matrix for each segment. Now this sounds like a nightmarish amount of work. Not so. The labels on the verbatims generally do not change across customer segments. What does change, however, are the importance numbers on those verbatims. So once a matrix is completed for one segment, 90% or more of the work is already done for the other segment matrices. Generally, all that has to be changed is the importance figures and the matrix is run again. All of our data should be on one of the several popular computer spreadsheet programs that will calculate the numerical results in microseconds.

DEPLOYING A CUSTOMER CHAIN OF VOCS

It is becoming more prevalent today to build products to satisfy a chain of customers within a market segment. Customer chains were discussed in Chapter 2. A typical chain for an overhead projector for the education market might be (1) the user (i.e., a teacher), (2) the buyer/purchasing agent, (3) a specifications writer for a school district or an entire state and, finally, (4) the dealer. All of these "customers" have their own individual as well as common needs. So, how do we deploy VOC and satisfy all four customers in the chain?

One method is to construct a Weighted Customer Importance Matrix using the process of Constant Sum in conjunction with the Nested Hierarchy Process both discussed in Chapter 6.

Weighted Customer Importance Matrix

What is it? — A matrix arraying specific VOCs against multiple customers in a customer chain.

Objective: — To calibrate specific VOCs weighted by their respective customer importance in a customer chain.

Purpose: — To isolate those Pareto 20% vital few VOCs that have the most significance for the final product design and sales potential.

Input: —VOC labels on each link in the customer chain. Documented VOCs relating to the specific customer. Note that one VOC may pertain to more than one customer link in the chain.

EDUCATION MARKET
Weighted Customer Importance Matrix

Customer Chain (importance)	Customer Weight	Need	Import. of need w/i group	Weighted import. of need
Dealer	0.2	A	5	1.0
	0.2	*B**	15	3.0
20	0.2	C	40	8.0
	0.2	D	30	6.0
	0.2	E	10 /Σ100	2.0
Specialist	0.5	F	10	5.0
	0.5	*B**	15	7.5
50	0.5	G	30	15.0
	0.5	H	30	15.0
	0.5	I	15 /Σ100	7.5
Buyer	0.2	J	10	2.0
	0.2	K	10	2.0
20	0.2	*L**	5	1.0
	0.2	M	50	10.0
	0.2	T	20	4.0
	0.2	U	5 /Σ100	1.0
User	0.1	N	10	1.0
	0.1	O	10	1.0
10	0.1	P	10	1.0
	0.1	Q	60	6.0
	0.1	*L**	5	0.5
	0.1	S	5 /Σ100	0.5
Σ 100				

* **Bold** letters represent needs falling in
more than one Customer Chain link.

8.2 Weighted customer importance matrix – education market.

Output: — A set of calibrated VOCs in a matrix format weighted by all links in the customer chain. This weighted list can then be used as the rows of the House of Quality or as the scored VOC input to the respective functions in the COPC matrix (Appendix C).

Instructions: — (See Figure 8.2)

1. Identify each customer link in the chain of customers. Write a glossary describing these customers if necessary.
2. Using the Constant Sum method (Chapter 6), allocate 100 points across the customers signifying their importance to product design and future sales. When finished, all points must sum to 100. To keep numbers smaller, convert the 100 points to two-digit decimals such that they sum to 1.

EDUCATION MARKET
Regrouped Descending Order Of Weighted Importance VOC's

Customer Chain (importance)	Customer Weight	Need	Import. of need w/i group	Weighted import. of need
Specialist	0.5	G	30	15.0
Specialist	0.5	H	30	15.0
Buyer	0.2	M	50	10.0
Dealer	0.2	C	40	8.0
Specialist	0.5	B *	15	7.5
Specialist	0.5	I	15	7.5
Dealer	0.2	D	30	6.0
User	0.1	Q	60	6.0
Specialist	0.5	F	10	5.0
Buyer	0.2	T	20	4.0
Dealer	0.2	B *	15	3.0
Dealer	0.2	E	10	2.0
Buyer	0.2	J	10	2.0
Buyer	0.2	K	10	2.0
Dealer	0.2	A	5	1.0
Buyer	0.2	L *	5	1.0
Buyer	0.2	U	5	1.0
User	0.1	N	10	1.0
User	0.1	O	10	1.0
User	0.1	P	10	1.0
User	0.1	L *	5	0.5
User	0.1	S	5	0.5

* **Bold** letters represent needs falling in
more than one Customer Chain link.

8.3 Regrouped descending order of weighted importance VOCs.

3. Assign VOCs needs to the particular customer to which they pertain. Note again, that some VOCs may pertain to more than one customer.
4. Within each customer row (cluster) repeat the Constant Sum process again for the other VOCs by distributing 100 points across the VOCs such that they sum to unity or 100 within each customer row.
5. Repeat steps (3) and (4) for the remaining customers in the chain.
6. Within each customer row, multiply each VOC Constant Sum importance rating by the respective customer weight.
7. Create a new matrix by regrouping the weighted VOCs in descending order of weighted importance (Figure 8.3). This new matrix is the Regrouped Descending Order of Weighted Importance.

The result is a weighted importance for each VOC calibrated by the weights of the customer chain links. In the case where a VOC falls in

EDUCATION MARKET
Combined Weighted Descending Importance VOC Matrix

Customer Chain (importance)	Customer Weight	Need	Import. of need w/i group	Combined Weighted import. of need
Spec	0.5	G	30	15.0
Spec	0.5	H	30	15.0
Spec/Dealer	---	B *	---	10.5
Buyer	0.2	M	50	10.0
Dealer	0.2	C	40	8.0
Spec	0.5	I	15	7.5
Dealer	0.2	D	30	6.0
User	0.1	Q	60	6.0
Spec	0.5	F	10	5.0
Buyer	0.2	T	20	4.0
Dealer	0.2	E	10	2.0
Buyer	0.2	J	10	2.0
Buyer	0.2	K	10	2.0
Buyer/User	---	L	---	1.5
Dealer	0.2	A	5	1.0
Buyer	0.2	U	5	1.0
User	0.1	N	10	1.0
User	0.1	O	10	1.0
User	0.1	P	10	1.0
User	0.1	S	5	0.5

* **Bold** letters represent needs falling in
more than one Customer Chain link.

8.4 Combined weighted descending importance VOC matrix.

more than one customer chain category, their weights are combined (in our example, needs "B" and "L") and all VOCs would be relisted in decreasing order of the combined weighted importance in a Combined Weighted Importance VOC Matrix (Figure 8.4). This results in a quasi Pareto list of VOCs which can be used to establish a cut off point below which those respective VOCs would not be carried forward to deployment.

Advantages

1. A detailed and mathematical method to decide which VOCs should be carried forward for deployment.
2. A way to reduce the number of VOCs to be used for QFD and COPC. That is, a way to decrease the size of the deployment matrices.

3. A way to determine those VOCs common to more than one customer.

4. A way to examine which customer links and their respective VOCs have the most influence on future sales.

Please note that Lou Cohen discusses this process in refined detail in his excellent book, *Quality Function Deployment, How To Make QFD Work for You.*[5]

STAKE HOLDER NEEDS MODELING

A similar method of displaying VOC across a chain of customers is the Stake Holder Needs Modeling developed by Larry Zeidner and Ralph Wood.[6] This, too, is a weighted scoring matrix using the Constant Sum method. As in Figure 8.2, Constant Sum is used to determine the importance weighting factors for each customer link in the customer chain (Figure 8.5). Then for each customer in the chain, 100 points are allocated across (down the column) the list of VOC verbatims. Each column must sum to 100. Some VOC verbatim rows may be empty with no points. This can happen if the verbatims were generated internally by the design team. Next the constant sum numbers in each row are multiplied by the customer importance weighting factor and these products are summed horizontally for each individual row. The last column of the matrix represents the weighted score for each VOC verbatim. As before, the matrix can be rearranged in descending order of weighted importance (Figure 8.6). The numbers in each column should be verified by real customers or, better yet, the customers should complete the matrix themselves in real time.

So, what is the difference between the two methods? The construction of the matrices is obviously similar. The StakeHolder's Needs Matrix (SNM) uses verbatims at a much higher level of indenture than the Weighted Customer Importance Matrix (WCIM), Figure 8.2. In order to construct the SNM, it is necessary to first do a data reduction using MPM discussed in Chapter 5, or Ranked Pareto Voting or Q-Sort both discussed in Chapter 6. The mathematics is the same. The WCIM is generally a two-level tree structure, whereas the SNM is a small matrix based on top level needs.

Note that in both methods all of the customers were from the same market segment, in this example, "education." As mentioned earlier one should not mix multiple segments in one analysis.

SUMMARY

For VOC to be useful it must be deployed into the product commercialization system. Just collecting and processing it are not enough. A struc-

Customer Chain Modeling Matrix
Education Market

VOC Verbatim	Customers				Weighted Customer VOC's
	User 0.10	Buyer 0.20	Specialist 0.50	Dealer 0.20	
A					0
B	10	10	10	10	10
C	10		20		11
D		40	30		23
E		5		10	3
F	40			50	14
G	5	5	5		4
H	20	5	5	20	9.5
I		25	20		15
J	15	10	10	10	10.5
Total	100	100	100	100	100

8.5 Customer chain modeling matrix – education market.

Customer Chain Modeling Matrix
Listed In Descending Order Of Weighted Importance

VOC Verbatim	Customers				Weighted Customer VOC's
	User 0.10	Buyer 0.20	Specialist 0.50	Dealer 0.20	
D		40	30		23
I		25	20		15
F	40			50	14
C	10		20		11
J	15	10	10	10	10.5
B	10	10	10	10	10
H	20	5	5	20	9.5
G	5	5	5		4
E		5		10	3
A					0
Total	100	100	100	100	100

8.6 Customer chain modeling matrix listed in descending order of importance

tured deployment tool is needed, such as QFD and/or COPC. Before these tools are used, however, a decision must be made as to which and how much VOC is to be carried forward. The tree diagram and nested hierarchy processes may be used for this determination. Deployment may create the problem of information overload if all verbatims are carried forward. Generally the Pareto 20% vital few are deployed which, in turn, keeps the dimensions of the QFD/COPC matrix at a workable size. That is, instead of one gigantic matrix, several smaller matrices are developed, each constructed by parallel teams. Caution must be used in translating the verbatims to be certain they are not translated out of context. Guidelines have been developed to help in this process. Finally, the HOQ relationship matrix is used to mathematically show the strength of the VOC — Product Requirement Relationship. The COPC matrix, on the other hand, is used to deploy verbatims to respective product functions that are used for technology ideation later in the process. Finally, within a particular market segment, a customer chain of VOCs can be deployed by weighting the customer relative importance in the chain, rating the VOC importance within each customer link, and factoring them by the customer weights. These calibrated VOCs are then deployed using QFD or COPC. Whether you are deploying a single customer or a chain of customer VOCs, we must be careful not to mix different market segments within the same deployment mechanism. Even though we can deploy a customer chain, all links of the chain must be in the same market segment.

BIBLIOGRAPHY

Shiba, S., Graham, A., and Walden, D., *A New American TQM, Four Practical Revolutions for Management*, Productivity Press, Portland, OR, 1993.

REFERENCES

1. Shillito, M. L., *Advanced QFD, Linking Technology to Market and Needs,* John Wiley & Sons, New York, 1994.
2. Daetz, D., Barnard, B., and Norman, R., *Customer Integration, the Quality Function Deployment (QFD) Leader's Guide for Decision Making*, John Wiley & Sons, New York, 1995.
3. Barnard, W. and Wallace, T. F., *The Innovation Edge, Creating Strategic Breakthroughs Using the Voice of the Customer*, Oliver Wight Publications, Essex Junction, VT, 1994.
4. Barnard, W., "Customer Focused Strategic Planning" Seminar, The Center for Competitive Edge, University of Dayton, Dayton, OH, July 1994.
5. Cohen, L., *Quality Function Deployment, How to Make QFD Work For You*, Addison-Wesley Publishing, Reading, MA, 1995.
6. Zeidner, L. and Wood, R., The Collaborative Innovation Process (CI), *Trans. 12th Symp. Qual. Funct. Deployment*, Novi, MI, June 2000.

9

TRACKING VOC INTO THE FUTURE

TRANSIENCE OF THE VOC

The VOC is transient, it changes with time. Labels change, as do importance ratings change. This can create problems in product design. In design, we cannot aim at a moving VOC target because doing so will increase the number of redesign cycles and quickly and significantly drive up cost. We must pick a static slice in time in a dynamic VOC world. We have to pick a date where design is to be frozen. All changes to the product beyond this date will be included in the next design model at a later date. This is the Japanese approach of introducing many models in rapid succession, each with small incremental changes/additions. Each model takes advantage of all prior accumulated experience to date. In the U.S., we have to hit a home run which prolongs the development cycle to get it right. In the final analysis we tend to miss the target; too much too late.

The VOC, as well as the QFD/COPC process in general, is a dynamic process that pulses forward and loops back as needed. The process should loop future signals back to the shifting present (Figure 9.1). The QFD and COPC matrices, then, are living documents that are updated over time. Keeping the matrix data updated makes it much easier and faster to design the next product model.

It is claimed that QFD and COPC compress the development cycle and commercialization process. The first matrix application generally results in moderate cycle time compression. The real significant cycle time gains come with the second and continuing matrix applications of the process. Unfortunately, most companies stop after round one.

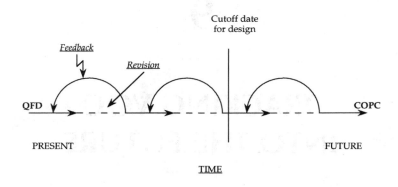

Figure 9.1 Pulse forward-loop back model. (From Shillito, M. L., *Advanced QFD Linking Technology to Market and Company Needs*, John Wiley & Sons, New York, 1994. With permission.)

FUTURING

In order to consider the future of VOC, it is necessary to work with both qualitative VOC and quantitative VOC. Qualitative VOC deals with labels and quantitative VOC deals with the importance of those labels.

The question is, will these labels remain the same over a particular time period? Will they change? Will some disappear? Will new ones come into play? The same questions apply to the numbers, usually the numerical importance of those labels. What we want to know is what will change, in what direction, how much, and how fast? Some of the tools of technological forecasting (TF) can help us create a window for the answers to some of these questions.

Futuring is performed using data from three time periods; the past, the present, and the future. We look at the past to determine trends. We structure the present to develop relationships and evaluate importances. We look toward the future to evaluate events, influences, impacts, and how we got there.

An important point to remember is that futuring does not produce a prediction but rather an integrated perception of what could be, not what will be. The tools of TF allow us to structure conversations to build windows into the future.

The futuring tools appropriate for VOC are the trend matrix, Delphi, Monitoring, Scenarios, impact analysis, and the Molecular Explosion Model. Please note that all methods to be described are highly subjective and do not proclaim to be based on an exact science. They are to be used as dialoging tools in a "what if" mode to get us to think about the possible future of specific verbatims. They may or may not lead to incorrect conclusions.

Extending VOC into the Future — Trend Matrix and Delphi

Whenever VOC is determined and documented for QFD applications, it is generally done in the present tense. That is, we derive the labels for customer needs and then rate their importance as they exist today. Since many QFD teams are involved with the design of future products, the team members are quick to realize that current importance of customer needs may not be the same in the future. Importance can increase or decrease or, perhaps, the need may disappear altogether. As former needs disappear, new ones may come into existence. In order to remain competitive, it is necessary to re-evaluate customer needs on a periodic basis. To do so requires a process and a structure to peer into the future.

A trend matrix (Figure 9.2) can be constructed to register team perception of importance time-phased into the future. Input regarding importance should come from the best sources. This may require contacting individuals outside the team to develop a trend for a customer need. These may include professional societies, academia, customers, information banks, and electronic data searches. Also it is necessary to be alert for new needs that don't exist today. A monitoring file is appropriate for starting a VOC database. The trend matrix is constructed by first listing the customer needs, usually from the HOQ or COPC matrix, and then recording how important those needs are today for the particular market, segment, and user. Generally a 1–to–5 scale is used to express current importance. Descriptors are derived for each numerical anchor point of the scale as explained in Chapter 6.

To indicate the trend in importance in those needs over time one can use a series of arrows. An arrow pointing up indicates the current need will increase in importance; a horizontal arrow indicates the importance will remain as is; an arrow pointing down indicates that the importance will decrease; a zero indicates the need will disappear.

I prefer to use arrows signifying direction because it is difficult to indicate future need with a rating scale. All that is important is the direction in which the need will be changing. That is, we want to know the direction of the arrow, not its length.

One useful method for collecting VOC information about the future is the Delphi method using a Delphi questionnaire.[1] This method was developed by the Rand Corporation in the 1950's and has many variations based on the original model. Delphi is a technological forecasting (TF) technique inquiry tool for looking into the future. It is used to ask people what events they see happening in the future, their likelihood of occurrence, and their

VOC Trend Matrix

VOC Needs	Current Importance	Future Importance	
		5 yrs.	10 yrs.
Productivity	3	↑	↑
Reliability	5	→	→
Maintenance	4	→	→
Cost/page	4	↑	→
Disposability	4	↑	→
"Green"-ness	3	↑	↑
Media interface	3	↑	↑
Standard interface	3	↓	O
Future	O	↑	↑

↑	**Increasing importance**
→	**Status quo**
↓	**Decreasing importance**
O	**Need is/will not be a factor**

Figure 9.2 VOC trend matrix. (From Shillito, M. L. and DeMarle, D. J., *Value its Measurement Design and Management,* John Wiley & Sons, New York, 1992. With permission.)

impact if they do occur. Figure 9.3 is an adaptation that can be tailored to collecting VOC data about the future. Questionnaires would be summarized and the summary data would be entered into the VOC trend matrix in Figure 9.2.

There are numerous ways to conduct a Delphi survey. Two types of questions that have worked well are, (1) what is the likelihood that a particular event will occur by a specific time frame, and, (2) what is the direction of current trends into the future.

Part A of Figure 9.3 asks respondents the likelihood of an event occurring within 5 years and 10 years. For this example, 5 years and 10

Delphi Questionnaire for VOC

PART A What is likelihood that:	5 Yrs: Short Term	10 Yrs: Long Term
1. Productivity will be at least 100 units/hr.?	90	100
2. Recyclable consumables / containers will be federal law?	85	100
3. etc.		

PART B Using arrows, ↑ increasing, ↓ decreasing, → no change, estimate the change in importance of each of the following needs (if you believe the need will disappear, use a zero):		
1. Productivity	↑	→
2. Reliability	↑	↑
3. Maintenance	↑	→
4. etc.	↓	o

Figure 9.3 Delphi questionnaire for VOC. (From Shillito, M. L. and DeMarle, D. J., *Value its Measurement Design and Management,* John Wiley & Sons, New York, 1992. With permission.)

years are arbitrary and would be adjusted according to the subject area studied. A rating guideline should also be included to help respondents estimate probability. For example: highly likely = 90 to 100%, quite likely = 65 to 90%, as likely as not = 50%, not very likely = 10 to 35%, and Unlikely = 0 to 10%. It is important that a category scale is used.

Part B of Figure 9.3 asks respondents to draw arrows in the answer space to represent their perception of the future trend of particular events.

Interactive Delphi Grid

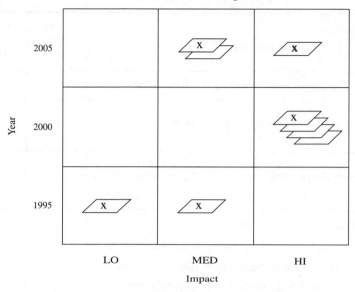

x = Probability of event occurring

Figure 9.4 Interactive Delphi grid. (From Shillito, M. L. and DeMarle, D. J., *Value its Measurement Design and Management*, John Wiley & Sons, New York, 1992. With permission.)

Arrow category descriptions are listed on the questionnaire for trending guidelines.

The original Delphi model used yet another questioning method. The original questioning technique asked people to estimate how many years they think it will take until a particular event occurs. For example, "How many years will it be until all new U.S. cars after 1995 have ABS brakes as standard equipment?" This type of question can also be used for VOC. Whichever variation is used, the wording of the questions is very critical to be sure you elicit the response you want.[2] The choice is yours.

Knowing the future direction of customer needs is helpful in selecting what technologies to use for future products. For example, if the VOC is kept up–to–date regarding technology, future generations of products can be speculated based on selection of latest technology and estimated importance of needs for the approximate time period of product introduction.

Another Delphi variation is an interactive grid mapping process. The process works on the same principle except that the various customer needs are written on cards or sticky pads. At the interview, the interviewee is asked to place the cards on a grid (Figure 9.4) where the y-axis represents time and the x-axis represents impact. If the interviewee develops other needs that are not in the starter deck of cards, new cards are written and are placed on the grid. The interviewee may also be asked to estimate the probability of occurrence on the card. The resulting grid is a map of when certain needs will occur, their probability of occurring, and the impact if they do occur.

MONITORING THE VOC

Monitoring is a TF surveillance technique that entails keeping current tabs on significant signals in order to assess change.[3] The VOC process is an excellent place and activity for discovering signals to watch for future significant changes.

The basic process entails establishing a file, or an information storage and retrieval system, and assigning responsibility for maintenance of the file. Using monitoring, VOC signals can be followed for changes. The most obvious questions in monitoring are: "Are significant shifts occurring in any of the VOC verbatims or categories? What other events are coming into play that could be related to or affect a particular VOC?"

Data are collected from the literature, trade magazines, and journals, as well as personal contacts and observations. Consideration should be given to data storage and retrieval, as simple notebooks and files may quickly become impractical. Monitoring is used to track signals and events in order to assess change. These signals could have a profound impact on the company or project if they ever reach a critical mass. The VOC process helps us discover what signals to monitor.

Monitoring and Delphi data also provides input to constructive scenarios about the market and customer.

Scenarios

One way of integrating VOC signals and information is to write a series of scenarios. Scenario writing is a qualitative forecasting technique that is used to project various futures from present conditions based on stated assumptions. Data from the trend matrix, Delphi inquiry, and monitoring provide excellent input for writing scenarios.

Scenarios may be written in many forms, lengths, and formats. Generally, a set of several scenarios is constructed as opposed to one most-likely scenario. The three most used are a pessimistic, an optimistic, and a most-likely scenario. They may be written in prose form or in a matrix format (Figure 9.5). Regardless of format, they should be believable, relevant, and thought-provoking.

VOC Scenario by Matrix Method

Scenarios for 20XX   Country _____
                        Market _____
                        Segment _____
                        User   _____

Assumptions: 1. SCSI interface
                        2. 500 x 500 pixel
                        3. etc.
                        4. etc.

VOC	Areas Affected in Company	Impact on Company			Impact on Product Design		
		O	P	M	O	P	M
• Send pictures by modem	• SW design • Image compression • R/D	➡	➡	➡	⬆	➡	⬆
• Ability to make electronic montages	• SW	⬆	➡	⬆	⬆	➡	⬆
• Store everything on 3-inch disk	• Design • HW/SW • R/D	⬇	⬇	⬇	➡	⬇	⬇
• Copyright violation	• Large	➡	⬇	⬇	➡	➡	➡

O = Optimistic   ⬇ = Negative impact
P = Pessimistic   ⬆ = Positive impact
M = Most likely   ➡ = Neutral; no effect

Figure 9.5 VOC scenario by matrix method.

VOC scenarios can be helpful in deployment through COPC and the HOQ as discussed in Chapter 8. For example, with help from marketing, the team could use VOC scenarios to write future advertising brochures and literature. Such scenarios can also be related back to the business plan and business strategy for upgrades and what-if simulations.

Paradigms and VOC

As we discussed in Chapter 1, paradigms can play a major role in shaping or changing VOC. Paradigms may keep VOC entrenched or change it completely! Either way, they do influence how we view the future and

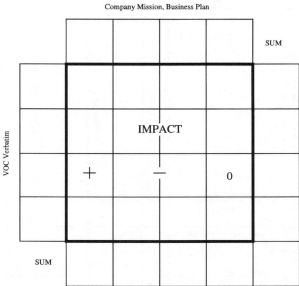

Figure 9.6 Generic impact matrix. (From Shillito, M. L. and DeMarle, D. J., *Value its Measurement Design and Management,* John Wiley & Sons, New York, 1992. With permission.)

VOC. This is why structured processes like the TF tools help surface and make paradigms visible in order that we can deal with them.

Impact Analysis

A useful tool for estimating the impact of changing customer needs (verbatims) is impact analysis (IA). IA is a subjective measurement quantification technique for evaluating the impact of external factors (in this case VOC verbatims) on a set of items. It is a matrix scoring method wherein raters use plus signs (+) and minus signs (-) and zeros to quantify their perception of interactions of items. It can be used in any situation where it is desirable to measure both the positive and negative forces that impinge on a system or set of alternatives.[4-6] Figure 9.6 represents a generic impact matrix for VOC, company mission, and business plan. This model is a simplification of the original, more comprehensive model developed by the author discussed at length in the references.

Impact Matrix 3-Hole Punch

PLANNING VOC VERBATIMS	MISSION			BUS PLAN		
	Create superior product value	Focus on customer satisfaction	Achieve market leadership	Expand functionality of punches	Expand into new market segments (exec)	Σ
6. Pierce multiple sheets 7. No jam	+	+	+	0	0	3
25. Pierce transparency 26. Material, no jam	+	+	+	+	0	4
28. Professional line with name plate	0	0	+	+	+	3
Σ	2	2	3	2	1	

+ = Will make it easier to achieve mission and business plan
− = Will make it difficult to achieve mission and business plan
0 = No influence

Figure 9.7 Impact matrix, 3-hole punch.

Figure 9.7 is a sample impact matrix of selected VOC item affects on a company mission and business plan. The basic elements of the mission and business plan are listed as column headings. Specific selected VOC items that are expected to change in the future are listed as row items. The matrix is used to express the impact of the rows (VOC) on the columns (plans). Note that the VOCs retain their original identification numbers.

In our example, VOCs were selected from a 3-hole punch project. In this case some were combined. To determine the impacts we begin one row at a time. "Pierce multiple sheets with no jamming." Will this have a positive, negative, or no affect on "create superior product value"? In this case we feel it will have a positive affect. That is, improving our product with respect to "pierce multiple sheets with no jamming" will make it easier to accomplish the particular mission item. Conversely, a negative impact would make it more difficult to accomplish the mission item. A zero is used for no affect.

The entire matrix is quantified in the same way. It is best to complete the matrix by scoring one complete row at a time until finished. Once quantified, the matrix columns and rows are algebraically summed to determine total overall impact. The column totals show the combined affect of all VOCs on each individual mission and business plan item. Row totals show the combined overall affect of VOCs across all mission and business plan items. The individual cell impacts of plus, minus, and zero are still preserved and can to used to determine which cells influenced the algebraic sum.

The impact matrix can be used, then, to estimate the affect of pursuing certain VOC items. That is, if the customer expressed a desire for certain things and these things will change over time, what will be the affect on our accomplishing our mission and business plan if we do exactly what the customer asks us to do? The impacts catch our attention and allow us to brief management on the results. We also have an audit trail for their derivation.

There are several ways to quantify an impact matrix. First of all, instead of simple (+), (-), and zero, one could use numbers from an impact scale such as ±9, ±3, ±1, and zero. The VOCs could be entered along with their respective importance ratings (for example the NHP importances from Figure 6.1 or 6.2). The scores would then be used as weighting factors to multiply against the impact scores to derive a weighted impact.

Implications of VOC Signals

Another way to track VOC is to determine its implications for the company — whether it continues to change or if it materializes. For example, let us assume we are in the attaché case design and manufacturing business. Let's also assume we have interviewed customers for VOC, and one verbatim that surfaced was "built-in stun gun in attaché." This sounds like a solution to a personal/physical security concern. It is also a new customer need for an attaché case, that is, personal security. This is an intriguing new feature for an attaché case and one we wish to explore further. How might we go about this? What are possible implications if we include such a device in our attaché?

A very useful tool for surfacing and measuring implications is the Molecular Explosion Model (MEM).[7] I first learned about this tool in 1973 while attending James R. Bright's Technological Forecasting workshop in Castine, Maine. The tool has had many names, among them impact wheel and futures wheel. Lehning[8] describes and uses her "future wheel" process in the larger context of futuring, that is, looking for consequences and implications. Wagschal[9] also uses the wheel in futuring for exploring consequences of future possibilities. Searle[10] also describes his impact wheel process in detail. Searle uses his impact wheel to distinguish the layers in a hierarchy of consequences and gives explicit instructions in its use. It is very similar to the one about to be described here. Vanston[11] also describes an impact wheel used as a normative (goal oriented) forecasting technique. Joel Barker,[12] the futurist, if not the originator, was one of the first to use the tool. He has greatly enhanced and refined it into a far more sophisticated technology which is part of his licensed Strategic Exploration Process. I must credit Mr. Barker for his progressive development of this excellent tool. I have chosen to use the name "molecular explosion model" (MEM) because of its final finished appearance. The MEM is used to determine the first and higher order impacts on some recipient that can result from an occurrence of some event. Figure 9.8 illustrates a MEM.

I will use the model described by Searle[10] to illustrate the MEM mechanism.

The process starts with a center or hub which contains the issue at hand. The issue must be stated very precisely. For our example the center is labeled "built-in stun gun in attaché."

To develop implications we start with the hub and ask what the impact on the company will be if this event occurs, good or bad, etc. We record these statements in separate circles around the circumference of the hub. Each circle is connected to the hub with a single line. A recorded statement must also be short and specific. A plus (+) or minus (-) sign may be recorded with each statement to signify the directions of the impact. Some teams choose to use a scale to indicate both direction and magnitude of the impact such as ±1, ±3, ±9. The correct way to show impact is the method that works best for the team. There is no right or wrong way.

Now that the team has completed level one, they repeat the process all over again on each of the new level 1 circles. This time the new (level 2) circles are connected to the level 1 circles with a double line. Finally, a third level impact is derived by expanding all of the level 2 circles and so on. Three lines connect level 2 circles to level 3 circles. Many times several level 3 impacts are expanded further as seen in Figure 9.8. Recording of the impact statements must be done in a circular manner as opposed to a linear chain of events. That is, expand MEM events in concentric circles. It is easy to fall into the trap of recording a level 1 event and then continuing to expand this event on out to a fourth or fifth level before going to the next level 1 event. Most teams will have exhausted their thoughts by the end of round 4. Depending on the subject and use, many times two levels are sufficient. The amount of detail and number of levels is determined by the subject and needs of the team.

How do we use this information? What we are looking for are events or a chain of events that can have a beneficial positive or a serious negative

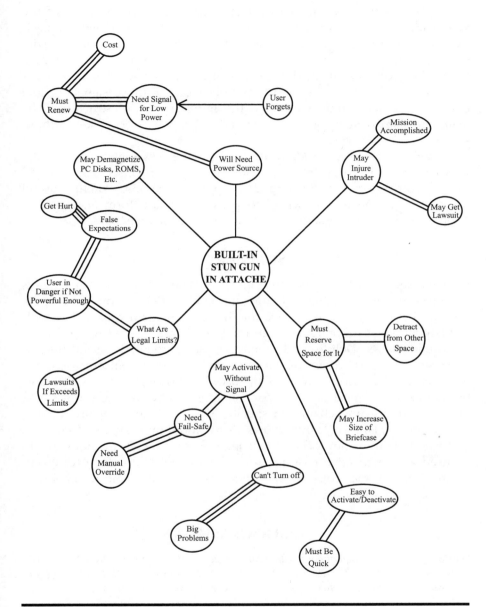

Figure 9.8 MEM diagram for attache case.

impact on the company. That is, something for which no one was prepared. We are looking for serious consequences that may result from some action or event. Many of these events surface during a QFD project. The MEM then serves as a testing ground to determine the impacts of the events before they occur. Many signals are discovered because of the systematic procedure for deriving the VOC. When an important signal is discovered during the process, it should immediately be highlighted with a yellow marker so they are not lost later on as more data is developed. When the process is finished, the team can return to those marked items and apply the MEM to envision the implications of those signals on the company, business unit, etc. Once the implications are structured, the team can then develop and recommend appropriate responses to those signals.

Other creative uses of MEM are to leave the wheel-like chart on the wall so other members and non-team members can observe it and add to it — sort of a "what's missing in the picture" exercise. Another useful exercise is to convert the wheel to prose/paragraph form and send to people over an electronic mail system and ask for responses.

SUMMARY

We have seen that VOC changes with time. When collected, it represents a static slice in time. In reality though, the VOC model is a forward looping process that brings new data back into the shifting main stream. The tools from Technological Forecasting can be used to trace VOC into the future. The trend matrix, Delphi, and monitoring are particularly useful for this purpose. Scenarios are an imaginative way to integrate information from these tools. Scenarios may also be used to update COPC, QFD, and business and technical plans. Impact analysis can be used to estimate the impact of trends and change in specific VOCs on the company mission and business plan. The MEM allows us to study implications of changes and events before they occur. Most importantly, the TF methods are to be used as a perceptive tool not a persuasive tool. We want to discover, in an impartial and objective a manner as possible, some insights into VOC that don't exist today.

BIBLIOGRAPHY

Martino, J. R., *Technological Forecasting for Decision Making*, Elsevier, New York, 1972.
Porter, A. L., Roper, A. T., Mason, T. W., Rossini, F. A., and Banks, J., *Forecasting and Management of Technology*, John Wiley & Sons, New York, 1991.

REFERENCES

1. Jolson, M. A. and Rossow, G. L., The Delphi process in marketing decision making, *J. Mark. Res.*, 8, 443-448, November 1971.
2. Salancik, J. R., Wenger, W., and Helfer, E., The construction of Delphi event statements, *Tech. Forecast. Soc. Change*, 3, 65-73, 1971.

3. DeMarle, D. J. and Shillito, M. L., Technological forecasting, in G. Salvendy, Ed., *Handbook of Industrial Engineering*, John Wiley & Sons, New York, 1982, 11.1.1 – 11.1.5.
4. Shillito, M. L. and DeMarle, D. J., *Value, Its Measurement Design and Management*, John Wiley & Sons, New York, 1992.
5. Shillito, M. L., "Impact Analysis," paper presented at James R. Bight's Technology Forecasting Workshop, Castine, ME, Industrial Management Center, TX, June 1977, 36.
6. Shillito, M. L., *Advanced QFD, Linking Technology to Market and Company Needs*, John Wiley & Sons, New York, 1994.
7. Shillito, M. L., VOC with a future dimension, *Trans. 6th Symp. Qual. Funct. Deploy.*, Novi, MI, 1995, 183-189.
8. Lehning, M. A., *Managing Change*, Tracking Trends, Inc., Omaha, Nebraska.
9. Wagschal, P. H., Futuring: a process for exploring detailed alternatives, *World Future Soc. Bull.*, September-October, 1981, 25-32.
10. Searle, B., The impact wheel: the empowerment experience, *1989 Annu. Devel. Hum. Resour.*, University Associates, San Diego, CA, 83-87.
11. Vanston, J. H., Jr., *Technology Forecasting: An Aid to Effective Technology Management*, Technology Futures, Austin, TX, 1982.
12. Barker, J. A., Author's conversations, Infinity Limited, Inc., Lake Elmo, MN.

10

VOC SYSTEM FROM A SEASONED PERSPECTIVE

HOW DOES IT ALL RELATE? THE VOC SYSTEM REVISITED

How does VOC, people, organizations, behaviors, data, time, product, business, strategy, business plans, and politics all fit together? We can view VOC as a Behavioral/Organizational/Business/Data system. The above elements operate as subsystems which, in turn, are ordered and dependent.

I have chosen to represent the VOC system elements in a matrix (Figure 10.1) whose columns each represent three levels of detail from macro at the top row to micro on the bottom row. All row levels are ordered in magnitude in the same direction.

All elements begin at the top and progress serially toward the bottom row. The upper row represents the strategic level, the second row represents the tactical level, and the third row the operational level. The fourth row represents pay dirt, delivery, and commercialization. Scanning across each row will outline what needs to be done for each element of the system and delivery. For example, at the top row, senior management works with speculation and opinion. They use macro tools, processes, and thinking to focus on the future. They deal at the total organization level using intuitive models to set strategy.

We can create another scenario by scanning across the next lower, or second, row. For the system to work smoothly the rows should progress uniformly to the fourth row. One should not move in an element (column) to the next lower level until all elements in the upper level of the column have been satisfied. Likewise, one should not move an element to the next lower level until all elements of that row have been satisfied at the same level as each other. Here is where the problems start. People,

Organization Involvement	Data Type	Tools / Processes	Time Orientation	Behavior	Models	Business	Product	Vertical VOC	Focus	Customer Contact	Tools
						VOC — Commercialization Elements					
Senior Mgmt.	Speculation	Macro	Future	Organization	Intuitive	Strategy	Functions	VOM	Strategic	Little	Macro / Qualitative
Business / Technical Mgmt.	Opinion	Intermediate	Near Future	Team	Trend	Business Plan	Needs	VOE	Tactical	Some	Qualitative / Quantitative
Individual Project	Facts	Micro	Present	Individual	Event	Deliverable	Features	VOC	Operational	Much	Micro Quantitative
						Commercialization					

Figure 10.1 VOC development activity coordination matrix.

teams, managers, etc., want to charge off on their own and do what they are good at. For example, I have seen teams start designing a product before the business plan was assembled, before the market segment was finalized, and before corporate strategy was finalized. They were told to just start building the product, and that the problems would be fixed and corrections made later on.

Do you realize how much this cost the company? Do you realize how much longer the product cycle was protracted? Then there are other companies who develop products first and then see if they can find a market for it or develop a business case around it, sort of VOC in reverse. There are different processes and programs to develop products and I am sure many companies have had successes using their own models. I do believe, though, that if new product development follows a VOC process similar to the matrix, the success rate will increase and the time to money will decrease.

Let us look at the various elements of the VOC system.

1. ***Organizational Involvement***: Who is involved at what level? The process should begin at the highest level in the company, senior management. They set the broad perspective. The next level down is business and technical management. They translate the strategic participation and technology strategies into product family strategies. Finally this information provides input for the product/program teams to develop specific line of business plans and product concepts and for the cross-functional technical teams to begin designing product.

2. ***Data Type***: The VOC data that is used ranges from speculation to facts. The upper management levels use more speculative data backed up with any hard data available. At this level there is little or no customer contact. Middle management works with opinion which has more specific backup, usually collected from the field with customer contact. At the engineering and production level, they work with more tangible data based on experience and customer specific probes.

3. ***Tools/Processes***: VOC tools used at the higher levels of management are macro in scope and point in strategic system directions. At the other end of the spectrum, the tools are more micro oriented and based on subsystems or product parts and pieces. The upper level uses more scenario planning. The middle level uses market and business research techniques which are more applied mathematics and involve some customer contact. The lower level uses specific data derived from customer contacts, which is put into a structure and quantified for importance.

4. ***Time Orientation:*** At the upper management or system level, VOC time is future–oriented and reflects years into the future. Whereas, at the project level, time deals with the present and the frantic countdown to product launch, which is measured in months, weeks or days.

5. ***Behavior:*** The way plans are carried out varies at each level. At the top level a few top level management people work together to plan the corporate strategy by using input and feedback across all levels. At the tactical level cross-functional teams seem to be the method for planning. Teams are also used at the product design level. The team projects also create much homework that is done at an individual level and aggregated into a whole.

6. ***Models:*** Models used to develop the VOC can be event–oriented, trend–oriented, and intuitive. At the operational level, the product builders use event models based on real time and customer contact. At the tactical level, planners tend to use trend type models based on historical data trends and their extrapolation into the future. These involve sales activity records by market segment, demographic records, etc. At the strategic level, management uses some intuitive models which they mix with trends and event feedback from the two lower levels.

7. ***Business:*** This column deals with the various elements of the business chain. Upper management sets broad corporate strategy and portfolios which are converted into a business plan or participation strategy at the tactical level. Also at this level, the product families and product concepts begin to take shape. At the operational level, final product design, manufacturing process, and delivery are formulated. Notice that all of these elements and levels must be in sync up and down the chain. The bottom must be connected to the top.

8. ***Product:*** The product can also be viewed from different perspectives. At the lowest level, teams deal with product features, which, in turn, dictate technology parts and pieces. Features are the physical fulfillment of customer needs. Needs are identified and used at the tactical level. Project people need to understand customer needs so they can make design decisions and tradeoffs for future designs. It is important in collecting customer information to distinguish between a need and a feature. Needs can be aggregated by function. The function level is used by management to set strategy. The needs rest in an appendix as backup for strategy.

9. ***Vertical VOC:*** VOC was described in Chapter 1. It is important that the various levels are in sync. Ideally, VOC flows from the top (macro) level down. This does not always happen. The important

point to address are any gaps in the VOC chain and to be honest with ourselves as far as what is missing to do the job.

10. **Focus:** Focus of the project is another way of looking at vertical VOC and time orientation. The higher in the hierarchy the more strategic the scope. As one descends the hierarchy the more focused jobs and efforts become.

11. **Customer Contact:** Senior management has little contact with customers and users. The exception is with million dollar type accounts where the president of the company is on a first name basis with the presidents/owners of customer companies. There is considerably more customer contact at the middle level where marketing and sales play a significant part. At the project level, there is even more customer/user contact in conjunction with marketing and sales. VOC and the project team members should be interfacing directly with customers, especially end users to determine customer/user needs. This is where the VOC collection methods discussed in Chapter 3 come into play.

12. **Tools:** Tools used in the commercialization process and product life cycle also progress from being very macro in scope at the top to being more specific lower down in the organization. The middle levels, marketing for example, use more quantitative tools and deal with statistical acceptance sampling processes and procedures. They do so because they want to verify within certain confidence limits how much of a particular metric a user desires. For example, "How much gas mileage do you expect from you car?" They use complex statistical procedures to derive the possible outcomes from samples that represent the whole population. At level three, the habitat of VOC, we want to get the names of the labels that marketing and statistical people want to verify. Therefore, if we do a poor job at identifying the labels on the customer/user needs, marketing could be doing a perfect job at working on the wrong thing! VOC, then is a precursor to marketing and quantitative research.

So what do you do with this VOC matrix? It is not a tool per se. It can be very useful for checking your project against the various VOC elements (columns). For example, you can place an 'x' at the appropriate column level for your project for each element. The level you mark is based on your best appraisal of your current project status.

Once you have marked each element, connect them all with a line. The ideal shape should be a straight line. A straight line signifies that all the VOC elements for your project are progressing uniformly. That is, you haven't put the cart before the horse. If your resulting line has many peaks or valleys, you have reason for some concern because they signify poor or little coordination of effort. The project is going to be protracted and the time to money prolonged. Information may not be used properly and the wrong product could be developed for the wrong market. One or two spikes or valleys is not too bad as long as action is taken to get everything in sync. It is easier to correct one or two. More than two corrections may be a major effort.

SO WHAT DOES IT ALL MEAN?

Throughout the first nine chapters the many parameters that must be considered in developing good VOC have been discussed. All parameters must be considered and all should be in sync with each other. Putting the cart before the horse can make VOC development and deployment difficult. Good coordination at all levels of the company are necessary. Doing a good job at coordination takes good communication and dialogue. In this chapter I have attempted to show how all of these parameters are related. The ideal state is for all of them to be in perfect harmony. The VOC coordination matrix is a mnemonic device to act as speed bumps in a company's haste to quickly develop VOC.

THE DEPLOYMENT FRAMEWORK FOR VOC

The two VOC deployment mechanisms already mentioned are QFD and COPC (discussed in Appendix C). The framework can be represented by a Venn diagram (Figure 10.2). Let us look at the intersection of the three circles. The intersection of research and development and manufacturing involves manufacturability. The people in R&D can invent new things, but many times it is difficult to scale the R&D model to manufacturing proportions and robustness. So, there is conflict between R&D and manufacturing. R&D develops new things but they may be difficult to manufacture. The intersection of manufacturing and marketing is delivery. Marketing is usually upset with manufacturing because they cannot get the finished product out on time. Manufacturing, in turn, is upset with marketing because marketing is usually changing the feature set or specifications. So manufacturing has to deal with a shifting and moving target. No wonder they cannot get the product out on time! Next the intersection of marketing and R&D involves product features. Marketing claims they know what the customer wants in the product (in many cases they do not) and so does R&D. Therefore, both think they should run the company. So, in all of the intersections it seems that no one likes each other very much. It is a nasty downward spiral with minimum communication and lots of battered egos.

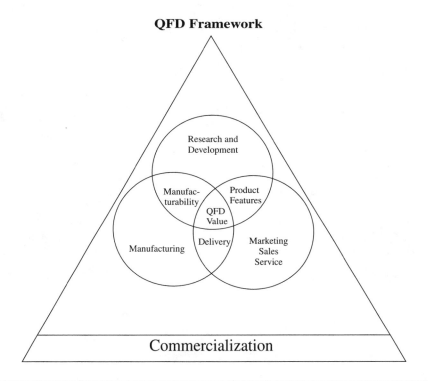

QFD Framework

Research and
Development

Manufac-
turability

Product
Features

QFD
Value

Manufacturing

Delivery

Marketing
Sales
Service

Commercialization

10.2 QFD framework.

QFD and COPC become the attractive force, structure, and glue to pull and hold all of these entities together in a non-threatening manner to develop a cohesive forward momentum to better fast commercialization and time to money. These deployment mechanisms (QFD and COPC) help teams accomplish this through non-threatening structured dialogue and participative decision making. They guide the deployment teams to a structured common focus that provides cohesion to the team with clear goals and structured deployment. That is, in a short time the process takes over and the walls of reticence and reserve begin to fade away and everyone is talking to each other because they become interested in the process.

The processes coupled with a good facilitator foster participation. In Figure 10.2 the Venn diagram has been placed inside two nested equilateral triangles pointing upwards to symbolize increased benefit to company commercialization, internal communication and, improved value to the customer. VOC is the engine and driver of the processes. How can you lose?

APPENDIX A

VOC FORMS

12 Questions and Sample Answers

Customer Morphology Worksheet

Voice of the Customer Table Worksheet

Customer Needs Matrix Worksheet

Customer Matrix Worksheet

Product Profile Matrix Worksheet

Pair Comparison Worksheet

INITIATING A VOC/QFD/COPC PROJECT

12 Questions Pre-project Assignment

Purpose

The purpose of the 12 Questions is to bring focus to a VOC/QFD/COPC project so that the team doesn't develop the wrong product. The questions primarily address the scope and nature of the project, start the process of defining the customer, and check the team's make-up in order to help the team be effective before they are efficient.

Use

The 12 Questions are issued to the team leader prior to the start of a study. The team leader, project leader, and process facilitator develop answers to the questions in an attempt to produce a straw-man document that can be used by the team to get a jump-start. The team then improves the answers and develops ownership of the final answers.

Outcome

Answering these questions will indicate what is known and what is not known about the subject of the study. Discussing and documenting these subjects is one of the most important parts of the VOC/QFD/COPC process. A poor job here can cause teams to be off-course, lose time, and develop excellent recommendations on the wrong product.

Linkage

Developing answers to these questions creates a focus for the team and the project. Answering the questions also helps create a link to the business plan or participation strategy and the company's strategic plan.

12 Questions

The 12 Questions are straight-forward, although the effort to derive the answers can be complex. A generic set of hypothetical answers is provided at the end of this document for your references.

1. Purpose
   - Why are we doing this study? What is the focus?
   - What is the team mission?
2. Completion date
   - When **must** this study be finished?
3. Decision maker
   - Who is the decision maker?
   - Who is the first person in the decision chain that can say "no" regarding the team output?
4. Scope
   - What **is** included in this study?
   - What **is not** included in this study?
5. Product
   - What product?
   - What model?
   - What generation?

- World class?
- Revolutionary?
6. Market/customer
   - Who is the customer we're trying to satisfy?
   - Country?
   - Market?
   - Segment?
   - User?
   - Chief buying influence?
7. Time horizon for the product. Window of opportunity.
   - This year or next year?
   - When?
8. Assumptions
   - Product?
   - Market?
   - Company?
   - Manufacturing - who and where?
   - Distribution?
   - Customer?
   - Other?
9. Business plan
   - Do the answers to the above questions fit the organization's business plan?
   - Do we (the team) have a copy of the business plan?
   - Are there spin-offs that will apply to other organizations?
   - Does a business plan exist?
10. Team members
    - Who is the team leader?
    - Based on the answers to the previous questions, do we still have the right people on the core team?
    - The core team remains for the life of the project; who are the members?
    - What background do we need?
    - What geography is represented?
    - Ad hoc members:
      - Who are they?
      - What background/expertise/information?
      - When do we need them?
      - How long do we need them for?
11. Purchasing drivers. Why would a customer even think about purchasing this product? What are the macro criteria the customer uses to make a choice?
    - Economics
    - Product performance

- Safety
- Ease of use
- Workforce capability
- Environment
12. Task/deliverable/function
    - What task is the customer/user trying to accomplish through buying our product?
    - What is the deliverable or output from using this product?
    - What is the basic function of the product? Why does it exist?

12 Questions — Sample Answers

Here are some sample answers to the 12 Questions:

1. Purpose?
    - Use the COPC process to generate a design for a high-volume widget.
    - The design must address cost estimate, product availability, and product architecture.
2. Completion date?
    - December 25, 20XX.
    - Year-end to support the high-volume core and to provide input to the AOP.
3. Decision maker?
    - John Doe.
4. Scope?
    - *Is:* widget through host interface and mechanical interface.
    - *Is not:* autoload; define a labeling system; higher application authoring software.
5. Product?
    - Electro-mecha-tronics widget.
    - Model two.
    - Generation three.
    - Evolutionary upgrade (not revolutionary).
6. Market/customer?
    - Country-worldwide.
    - Market-OEM widget manufactures; company lines of business; major widget reseller chains; value-added resellers.
    - Segment-desktop computing.
    - Workstation users.
7. Time horizon for the product?
    - June 20XX.

8. Assumptions?
    - Orange book media compatible.
    - Minimum 10k units/month.
    - $5\frac{1}{4}$, half-height.
    - SCSI interface.
    - Will be manufactured on-site and not contracted out.
9. Business plan?
    - "Yes" to all business plan questions.
10. Team members?
    - In addition to core team (comprised of Joe, John, Sue, and Patrica), we will need an expert in media manufacture when this subject arises (approximately 6 weeks).
11. Purchasing drivers?
    - Higher productivity.
    - Increased reliability.
    - Reduced access time.
    - Disk compatibility.
    - Smaller footprint.
12. Task/deliverable/function?
    - Task: read and write data on widget.
    - Output from product: widget with information.
    - Basic function: read and write data.

Customer Morphology Worksheet   FORM __

Where is product used?				
Who uses product?				
Who makes buy decisions?				
CBI				
What method is used?				
H/W Interface?				
S/W Interface?				
Whose product currently used?				

Figure A.1 Customer morphology worksheet.

Voice of the Customer Table

Interviewee: _____
Interviewer(s): _____

Market Segment(s): _____
User(s): _____
Product: _____

Customer Verbatim	Reworded Data	I/E	Need	Solution	Feature	Other ------>

Figure A.2 Voice of the customer table.

Customer Needs Matrix Worksheet

FORM __

Needs	CUSTOMERS			

Figure A.3 Customer needs matrix worksheet.

Customers for Product _____

Customers							

Macro Requirements							

Customer Matrix Worksheet

Figure A.4 Customer matrix worksheet.

FORM ____

Product Profile Matrix Worksheet

VOC NEED	Barely Acceptable	Tablestakes	Fully Satisfied		Wow!
	1	2	3	4	5

Figure A.5 Product profile matrix worksheet.

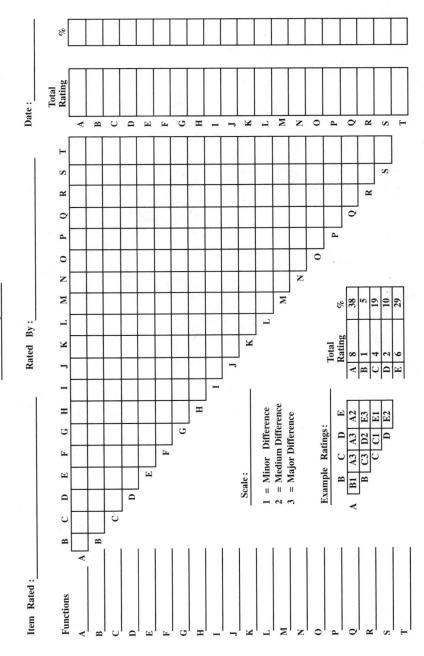

Figure A.6 Pair comparison worksheet for value measurement.

APPENDIX B

KANO COLLECTION AND INTERPRETATION METHOD

As we have seen, there are many methods one can use to investigate VOC. One particular method that is used to determine types of customer needs is that developed by Noriake Kano of Tokyo Rika University.[1,2]

His famous graph (Figure B.1) is referred to in almost all books written on this subject. The x-axis of Figure B.1 indicates the degree of functionality of the product, from dysfunctional (physically unfulfilled condition) to functional (fulfilled). The y-axis indicates how satisfied the customer is, from satisfied at the top to dissatisfied at the bottom. Kano uses this graph to explain VOC. For example, the bottom curve labeled "must be" represents VOC verbatims that are taken for granted. "I expect my car to start; I expect it to be safe; I expect the windshield wipers to work," and so on. These features are needed to play the game and they better be of the best quality and performance. These features cannot increase customer satisfaction but you can lose a great deal if they are absent or perform less than average. These are table stakes. The company also gets no credit or "brownie points" for exceeding the norm.

The next curve labeled "one-dimensional" is where marketing and business research enter the picture. This curve is based on the premise that customer satisfaction is proportional to how functional a product is, that is, the less functional the product the less satisfied the customer and visa versa. Some companies call these "satisfiers." The more fulfilled the requirement is, the more satisfied the customer. For example, the better gas mileage and better acceleration a car has the more satisfied the customer is. This is commonly referred to as "more is better."

The upper curve labeled "attractive" represents the situation where the customer is more satisfied when the product is more functional but not necessarily less satisfied when the product is less functional. This many times is the world of hi-tech. They are exciters that are on the R&D shelf that the customer is not aware of, but if they are incorporated in the product they will be delighted. Examples of delighters are ABS brakes,

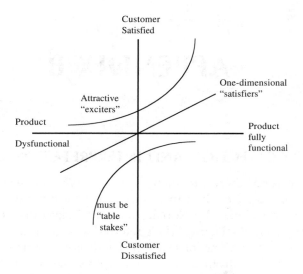

Figure B.1 Kano graph.

air bags, global positioning apparatus for a car. Once these exciters are incorporated, they quickly migrate through the "satisfiers" to the "must be" elements. An example is air conditioning in a car in the 1950s. Only the wealthy could afford it. Once it became more affordable it migrated quickly to "must be." A very large percentage of cars have air conditioning as standard equipment today. The company that can develop and introduce "exciters" quickly while increasing the "satisfiers" and maintaining highest quality in the "must be's" is the company that is going to be highly successful into the 21st Century.

KANO SURVEY

What is it? A special questionnaire with a standard set of answers for all questions for answering a bi-directional question.
Objective: To determine and classify whether or not a customer verbatim is a "must be," a "linear satisfier," or an "exciter."
Instructions

1. Decide which questions to ask.
2. Design a bi-directional answer sheet for each individual question (Figure B.2).
3. Tally all responses on a collection matrix (Figure B.3 and B.4).
4. Normalize tallies (Figure B.5).
5. Use the Kano overlay (Figure B.6) to classify response.

Customer:_____   Interviewee _____

Question:

(+)   If the copier delivers one piece of paper,
      how do you feel?

(-)   If the copier misfeeds or multifeeds,
      how do you feel?

Question (+)		Question (-)
	1. I like it that way	
	2. I must be that way	
	3. I am neutral	
	4. I can live with it that way	
	5. I dislike it	

Figure B.2 Kano questionnaire and answer sheet example.

Question #1, Paper Feeds
n = 1

		(-)				
		1	2	3	4	5
	1					
	2					X
+	3					
	4					
	5					

Figure B.3 Kano collection matrix.

The Kano graph is quite useful as a communications device about customer wants and needs. Customer requirements may also be collected and classified by a special questionnaire developed by Kano. The

Tally Sheets, Question #1, Paper Feed
n = 88

		(-)				
		1	2	3	4	5
	1					
	2			2	6	1
+	3			1	3	42
	4			1	1	21
	5					10

Figure B.4 Kano tally matrix.

Tally Sheet, Question #1, Paper Feed
n = 88

		(-)				
		1	2	3	4	5
	1					
	2			2.2%	6.8%	1.1%
+	3			1.1%	3.4%	47.8%
	4			1.1%	1.1%	23.9%
	5					11.4%

Figure B.5 Normalized kano tally matrix.

questionnaire uses five basic answers in each of two ways. The first question asks how you feel if a particular feature is present in the product, process, or service. The second question asks how you would feel if that feature were not present in the product. The five basic answers are:

1. I like it that way.
2. It must be that way.
3. I am neutral.
4. I dislike it but I can live with it that way.
5. I dislike it, and I can't accept it.

		(-)				
		1	2	3	4	5
	1	Q	E	E	E	D
	2	R	I	I	I	M
+	3	R	I	I	I	M
	4	R	I	I	I	M
	5	R	R	R	R	R

E = Delighter
M = Must have (take it for granted)
R = Reverse (funtional vs. disfunctional)
L = Linear satisfiers
Q = Questionable result (contradictions)
I = Indifferent

Figure B.6 Kano tally matrix overlay.

Figure B.2 illustrates a Kano questionnaire and answer sheet. First, the question about a copier is asked in two ways (one positive and one negative). The answer for the positive question is checked in the left column and the answer to the negative is checked in the right column. Notice both questions use the same answers. This questionnaire pertains to just one product feature, paper feed, and would be given to numerous customers to answer.

Figure B.3 illustrates the collection matrix for tallying answers across all interviewees. Notice that the positive question answers are the rows and the negative answers are the columns.

Our answer to the copier paper feed is placed in cell (2,5) because answer 2 was selected for the first question and answer 5 was selected for the second question. After interviewing all our customers, the final tally sheet might look like Figure B.4, for 88 interviewees for just one question. The tally would then be normalized to percentages and would look like Figure B.5.

How can we use this information to distinguish between "must be's," "satisfiers," and "exciters"? To determine this Kano designed an overlay for the tally matrix, Figure B.6. Imagine that the overlay is made from transparent material. When looking through the overlay at the tally matrix one can determine what type of response corresponds to each cell. For example, "linear satisfiers" fall in cell (1,5); "must be's" in (2,5), (3,5), (4,5),

Questions/Needs	D	L	M
1. Paper feed			X
2. Etc.		X	
3. Etc.		X	
4. Etc.	X		
5. Etc.			X

To House of Quality →

D = Delighter
L = Linear satisfier
M = Must be

Figure B.7 Kano question summary sheet.

"delighters" and "exciters" in (1,2), (1,3), and (1,4). The "indifferent" category means the customers are neutral. "Reverse" and "Questionable" indicate a problem with the question or the data gathering.

The sum of percentages for each type of need for our copier paper feed example are:

Linear	Must Be's	Exciters
1.1 %	1.1	2.2
1.1 %	47.8	6.8
	23.9	
	11.4	
2.2 %	84.2 %	9.0 %

So, 1.1% of the respondents felt that paper feed was a "linear satisfier," 83.1% are "must be's," and 9.0% are "exciters." Paper feed, then, is clearly a "must be."

Such a questionnaire and tally would be used for each question asked. Obviously, it is important that you are asking the vital few important questions. Results for all questions asked are posted to a question summary sheet as in Figure B.7. The results in these three columns are added to the House of Quality rows next to the corresponding importance rating column for each verbatim.

The Kano inquiry method is used to determine that balance of "must be's," "linear satisfiers," and "exciters" in a product. In general, "must be's" must be adequately satisfied, "linear satisfiers" must be competitive, there should be enough time-released "exciters" to remain competitive or differentiated.

SUMMARY

According to Glenn Mazur,[3] President, Japan Business Consultants, and translator of Kano's book, Kano uses his process in a rapid prototyping stage where problem and/or opportunity statements are brainstormed for possible solutions. The design team goes to the customer with the prototypes and asks the double–ended questions for each prototype process evaluation and by-passes product design and development. His process works well with high tech or revolutionary products. The Kano process has more to do with customer need than product development and is used in concept generation and not necessarily the House of Quality.

REFERENCES

1. Shiba, S., Graham, A., and Walden, O., *A New American TQM, Four Practical Revolutions In Management*, Productivity Press, Portland, OR, 1993.
2. Clausing, D., *Total Quality Development, A Step-by-Step Guide to World-Class Concurrent Engineering*, ASME Press, New York, 1994.
3. Mazur, G., President, Japan Business Consultants, Ann Arbor, MI. Personal conversations with the author.

APPENDIX C

CUSTOMER-ORIENTED PRODUCT CONCEPTING (COPC) — A DEPLOYMENT MECHANISM

Introduction

There are two formal structured methods to deploy VOC into the system, product, and company. One is Quality Function Deployment (QFD), which the writer assumes is already familiar to readers, and Customer Oriented Product Concepting (COPC), a variation of QFD.

QFD is generally problem solving oriented (get the rust out of the car door) and is used to establish customer and product specifications and/or technical requirements. QFD is many times focused on only a part(s) of a product. COPC is focused on the entire product. QFD works nicely when upgrading or modifying an existing company product. It is more difficult to use with non-existing products, that is, products the company never made before. COPC, however, was designed for use with non-existing products. It is based on the functional approach to product design.

Producing a product on the first try that has high end-user value should be a goal of any manufacturer. Such a desire is universal but, unfortunately, not often achieved. Product design is too often executive– or pro-ducer–driven as opposed to customer–driven. Such an approach usually leads to massive redesign and/or post-introduction problem solving. Often lacking is sufficient homework in the conceptualization or preliminary design stage in the front end of the product life cycle. This lack of homework merely increases product cost and delivery time.

Definition

A method for assisting design concepting is Customer-Oriented Product Concepting (COPC), which is an interdisciplinary team process used to derive recommendations for product design in a way that:

1. End-user musts and wants are identified and quantified for importance.
2. Company and other manufacturers product features are evaluated for current and future performance (competitive and performance analysis).
3. Product design features are correlated with marketing and business plans.
4. Appropriate technology or methodology is used to provide necessary product functions for accomplishing the user's task.
5. Appropriate manufacturing methods are utilized to build product.

These, in turn, are integrated in a matrix structure to assist one in concept selection so that:

1. Products satisfy user needs in performance, price, and delivery.
2. Products satisfy company needs and plans.

A customer purchases a product in order to accomplish some task within certain performance requirements. The product provides utility to the user, utility, in turn, is provided by product features and functions. The manufacturer, therefore, produces functions by designing the proper features and performance into a product that the customer is willing to purchase. Value is determined by how well the product allows the customer to perform his task for the price paid. In this respect, value is determined by the user, not the manufacturer. Selling price is directly related to user-perceived product utility and performance and is not related to manufacturing costs.[1] COPC is a method used to design a product with value added to both the user and the producer at a cost, quality, and price that is acceptable to both. The COPC process is especially useful for concepting consumer-type products, services, and systems.

COPC Philosophy

The foundation of COPC is based on the following tenets:

1. We must understand the customer:
   ■ They purchase function.
2. We must understand the product:
   ■ It provides function.
3. We must understand technology:
   ■ It supports and supplies function.
4. We must innovate through function:
   ■ Function opens the door to creativity.

5.We must communicate through an integrated rigorous process:
- Because we want to build the right product right the first time at the right price.

The Process

The process about to be described is an integrated model that combines (1) applied behavioral science and stake building philosophy to initialize the process and (2) a matrix incorporating value measurement, function definition, competitive analysis, a function-technology morphology, and elements of QFD. The team–deliverable result from using the COPC process is a series of recommendations (technology paths) representing different product concepts that have been screened by customer and manufacturing criteria. The process begins by the team addressing study purpose, decision maker, scope, study completion date, correct study team members, and assumptions. These issues are covered in Chapter 2 in more detail.

The team consists of members with diverse interdisciplinary backgrounds, such as marketing, sales, customer service, design engineering, manufacturing, and quality assurance. Acceptance and credibility of results can be affected by who is on the team and who is not. Unfortunately, power and politics are real issues to contend with. It is recommended to use a core team of knowledgeable people throughout the project. Many problems can be encountered if the makeup of the group frequently changes. For example, considerable time can be lost just getting new members up to speed in both content and process. Also, ratings and evaluations will become much less consistent.

The COPC process is used to design one product. It is not used to develop a product strategy for a family of products. If the product serves many different customers, a separate COPC should be performed for each individual user. It is also based on the assumptions that the company or business unit strategy is clear, and that the country, market, segment, buyer, and user have been clearly defined and documented by the business unit (a big assumption indeed!). If the above strategy and marketing documentation is not available or doesn't exist, the COPC team must develop the data themselves. If this is the case and the team has developed this data, it must be presented to upper management and the business unit for verification before progressing further in the process. Sufficient time must be allocated in the COPC process for verifying (or developing) country, market, segment, buyer, and user, because markets can be complex. Too many times answers to these items are taken for granted. This merely increases the chances of the COPC team designing the wrong product. Caution must be exercised on these topics because marketing and sales can be offended or embarrassed, especially if they really don't know the answers! A structured process like COPC brings to the surface many gaps in knowledge and information across many areas from distribution to manufacturing to marketing. This can, of course, be threatening to those who speak in mysteries with a high fog index and whose career has been founded on deception and turf protection. Consequently, it is advantageous if the process facilitator is experienced in the behavioral science techniques such as interpersonal skills, team building, and leading groups and workshops.

Constructing the COPC Matrix

The matrix is composed of three parts: (1) product functions and components, (2) the marketing/customer evaluation, and (3) the manufacturing/technology evaluation. An example matrix using a videocassette recorder (VCR) as the product to be designed will be used (see Figure C.1).

The following background information is offered to inform you more about the example product. Our product competes with all the myriad other VCRs on the market. Our model is used to record television signals as well as playback the programs. It is also widely used to playback other prerecorded videotapes, such as those rented or purchased at videotape rental stores. The following hypothetical marketing data are defined.

> *Country:* U.S. only.
> *Market:* Video.
> *Segment:* Home entertainment.
> *User:* Family.
> *Decision makers:* Parents.
> *Chief buying influence:* Primary income producer.

CUSTOMER-ORIENTED PRODUCT CONCEPTING PROCESS

Part 1: Product Functions and Components

Step 1: Define Basic Function

Purpose: To establish the reason for existence of the product. To begin building the matrix, the interdisciplinary team first defines the task that the user wants to accomplish by purchasing the product. To define the task or deliverable, the team members envision themselves as the user and ask why they are purchasing the product. For this example, the customer task is "play video tapes on the TV set." The team then defines the deliverable produced by the product, in our example, "an electronic (TV) image." Based on the user's task and product deliverable, define the

Customer-Oriented Product Concepting

PRODUCT: VCR
TASK: Play Video on TV
DELIVERABLE: Electronic (TV) Image
BASIC FUNCTION: Display Electronic Image

COUNTRY: U.S. Only
MARKET: Video
SEGMENT: Home Entertainment
USER: Family
DECISION MAKER: Primary Income Producer

MARKET/CUSTOMER

Operational Functions	Customer Requirements: Features	Importance	Competitive Analysis: Current Us	OM1	OM2	OM3	Desired Us	Improve Ratio	Sales Point	Planning: Score	Percent Score
Load Tape	Ease to Load	10	5	8	7	10	10	2.00	1.5	30.00	58.7
	Ease to Orient	10	9	9	9	8	9	1.00	1.2	12.00	23.5
	Instructions	8	7	8	8	8	8	1.14	1.0	9.12	17.8
										51.12	100.00
Transport Tape											
Record Image											
Playback Image											
Rewind Tape											
Remove Tape											

MANUFACTURING/DESIGN

Manufacturing Criteria: Mfg Criteria	Percent Weight	Technologies (How To): Tech 1 Mfg	Tech 1 Cust	Tech 2 Mfg	Tech 2 Cust	Tech 3 Mfg	Tech 3 Cust
Cost	15	5	7	5	10	5	10
Dev Time	10	3	9	5	9	5	10
Durability	15	5	5	5	6	5	9
Time to Complete	5	1		5		4	
Quality	20	5		4		4	
Reliability	20	4		4		4	
Maintainability	15	4		4		4	
	100	425	711	445	905	440	982

Figure C.1 Customer-oriented product concepting matrix (VCR example). (From Shillito, M. L., *Advanced QFD Linking Technology to Market and Company Needs*, John Wiley & Sons, New York, 1994. With permission.)

overall basic function of the product. The basic function is the prime reason for existence of the product. It is what makes the product work or sell. It is what allows the customer to accomplish the task. As in traditional VE, the basic function is described in two words: one verb and one noun. Personal analogies are helpful in defining functions. That is, you actually pretend that you are the product itself and ask, I am a _____, what do I do? Why do I exist? The answer must be stated in the verb-noun format. In our example, the basic function of the VCR is "display (electronic) image." Some other examples of basic functions are wire, "transmit signal," screwdriver, "transmit torque," wall panel, "partition space," slide rule, "display analogs," refrigerator, "remove heat."

Step 2: Define Operational Functions

Purpose: To establish the operational functions that must be performed to accomplish the basic function defined in Step 1. The operational functions that must be performed to allow the customer to accomplish the task and obtain the deliverable are defined. The basic question to be answered is, "What are all of the necessary operational functions that must be performed in order to accomplish the basic function (and allow the user to accomplish the task)?" Operational functions are also defined in the verb-noun format. They are listed, where practical, in sequential order of operation, the way the product is produced and used today. This is equivalent to a linear time-sequenced function flow. This linear format is dissimilar to a traditional Function Tree (Chapter 3), where functions are ordered by cause and consequence and not by time sequence.

Operational functions are defined at the highest (macro) level of aggregation. Their number should be approximately 6 to 12. Personal analogies are again helpful in operational function definition. The process is, "I am a _____. My basic function is _____. How do I _____? In order to permit my customer to accomplish their task, I must (function), (function), (function), . . ., (function)." Operational functions are listed as the product performs or operates today. This function flow may not be valid for future designs that may use different technologies from today. Worry about that later. This is why you are building the matrix. In our example, the operational functions are load tape, transport tape, record image, playback image, rewind tape, and remove tape. Note that all functions have been listed. We included the function "record image" to account for the customer task of recording something. This function would not be used by the customer if the VCR is used only in a playback mode. However, we include it because the customer will also be recording TV shows. The basic function, however, is still display (electronic) image. A secondary function happens to be "record image" and is one way of acquiring an image to display. The other way to acquire an image is to rent or purchase a prerecorded videotape.

Listing operational functions works best with processes, machines, procedures, and services. For products like packaging, consumables, durable goods, and so on, it is easier to list major components first and then convert the components to functions at a later time. For example, a 35-mm film package might be listed as case, box, plastic can, can lid, case graphics, box graphics, can label, can label graphics, carton physical characteristics, or instructions. Underneath the component name would be listed its function(s). Typical functions might be: enclose boxes, enclose film cans, enclose film cassette, exclude elements (dust, water, dirt), maintain seal, convey information, add appeal, maintain shape, protect contents, etc. Sometimes two separate columns are used in the matrix, one for components, the other for functions. Listing the function is especially important for the creativity phase, where the team brainstorms to function and not components. Determining the basic and operational functions is not so simple a task for the team. Function definition is a new language to which participants must become accustomed. The function definition provides the structure for completing the matrix. It acclimates the team members and provides focus to concentrate on what the product must or must not do. Remember, the customer buys functions, not product.

Part 2: Marketing/Customer Evaluation

Step 3: List Customer Features by Function

Purpose: To list for each function all of the features and wants that the customer may encounter through the use of the product. Once all functions have been defined and sequenced, Part 2 of the COPC matrix is started. A list is made of all of the features or customer requirements pertaining to each individual function. In our example, some, but not all, of the features of the function "load tape" might be "ease to load," "ease to orient cassette," "clear directions," and "load in low light." Direct quotes from customers are great.

Customer features can be obtained from marketing intelligence, research data, focus groups, surveys, interviews, internal company sources, and all of the collection and structural techniques discussed earlier. The ideal source would be to invite and pay customers to be ad hoc members of the team! Typical categories of features are ease or difficulty of use, convenience, dependability, availability, appearance, information/instructions, maintenance, and service. Tom Snodgrass of the University of Wisconsin, at Madison, and president of Value Standards, Inc., has developed four categories of functions that have been used with considerable success in his customer-oriented product design method.[2] They are assure dependability, assure convenience, satisfy user, and attract user. These categories are also helpful as stimulators for thinking about features. Some functions may be invisible to the user, consequently these invisible functions may not have customer features listed in their row. What many teams do in these cases is list all customer needs that can be impacted by these functions. In this case, technology selection will be based on most favorable impact on customer needs.

It is best to record the features in the customer's own words when possible. If customer quotes are used, it is also recommended that a glossary of terms be established that includes precise translations of the features into terms that are more meaningful to the team and technical community. For example, the customer might say he "wants a sharp image." This is important to know, but the technical community needs to know how sharp is sharp. The descriptor would be recorded both on the COPC matrix and in the glossary of terms along with a descriptive translation. The feature as translated in the glossary might read, "The image on the TV screen should have clear definition around the edges. Perception of sharpness may be influenced by contrast." The glossary is especially useful if there is turnover in team members or if there are ad-hoc members. It helps get members up to speed.

The question of what to do with things like government regulations/standards, international standards, and other regulatory requirements arises quite often. These standards are more than customer wants. They are givens and absolutes. They cannot be overlooked. To always keep them visible one can add them as a grouping in a separate row(s) at the bottom of the list of customer functions and needs. The functional equivalent can be labeled as satisfy regulations. There is no compromise with regulatory requirements. They are not brainstormed or tested, but they need to be resolved. Technologies, in addition to scoring them against customer needs and manufacturing criteria, must be checked to see if they fulfill 100% of the regulatory requirements. This is equivalent to checking technologies for compliance with customer musts. Technologies are not rated against these standards. Instead, it is a dichotomous decision where compliance is labeled either 'yes' or 'no'. Those technologies that do not satisfy regulations are either eliminated for consideration or modified until they do fit.

Step 4: Quantify Customer Features for Importance

Purpose: To determine how important each feature is to the customer. After listing all of the features for all functions, they are quantified for perceived importance to the customer. One method that can be used is to establish a simple rating scale, say, 1 to 10, or 1 to 5. If a scale is used, descriptors should be written by the team for at least three or four anchor points in the scale (e.g., 1, 5, 10). The descriptors should, as best as possible, be stated in the words of the customer. Such a rating scale might be as follows:

Rating	Descriptor
10	I must have this feature. I expect it and would definitely switch brands and pay more to get it.
8	I would like to have it: all else being equal, I would probably change brands or pay more to get it.
5	It would be nice to have; it would make me happy, but I wouldn't go out of my way to get it. I might switch brands to get it but would not pay more to get it.
1	I am apathetic about this feature; it really doesn't influence my buying decision.

Descriptors written by the team members are used in order to promote consistency across raters. For example, without scale descriptors, what one person rates an 8, another person may rate a 10, and so on. Developing the descriptors encourages a dialogue among team members that results not only in more consistent ratings, but a sharing of viewpoints that might not have surfaced. In turn, this dialogue leads to better understanding. Caution must be observed, because there is a tendency when establishing rating descriptors to state them more in marketing terms like "must have this feature in the product to have a superior competitive advantage." This is a producer-oriented phrase. The actual user of the product could probably care less about whether or not the company's product has a competitive advantage to the producer. The user is concerned about their own competitive advantage. Rating scale descriptors must be tailor-made by the team for each project/product. There is no universal rating scale!

The actual rating should be discussed verbally as a group. Numeric flash cards or an electronic voting system can be used to get discussion started. The full-scale range of rating numbers (1,2,3,4, . . . ,10) is used for rating. It is advisable to have a team recorder/secretary record pertinent comments resulting from team discussions that lead to the final team rating. For example, it is not uncommon to have a bimodal or even a rectangular distribution of ratings. When this happens, the facilitator asks those who had high ratings to share their viewpoints leading to their ratings. Likewise, those who had low scores share their views. After the ratings discussion, the team is usually asked to vote again. The discussions and feedback generally lead to a convergence of votes in the second round. There is considerable information generated during these rating discussions that can be valuable later on. Such notes document the rationale behind a rating. This is especially important months after the team sessions when memories begin to fade.

What happens if the study team wants to list more than one customer for determining importance of customer needs? Will all customers have the same needs? Will each customer have his own measure of importance for each need? Our experience shows that the labels on the customer needs generally do not change across customers. What does change across customers is the importance of those needs. One way to capture all of this is to have an importance column for each customer. A separate importance rating would be given to each. In addition, weighting factors could be assigned to each customer according to their importance, volume of business, and so on. To do this 100 points would be allocated across the customers instead of using a rating scale. The weighting factors would then be multiplied by the importance ratings. The products would be summed for each customer need row. The final sum of products would then represent an overall weighted importance across all customer importance columns. It is then possible to interpret the customer matrix to better understand the weighted importance scores. Caution is advised if you include a large number of customers, say more than 3 to 5. Including every possible customer can dilute the overall weighted importance score so it becomes almost meaningless. The best way is to have a separate matrix for each customer.

It is obvious that marketing, customer representatives, or service and repair people should participate in rating the features for importance. The ideal state for determining customer importance would be to interview real customers or have them participate in the team exercise. This could prove difficult depending upon confidentiality and product disclosure. Having the right people participate in this exercise will also enhance the credibility of the COPC project. Another advantage resulting from customer feature identification and quantification is that gaps or missing information readily surface. If answers are missing, question marks are inserted and the topic is addressed later. The gaps in information can be very useful input for designing surveys or focus groups to obtain the needed information. Therefore, identified missing information can be just as useful and important as known information. Information gaps that surface highlight the fact that "we didn't know we didn't know the information was missing."

Step 4a: Optional Rating Method

An optional and often-used method for rating importance is Direct Magnitude Estimation, discussed in Chapter 6.[3] It entails locating the most important feature in the feature group being considered and giving it the highest rating, say, a 10 (assuming a 1 to 10 scale is used). All other features are rated relative to this feature. For example, a rating of 3 would be about one-third the importance of a 10. It is possible and legitimate for other features to also have a rating of 10. Regardless of which rating method is used, it is important that the ratings reflect only one customer/user. One set of feature ratings can not be used for a family of products representing different users. If this is the case, separate importance ratings must be performed for each individual user. Very often the majority of the ratings are the same, but it is still important that every rating is considered. Scale descriptors should also be checked for appropriateness for rating each user or product combination. It may also be necessary to add, delete, or change feature descriptions.

Step 5: Conduct Competitive Analysis

Purpose

1. To quantify how well current company product satisfies each feature (current state).
2. To quantify how well competitor's products satisfy each feature (current state).
3. To quantify how well company product should satisfy features in the future (future state).

After developing and quantifying all features and functions for customer importance, a competitive analysis is conducted regarding the performance of company and other manufacturer's current product against each feature. The importance of the feature to the customer must not enter into this comparison. How important a feature is has nothing to do with how the products really perform.

To begin the analysis, a simple rating scale is used wherein the basic question being asked is, "How well does this current product satisfy this feature?" A rating scale is established to estimate how well products satisfy each feature. A typical scale is 1 to 10, or 1 to 5. Descriptors are written by the team for at least three numerical anchor points. A satisfaction rating might be as follows:

Rating	Descriptor
10	Fully meets customer need. In some cases may even exceed expectations. Wonderful!
5	Satisfactory; not exceptional; not a problem or concern. Okay.
1	Unsatisfying; causes aggravation; customer may switch brands to avoid/eliminate this problem. Major problems.

As before, the scale and descriptors must be developed by the team so they have a scale that is meaningful and comfortable to them. The above scale is for example only.

All major competitors are listed. Sometimes there are too many competitors to list them all. Hence, only the most important are selected. Using the full rating scale range (e.g., 1,2,3,4, ...,10) the current company product and the competitor's product are scored for performance or fulfillment of each feature. If possible and where practical, real products should be available for comparison and evaluation. Scoring can be started with numerical flash cards or an electronic voting apparatus. It is important that team scores be discussed, especially if there is wide variation in scores. Scoring products according to feature provides a competition benchmark for current company product. This benchmark will be used to rescore where the company (team) desires to be, feature by feature, at some date in the future. The same rating scale is used. The future time horizon is established by the team and heavily biased by marketing. This will usually be the product introduction date. Future-state rating should reflect the company's current standing with competitors' product and, in this case, the perceived importance of the feature to the customer. The basic question being asked when rating company future product performance is, "Given our current product performance in relation to the competitor's, and, based on the importance of this feature to the customer, where do we desire to be in the future with respect to this feature?"

When doing the competitive analysis, and product current and future performance, only one feature is rated at a time. That is, company current product is rated for feature performance. Then, immediately, the other competitor's products are rated for the same feature while thoughts and discussion are still fresh in team members' minds. After rating company and competitors' products for that particular feature, the team proceeds to rate company future desired performance.

Doing all of these ratings consecutively by row helps maintain the mind set and reference base for the feature. It is less confusing than rating one entire column (company) at a time across all features. When scoring where company product is desired to be in the future, don't fall into the trap of thinking that there must be an improvement for every feature. The performance of many features will remain the same. Be realistic! There is a tendency to overachieve or over design. It is possible sometimes to have a performance rating greater than 10. This may set a new standard, or it may remain overkill. Here, as with feature importance ratings, recording of comments from team dialogue necessary to score the products is very valuable.

Rating desired company future performance is generally done by using the current company products as the reference. Sometimes this may not be so simple. For example, the current company product may be a manually operated product whereas all competitor's products are automatic operation. In this case, what is the reference base? What some teams have done in the situation is to do two comparisons to produce two desired future scores. The first comparison is with the company's current manual product. The second comparison is based on the average across all competitors scores as the reference base. Both desired future scores can be useful. Reference with the current manually operated product gives an indication how much the company has to change based on current design and current manufacturing methods. The other score indicates how much the company has to change the product based on the average competitor's product. Both scores can be used to compute two improvement ratios, discussed next in Step 6.

Step 6: Calculate Improvement Ratio for Features

Purpose: To compute a ratio signifying how much change is desired for current company product for each feature. In order to determine the amount of improvement needed for each feature, an improvement factor is computed. This can be done two ways. First, an improvement ratio can be calculated for each feature by dividing the desired future performance rating by the current performance rating. The resulting ratio is the amount of improvement needed for each feature. The ratio highlights those features needing attention and improvement in relation to customer need and competitive standing. There has been some controversy about computing a ratio. The argument has been, for example, that an improvement ratio of 9 divided by 3 is much more important than an improvement ratio of 3 divided by 1. The ratio does not really reflect where along the continuum of change and competitive position the ratio lies.

An alternative to the ratio is to use the arithmetic difference between desired future state and the current state. Using this method with the same above numerical example creates an improvement rating of 9 – 3 = 6 and 3 – 1 = 2, respectively. The feeling has been that the arithmetic difference maintains the focus of improvement and, in addition, places emphasis on the more important changes.

To avoid situations where the arithmetic difference might produce a zero, a 1 can be added to all resulting arithmetic differences. Thus, 1 + (future state – current state) = change factor.

Step 7: Quantify Market/Sales Point (Leverage)

Purpose: To quantify how much advantage marketing may have if changes are made for particular features. Marketing and sales team members are asked for additional input called market leverage or sales point. Additional ad hoc marketing personnel may have to attend the team meetings to give additional input, or the marketing team member may canvass pertinent personnel outside of team meetings and bring the data to the team at a later date.

The basic question being asked of marketing for each feature is, "Given the importance of this feature to the customer, and considering the amount of improvement (improvement ratio) needed, if we in fact make a change in this feature, can marketing take advantage of it?" The questions are answered with numbers from a rating scale. The following sales point rating scale has been used.

Rating	Descriptor
1.5	Significant market leverage if change is made; most likely would mention it in advertising.
1.2	Some market leverage: technical representatives would have advantage on customer premises.
1.0	Status quo; no significant leverage; no negative impacts.

The ratings 1.5, 1.2, and 1.0 have been researched, studied, and used thoroughly over time. They seem to be empirical. These ratings have been carefully developed by the Japanese in their efforts to develop and apply the QFD process.[4] They provide sufficient information and, at the same time, lessen the impact of this rating on prior ratings of customer importance and improvement ratio.

Again, marketing must participate in this evaluation. If the team does this rating without marketing input, the COPC project will lose credibility. There have been cases where the sales point quantification step has not been used. Sometimes the customer importance rating, improvement ratio, or the competitive analysis is sufficient. To use or not to use sales point is a judgment call by the team on a per-case basis.

Step 8: Compute Feature Score

Purpose: To combine customer importance, improvement ratio, and market leverage into one figure to represent the merit of each feature for each function. The feature score is a product of three numbers:

(Feature importance to customer) × (Improvement ratio) × (Sales point)

= Feature score

After raw feature scores are computed for each feature, they are normalized to a percentage by dividing the total of all raw scores across all features for one function into each individual feature score. Note that normalizing is done separately for each individual function and is not based on the grand total of all scores across all functions.

The product of these three ratings, the feature score, draws attention to those customer features needing the most attention in designing a product based on customer needs. The purpose for normalizing is that these percentages will be used as a weighting factor for multiplying technology scores later in Part 3 of the matrix.

At this point in the matrix, we now have quantified customer features and functions. We have addressed the question, "What are we trying to do for our customer?" This is very useful information, but to stop here would be an incomplete analysis. What we have at this point is an identification of those features that will play an important role in designing the product from the customer's perspective. We now need input from the company and manufacturing.

Part 3: Manufacturing/Technology Evaluation

Step 9: Develop Technologies (Methodologies)

Purpose: To generate for each individual function a list of ways, methods, or technologies that might be used to accomplish or perform the functions. It is now time to configure product concepts. To do this, we array against each operational function all of the known or possible ways of performing the function. This entails listing all of the technologies, methods, and procedures that might be used to construct a new product concept. One function is expanded at a time. Brainstorming or other creativity techniques are used to generate a list of all possible options that might be used. Each function will, in fact, require its own individual mini-creativity session. The usual rules of creativity apply — go for quantity, no judging of ideas, hitchhiking is welcomed, and so on. The team is first encouraged to have a brain dump of all of the obvious off-the-shelf ideas for achieving the functions. After this purge, the team then develops more new and unique ideas. Function-technology expansion is continued until the team feels they have saturated or exhausted the function-technology possibilities. The creative expansion process is done verbally as a group, so all team members benefit from interaction. It also encourages hitchhiking on other's ideas. Sketching ideas on chart pads also helps. Some teams have even added sketches on the COPC matrix.

It is during this technology expansion that the team finally gets into the nuts and bolts technology of building the product concept. It is now time for designers, manufacturing engineers, researchers, and others to contribute their content knowledge to build a product concept. It has been suggested that the technology brainstorming be performed immediately after generating the operational functions in Step 2. The feeling is that doing the importance ratings, competitive analysis, improvement ratio, and sales point before the creativity session may inhibit the individual's creativity. The correct procedure is the one that the facilitator and team feel most comfortable with. Again, the COPC facilitator must have facilitating and interpersonal skills to handle these situations. I personally have not found this to be a problem.

After this creativity step has been finished for all operational functions, the team will have created a function-technology morphological matrix.[5] This is a useful matrix. It can be considered a technology library cataloged by functions. It will provide the landmarks to chart a concept path to future design. The mechanisms for charting the path will be discussed next.

Step 10: Establish Manufacturing-Type Decision Criteria

Purpose: To document and quantify a set of manufacturing-type criteria to use for selecting technologies. After expanding all the functions for technologies, it is now necessary to choose one technology for each function to create a technology path through the matrix. Each different combination of technologies creates a different path and thus creates a different concept.

How does one choose which technology to use for which function? It will eventually be done by scoring and weighting the technologies against two sets of criteria: one for the marketing/customer features, which we have already developed, quantified, and normalized, and one for manufacturing and design, which must now be developed.

A set of manufacturing/design decision criteria will be established for each function. Typical criteria are: development cost, operating cost, installation cost, development time, time to completion, quality, reliability, maintainability, ease to automate, unit manufacturing cost, manufacturability, serviceability, technology risk, performance, upgradeability, hardware interface, software interface, safety, patentability, front-end load, simplicity of design, simplicity of operation, availability of materials, and quality-of-work life (QWL). After identifying and defining the criteria, they are weighted by the team for relative importance. This is done by allocating the team 100 points to distribute across the criteria such that the total sums to 100. The team does this by verbal interaction as opposed to individual distribution. The interaction necessary to reach group agreement is very information rich and worth the time. Sometimes the discussion can become very heated with strong arguments. This sum-to-unity method is more representative of the team's decision criteria than scoring each criterion individually on a scale (e.g., 1 to 10, 1 to 5) and then normalizing them to a percentage by dividing each individual criterion score by the sum of all scores. The problem with a rating scale is that all criteria are important and the corresponding ratings end up as 8's, 9's or 10's, or 3's, 4's or 5's. That is, they all end up at the higher points in the scale range. With the 100-point sum-to-unity method, the team is forced to deal with tradeoffs across criteria; what they add to one criterion they must take away from another. This trade-off gives a more realistic picture of relative importance. All the criteria are important, but we want to know which are more important than others.

It is important that decision criteria be as mutually exclusive as possible in order to reduce confounding and interaction. For example, the criterion "waste" can be a subset of the criterion "operating cost," and using them both can give double accounting to operating cost. Experience shows that the ideal number of criteria is 10±2. More than 12 criteria increases the chances for subsets and multiple accounting.

These weighted criteria will be used as a set of weighting factors to multiply times technology scores to produce an overall weighted technology feature score that can be used for choosing appropriate technology. Next, how do we score the technologies?

Step 11: Score Technologies

Purpose: To quantify how well each technology satisfies (1) the customer features and (2) the manufacturing decision criteria. Thus far in the process, two sets of criteria and their weighting factors have been established. They are customer features and manufacturing criteria. The next step is to rate each technology against both sets of criteria. A rating scale is established to allow team members to quantify how well the technology satisfies the manufacturing criteria and the customer features. The basic question asked is, "How well does this technology satisfy the criterion?" As seen before, a typical rating scale is 1 to 10. Descriptors are also written for several anchor points. A typical scale might be

Rating	Descriptor
10	Satisfies feature/criterion in all respects. Ideal.
5	Satisfies feature or criterion. Okay.
1	Satisfies feature/criterion little or not at all.

The team decides which to rate first, customer features or manufacturing criteria. It is easier if the technologies are all rated against one set of criteria or features at a time. After scoring all technologies for customer features, the scoring process would then be repeated for the manufacturing criteria or visa versa.

This is less confusing than scoring the technologies for both customer features and manufacturing criteria at the same time. Also, when rating features and criteria, it is best to do so one row at a time. That is, rate all technologies for function 1 and feature 1, then rate them all for function 1 and feature 2 and so on. The same procedure would be used for rating against manufacturing criteria; function 1 and criterion 1, function 1 and criterion 2, and so on. Scoring one row at a time is much easier, because it provides a mental reference base that makes comparison easier. The same rating scale and descriptors are usually used to rate both sets of features and criteria, although separate scales could be established for each.

Step 12: Compute Technology Scores.

Purpose: To calculate both a customer feature score and a manufacturing criteria score for each technology to provide a basis for comparing the attributes and merits of technology options for each function. At this point, each technology cell in the matrix has two sets of ratings, one for customer features and one for manufacturing criteria. These two sets of ratings will be multiplied by their respective weighting factors. Their products will be summed to produce two separate total weighted scores. That is, the customer feature score is obtained by summing the products of the individual normalized customer feature scores, developed in Step 8, and the technology feature score, developed in Step 11. Likewise, a manufacturing criteria score is calculated by summing the products of the individual manufacturing criteria weighting factors, developed in Step 10, and the technology manufacturing score, developed in Step 11. This process is repeated for each technology for each function row.

At this point there is a natural tendency to combine these two sums into one overall technology cell total score. The two summed scores for each technology should be kept separate. Combining them consolidates too much information. Important signals are easily missed. With one overall score, you are inclined to choose the technology with the highest combined score, which many times is not the best choice. Both scores are needed to search for tradeoffs and to balance the right combination of technologies for customer and company.

Step 13: Create Technology Paths

Purpose: To choose one technology in each function row to create a technology path representing the best combination of options for both customer and manufacturer. The matrix has now been completed both qualitatively and quantitatively. The team is in a position to start choosing technologies to form a technology path across functions. The path is really a concept and not necessarily a detailed design. The path will be based on the best combination of function technology scores. Strong and weak points of each technology become obvious. The scores allow the team to discuss and choose the best combination of technologies that best satisfy both customer and manufacturer needs. Tradeoffs will have to be made. Each different combination of technologies represents a different concept. At first glance, you might expect that there are an infinite number of possible paths through the various combinations and permutations of technology cells. In reality, this is usually not the case, because there are combinations of technologies across function rows that are illogical or impossible for both customer or manufacturer criteria.

For example, sometimes it is electro-mechanically or physically-chemically impossible to connect certain technology combinations. In any case, there are still many options available, and picking the best combination of technology scores will help surface options and identify the most likely candidates. To begin, several paths are created that have different objectives. For example, a least-cost path could be constructed by connecting the lowest-cost technology in each row regardless of whether they are logical or optimum combinations. This path becomes the least costly concept that could ever be achieved and still meet customer and manufacture needs. It is highly likely that this path may be technologically impossible to achieve, but, if it were possible, it would be the lowest-cost alternative. The cost of this path then becomes the target cost. The same principle can be used to construct other paths for best quality, reliability, maintenance, QWL, and so on.

Selection of technologies may not be easy. Constructing the various paths begins to bound the various options. Some technologies will consistently surface for all paths. This does ease the selection process. A graphic device used to summarize the number of path options is the strategy matrix.

Each row of the strategy matrix represents a separate path (option). The actual names of the selected technologies are written in the strategy matrix cells. The columns of the matrix show the boundary of path options. By scanning the function columns of the matrix one can easily locate technologies common across strategy path options. Discovering such common technologies can prove very valuable. Figure C.2 illustrates a strategy matrix of path options. Note for this example that for the function "locate sheet" that the technology "fixed edge" is common to four of six options that have so far surfaced.

With some products, selection of one technology is confusing. What happens is there is an interdependency among different function technologies. That is, whichever technology is selected for function x will constrain what technologies can be selected from function y and z, and so on. Some teams select the technology for the most important function and let this selection determine the technology selections for the remaining

Strategy Matrix 3-Hole Punch

Market Segment: School

STRATEGY	LOCATE SHEET	PIERCE SHEET	ADJUST HOLES	COLLECT WASTE	ASSURE CONVENIENCE	AESTHETICS
Best Customer	Adjustable stop	Lever with high fulcrum	Click stop	Snap-fit bottom	Drill	Today's design
Best Company	Fixed edge	Today's design	Permanent settings	Plastic pull-off	Heavy-duty mechanical punch	Today's design
Best UMC	Fixed edge	Today's design	Permanent settings	Plastic pull-off	Today's design	Today's design
Best Reliability	Fixed edge	Lever with high fulcrum	Permanent settings	Hinged bottom	Heavy-duty mechanical punch	N/A
Best Manufacturing Ability	Fixed edge	Today's design	Permanent settings	Plastic pull-off	Today's design	N/A
Best Quality	Adjustable stop	Level with high fulcrum	Adjustable stops with screw fastening	Hinged bottom	Drill	Burnished stainless

Figure C.2 Strategy matrix, 3-hole punch.

Function Summary 3-Hole Punch

Function: Adjust Holes
Dependencies: Pierce sheet, collect waste, assure convenience
Decision Criteria: UMC

Market Segment: Schools

TECHNOLOGIES	ADVANTAGES	DISADVANTAGES	NOTES
1. Click stops	• Easy to move • Easy to set • Easy to access	• Can drift out of sync or position; must continually readjust • Higher UMC • Lower reliability	• Use stronger spring tension on ball bearing; will increase UMC
2. Permanent settings	• Lower UMC • Easier manufacturing • Totally reliable • No purchased parts	• Limit to just one 3-hole format for customer	• Marketing will have difficulty selling this design • Schools have many varied material formats
3. Adjustable stops with screw fastening	• Customer has unlimited selection of material–hole formats • High quality	• Higher UMC • Screw settings can come loose • Less manufacturable • More purchased parts	• Must find reliable supplier • Must invest money to research/develop better screw settings

Figure C.3 Function summary, 3-hole punch.

functions. To do this, they assign importance weighting factors to all functions using the 100 point sum to unity rule. They then let the higher weighted functions guide their selection of technologies.

Step 14: Select the Best Technology Path

Purpose: To select the path(s) that will become the final recommendation(s) for product design. The team narrows down the options. After presentation and recommendations, the concepts are eventually turned over to design and manufacturing who will start prototyping, testing, and designing. It is not uncommon that two paths are developed for final recommendation, one for "today" and one for "tomorrow." The today path is based on the best combination of technologies that fit into current time constraints to get the product out on schedule. The tomorrow path is clearly the best choice, but still requires some research or development that will not permit meeting current schedules. It is this path that sets future direction for marketing and manufacturing. It is also the concepts that will bring added value to customer and company and that will allow best fit with the company strategic plan. All of the other least-cost and quality paths will still be retained for reference for presentation to management. Retaining these paths in an appendix will document and support current decisions. They can be used to show management that all possible options were considered in deriving the current recommended concepts.

COPC Strategy Matrix

What is it? — A strategy matrix summarizing the most likely technology paths to be considered for further discussion, analysis and presentation.
Objective: — To summarize the entire COPC Matrix on one small concise document.
Input: — COPC Matrix.
Output: — A strategy matrix.
Instructions: (See Figure C.2)

1. Select desired strategies. Most common are best customer path, best company, lowest cost, best reliability, best manufacturability, best quality, etc.
2. List functions as column heading on a matrix.
3. List strategies as row labels.

4. Select the corresponding technology from the COPC Matrix for each function that fits the strategy and write it in the appropriate cell of the strategy matrix.
5. One path that many teams plot is for the competitor's current design.

Advantages

1. The matrix may be used to look for common technology across functions.
2. It may be used to look for a technology profile across strategies.
3. It summarizes in concise form a product concept that has been evaluated against customer and company constraints. This summary is used in commercialization process gate reviews as well as mapping to a business plan.

Each row of the strategy matrix represents a different strategy. Each column lists the various technologies for each function according to the strategy.

The columns are used to locate technologies common to various strategies. Figure C.2 illustrates a strategy matrix for a 3-hole punch. Note for this example for the function "locate sheet," that "fixed edge" satisfies four out of six strategies. Unfortunately it is not the best for customer or quality. For "collect waste", "plastic pull-off" satisfies three strategies and "snap-fit bottom" satisfies the customer. However, "snap-fit bottom" and "plastic pull-off" are very similar and perhaps a hybrid combination can be devised.

The strategy matrix is used as a dialoguing method to discuss strategy and technology for final recommendation.

COPC Function–Technology Summary

The Function-Technology Summary extends the Strategy Matrix by listing the advantages and disadvantages of selected technologies and by highlighting consequences of decisions regarding possible technology selection.

What is it? — A summary of advantages and disadvantages for selected technologies.
Objective: — To highlight consequences of decisions and discussions regarding possible technology selection.
Input: — COPC Matrix
COPC Strategy Matrix
Output: — Advantages/disadvantages of technology strategy.

Instructions: (See Figure C.3)

1. For each selected technology for a given function, list the advantages, disadvantages, and appropriate notes (i.e., how might we overcome disadvantages, tradeoffs; what are other impacts? Etc.). Draw sketches if necessary.
2. List what other functions are dependent upon or are affected by the current function. Also, list the other functions the current function is dependent upon.
3. Use this summary in conjunction with the Strategy Matrix as discussion tools for final technology selection.

Advantages

1. There is an audit trail for technology selection.
2. It provides a basis for a recommendation for a management decision.
3. It highlights elements necessary for implementation and further action.
4. The matrix and the data provide the logical needed input to begin a Failure Mode Effects and Criticality Analysis (FMECA).

Okay, You've Built the Matrix, Now What?

At this point, several technology paths have been developed. However, there may be gaps in information. For example, there may still be questions about some of the importance ratings or some parts of the competitive analysis. These kinds of questions frequently arise. So, it will be necessary to verify some of the COPC matrix information. Many times verification will require customer data collection of some sort.

The COPC process helps define areas of needed information and directs the surveys and data gathering into areas of greatest payback. In this respect, the data and signals developed in the COPC process provide the input to design better questions for focus groups and customer surveys. I recall a classic case where a focus group questionnaire was developed independent of the COPC project. At the last minute, a representative from business research decided to review the questionnaire with the COPC team. Much to everyone's shock and amazement, more than 50% of the focus group questions were inappropriate and way off target. Little would have been gained had the original set of questions been used. After this embarrassing discovery, the market intelligence representative participated on the COPC team almost to project completion. The result was an almost completely revised set of focus group questions.

In some COPC applications, prototype products have been built and used at focus groups. Focus groups may involve videotaping customer reactions from a behind a two-way mirror. By observing a focus session, a COPC team can obtain first-hand information on customer reactions to the prototypes and/or to a prepared set of questions. The data from the interviews, questionnaires, and focus groups are summarized. The summary information is mapped back into the original COPC matrix. Importance and/or competitive analysis ratings are revised and updated. New features or criteria are added as necessary. The technology scores are recalibrated to reflect the data updates. The original technology paths are checked for validity. New technology paths may also surface. The matrix is fine-tuned to the point where a decision can be made on the technology path(s) to recommend.

The matrix should be continually updated and considered a living document. If the matrix is properly updated, the COPC process is self-correcting. Feedback loops often require the team to go back and update prior data, which, in time, provide some missing links and course corrections.

Can We Win?

The output from a COPC application is a product concept(s). This concept has been checked for its fit with customer and company needs. The concept represents the team's best estimate of what it will take to play the game. The following questions are appropriate to ask once a concept path has been established:

1. What will it take to play the game? Does this concept fit that profile?
2. Can we play? Do we want to play?
3. Can we win?
4. How do we compare to our competitors' design? Can they win?
5. Why should a customer buy this product (concept) as currently perceived?
6. Mr. Manager, this is what it will take to play the game, do you still want to play?

COPC is used at a tactical level in the company and employs a macro level of detail. The above questions are also macro level and are used as a "quick hit" for middle/upper level managers to check their overall business decisions regarding the product at the very early stages of the product life cycle.

So often, companies do not ask these question early on in the product life cycle. The reason is that they generally do not have a mechanism (like COPC) for doing so.

How Does COPC Relate To The Business Case?

I discussed the need for a design team to have access to the company business plan when developing products. Because COPC is a design process whose output is a product concept it should certainly connect with the business plan. The recommended product concept should be checked with the business plan to be sure both are congruent with each other. Such a comparison can work both ways: does the concept fit the plan and does the plan fit the concept? Use of the COPC process can provoke the dialogue for challenging the focus of the business plan.

The technology path(s) information can be used as input to a decision and risk analysis (DRA) process for building a business case. Some of the technologies surfaced in the COPC process become candidates for Research and Development projects. These projects are generally approved based on their fit to a business case. DRA and portfolio analysis are quite often the processes used to derive the business case. The COPC process integrates very nicely with this type of methodology. That is, the use of the COPC process results in a concept/design and the application of DRA can help one develop a business case based on the COPC design both favorably and unfavorably. I have lead several COPC projects where the concept did not fit the business plan. We went back to the matrix to try another path option. In some cases all the options we derived still did not fit the business plan. In this case the project manager and the company did not have a viable product! The result was a 4.5 million dollar prevented expenditure, because, under normal modus operandi, the team would have spent another two years to make the product work and spend all of the 5 million dollars allocated to the project! So, beware, COPC can also kill a product or project when done correctly. COPC outcome can work both ways.

General Observations Of The Process

The process of building the matrix is fairly straightforward. The behavioral and scoping activities to initiate the process are more complex. The perceived simplicity of the matrix can also be a detriment, because many teams believe they can run the process and build the matrix themselves. The entire process from launch to finish is best done with a neutral third-party facilitator to lead both team building and process. Otherwise, the teams can easily get mired in turf protection, drown itself in details, get lost in the woods, and quickly rush to solve unclear problems and shortcut the process. The process facilitator provides the COPC model and keeps the team on track. The facilitator's function is to keep the team well focused and make decisions on how long to dwell on a particular problem. This person does not get involved in content discussion and ratings but does ask devil's advocate questions while, at the same time, keeping the pace moving.

Meeting length and frequency are important. As with the other processes discussed in this book, the initial launch meeting is best scheduled for a full day. Regularly scheduled follow-up meetings should be 3 hours long and held at least once per week (twice a week is better) until the COPC project is finished. Because of the complexity and detail in designing products, infrequent meetings less than 3 hours do not work as well as longer duration meetings. Team members spend too much time getting back to speed to where they previously left off in the process. It has been my experience that 2-hour meetings are too short (it takes about 1 hour to get going). Four-hour meetings are too long. The fourth hour is nonproductive because the team members are brain-dead.

Using the right number and blend of core team members is important for developing a well-rounded knowledge base and for minimizing the effects of bias and political influence. Keeping the same people on the core team throughout is very important. It takes time to develop team cohesiveness and a team benchmark/framework for making judgments. Excessive changes in core team membership fractures the team bond and the mental reference base used in decision making.

The credibility of the COPC process and output is highly dependent on the consistency of team decisions, ratings, and applications of the process. Group consensus is the preferred method of decision making. However, where reaching consensus may take considerable time, the process facilitator should guide the team to proceed with a majority decision and write a minority report. Good meeting notes should be compiled so that the reasons behind group decisions can be retraced if changes have to be made at a later date. Many facilitators maintain an ongoing list referred to as a "parking lot" for recording ideas, questions, and action items that surface prematurely out of sequence in the COPC process. This is very helpful and helps bring focus on these issues later at a more appropriate time. The parking lot list of items is always kept visible at all team meetings either on wall charts or typed notes.

The COPC matrix is to be considered a living document that is continually updated with both qualitative and quantitative information. Product variables, customer needs, environments, and technology change with time. The matrix should be updated accordingly. Building the matrix on an electronic spreadsheet greatly simplifies the updating process. We have even constructed matrices real-time during the team meetings using a lap-top computer. An electronic projector coupled to the computer to project the computer image on a room-size projection screen has also proven very useful.

With the matrix on a spreadsheet, the team now has the opportunity to more easily interact with other team members and decision makers in a simulation mode. Numbers can be changed and scores recomputed instantly in a "what if" capacity. This is very appealing, especially to decision makers, and such interaction serves as stake building to foster ownership in the process, which in turn increases chances for acceptance of recommendations.

An interesting variation in using the electronic spreadsheet is to use it with customers/users. The entire COPC matrix would be developed by the team and put on the spreadsheet. Customers would then be asked to interact with the matrix. They can verify the customer needs by entering their numbers for their importance of the needs. They also would add additional needs that have not been included in the team-generated matrix. After direct customer input, the program would be run to recalculate technology scores. The on-line customer interface is particularly useful for those kinds of products that must be tailor-made for specific customer needs. In this case, the technologies in the matrix may be various interchangeable modules that can be integrated to form various customized configurations. The customer's importance ratings would highlight those modules best suited for the customer application.

In this respect, the glossary of terms is very useful. It provides a consistent language in the midst of change and amendments. The scoring and rating processes require a good understanding of the item(s) under discussion. Experience shows that considerable time can be lost due to confusion when terms are not specifically defined. Good, recorded definitions not only speed up the rating processes but promote better consistency as well. Communication is improved through a better shared understanding of information. Believe it or not, information can sometimes be a barrier to initiating a COPC process. We refer to this as information paralysis. This is the condition where teams think they know nothing about customers and product performance parameters. They believe conducting customer surveys and collecting data have to be done before beginning a COPC project. The belief is usually unfounded, because it is highly unlikely that intelligent people involved in the sale of a product know nothing about its use and performance. The COPC process draws out the collective knowledge of the team and brings all team members to a higher level of knowledge.

Function Correlations

An intercorrelation matrix may be added to the left side of the COPC matrix. The intercorrelation can be used with the function rows, see Figure C.4. Such a function roof can highlight any sensitive function

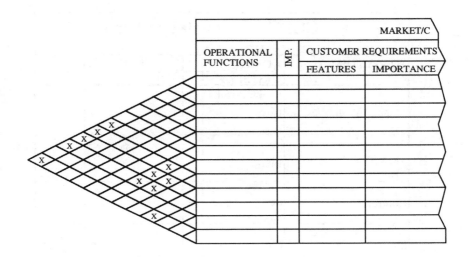

		MARKET/C
OPERATIONAL FUNCTIONS	IMP.	CUSTOMER REQUIREMENTS
		FEATURES	IMPORTANCE

Figure C.4 COPC matrix with function correlations. (From Shillito, M. L., *Advanced QFD Linking Technology to Market and Company Needs,* John Wiley & Sons, New York, 1994. With permission.)

intercorrelation. These intercorrelations may be helpful when considering various technology path options.

In addition to intercorrelations, functions may also be rated for importance by using any of the rating schemes discussed so far in this book. The two schemes can be used together to judge the importance or sensitivity of functions. If a function rates highest in importance and also affects many other functions we now have another signal to watch for when choosing technology to deliver that function. Conversely, if a function rates low in importance but affects almost all other functions, we immediately have a signal that something does not seem quite right. The point is that function intercorrelations and the importance ratings put us in a position to ask some important questions that may have never been asked before. It allows us to discover tradeoffs.

There is considerable depth to a COPC matrix and all its various labels, tools and ratings. COPC consists of tools within a tool. The depth of dialogue potential is directly proportional to the depth of the COPC matrix and its tools.

An Alternative Method For Constructing A COPC Matrix

Instead of building the COPC Matrix as a single matrix, it can be split into two separate matrices, the technology matrix and the customer matrix.

COPC—Technology Matrix							
SUBSYSTEM	COMPANY CRITERIA	I	TECHNOLOGY				
Manage Media	People Avail. Cost Risk						
Move Print Head	Etc.						
Control Print Head	Etc.						
Etc.	Etc.						

(left vertical label: Company Technology Filter)

Figure C.5 Alternate technology matrix. (From Shillito, M. L., *Advanced QFD Linking Technology to Market and Company Needs,* John Wiley & Sons, New York, 1994. With permission.)

The technology matrix would contain the operational functions as explained and derived in Step 2, the manufacturing criteria (Step 10), and the brainstormed technology (Step 9). The criteria would be scored for importance (Step 10) and the technologies would be rated against the criteria (Step 11). Technology scores would be calculated (Step 12) and technology paths would be developed that best fit the manufacturing criteria (Step 13). You will notice that this matrix is identical to the right half of the regular COPC Matrix (Figure C.1) as described earlier. Figure C.5 illustrates the first matrix, the technology matrix.

In Matrix 2, the customer needs matrix, we introduce customer needs similar to the left side to the standard COPC Matrix. (See Figure C.6) However, this matrix will be constructed differently than previously described. The alternative method involves developing a modified Pugh matrix[6] wherein the complete technology paths from Matrix 1, will be rated against the customer needs. Selected paths from Matrix 1 are entered as column headings in the Pugh Matrix. To estimate how a product (path) satisfies customer needs it is better to use a wholistic approach and consider the entire technology path. All operational functions do not perform in isolation in a product. We must consider the interaction of all functions and technologies in concert. After all, this is how the customer will use them.

Customer (Modified Pugh) Matrix

CUSTOMER CRITERIA	IMP	REFERENCE	TECHNOLOGY PATH					
			P 1		P 2		P 3	
Speed	15		5	+	3	+	5	+
Quality	15		3	+	3	o	5	+
Reliability	20		3	o	4	o	4	o
Etc.	5		4	-	4	+	5	+
Etc.	5		2	o	3	-	4	+
Etc.	10		1	o	3	+	5	+
WGT.SCORE			220		235		285	
RAW SCORE			18		20		28	
$\Sigma +$				2		3		5
$\Sigma -$				1		1		-
Σ o				3		2		1
Sum				1		2		5

(Left margin label: Customer Filter; center column label: REFERENCE)

Figure C.6 Modified Pugh (customer) matrix. (From Shillito, M. L., *Advanced QFD Linking Technology to Market and Company Needs,* John Wiley & Sons, New York, 1994. With permission.)

To construct the modified Pugh Matrix we list the customer needs as one list rather than clustering them by operational functions. The team rates the customer needs for importance as in Step 4. The scores are then normalized so their sum equals 100%. This information is entered in the far left column. Next the reference or target product is listed in its own column. The next columns represent the selected paths from Matrix 1 (Figure C.5). For example, Path P1 could be the best quality/reliability path, P2 could be the least cost path, P3 could be the best performance and so on.

Two operations are now performed on the technology paths. First, paths will be scored as to how well they satisfy the customer needs (similar to Step 11), and second, paths will be rated how they compare to the chosen reference product (many times the competition's).

First, a satisfaction rating scale is derived for rating the paths for each customer need. Using this scale the paths are rated one row at a time. A path column score is derived by summing the raw column ratings or by multiplying the normalized customer need importance by the corresponding path ratings and summing the products for a weighted column score. Which option to use is left to the reader. These totals will give the team an overall reference as to how well the paths fit or satisfy the customer needs. Individual cell scores will indicate any specific strengths or weaknesses of the paths.

The next operation is to compare the individual paths with the reference product. This is done by entering plus (+), minus (-), or zero (0) ratings. If a path is better than the reference product for a specific customer need, a plus sign is entered in the respective cell. If the path is worse, than the reference a minus sign is entered and if it is equal to the reference, a zero is entered.

Each path column is now summed for the total (+), (-), and (0) as well as the algebraic sum. What the team now has is a reference document illustrating how well a particular path satisfies customer needs as well as how it compares to the reference, usually the competitors, product.

Because the paths came from Matrix 1 (Figure C.5) we know the technology has already been studied in relation to the company needs. Matrix 2 (Figure C.6) incorporates the integrated technologies and allows comparison with customer needs and competitive position.

Earlier in Step 3, the issue of standards, regulations, and other dichotomous constraints was discussed. These regulations are grouped together and considered by themselves. With our current model of using the entire path we could construct a separate regulations matrix to work with regulations.

In a third matrix (Figure C.7), all regulations would be listed in the far left column similar to the customer needs matrix above. Likewise, the paths would form the rest of the columns. No reference product would be listed. The paths would be checked to see if they comply (yes or no) with each individual regulation. Symbols, letters, or words can be used to indicate compliance or noncompliance.

In Chapter 9, the need for and some methods for looking into the future were discussed. One of those methods is a trend matrix (Figures 9.2 and 9.3) This simplistic device incorporates arrows to indicate the direction of a change. This method could also be used here to create a customer trend matrix (Figure C.8). To do so, the customer needs and their corresponding importance from Matrix 2 (Figure C.6) would form the left columns in Matrix 4 (Figure C.8). Two additional columns would be added representing two future time periods (in our example 5 years and 10 years) in the future. To indicate the trend in the importance of the customer needs the team uses arrows. An up arrow indicates the importance of the need will increase, a down arrow means the importance

Regulations Matrix			
STANDARDS, REGULATIONS	TECHNOLOGY PATH		
	P1	P2	P3
110/200 voltage	Y	Y	Y
Effluent	Y	N	Y
Ozone Emission	Y	Y	Y
Etc.	Y	N	Y
Etc.	Y	Y	Y
Etc.	Y	Y	Y
Etc.	Y	Y	Y
Σ Y	7	5	7
Σ N	0	2	0
FULL COMPLIANCE?	Y	N	Y

Figure C.7 Regulations matrix. (From Shillito, M. L., *Advanced QFD Linking Technology to Market and Company Needs,* John Wiley & Sons, New York, 1994. With permission.)

will decrease, a horizontal arrow means the importance will remain the same, and a zero means the need will disappear or no longer be important. If new perceived needs will come into being they should be added to the matrix.

The four matrices may now be used together to set technology strategy for the future as well as design product for today and the near future.

Attributes Of The Process

The process of initializing the matrix activity, constructing the matrix, and choosing a concept path provides a vehicle for dialogue that has many advantages.

1. It is probably the first time marketing, research, manufacturing, and other individuals involved have a mutually developed common-source reference base displaying all of the parameters necessary in making design decisions.
2. Both vertical and horizontal company communications are enhanced.

Customer Need Trends			
CUSTOMER Needs	CURRENT IMPORTANCE	FUTURE IMP.	
		+ 5 yrs.	+ 10 yrs.
	5	→	→
	3	↑	↑
	3	→	↑
	5	→	→
	4	↓	→
	3	↑	→
	3	↑	→
	5	→	→

Figure C.8 Customer needs trend matrix. (From Shillito, M. L., *Advanced QFD Linking Technology to Market and Company Needs,* John Wiley & Sons, New York, 1994. With permission.)

3. Because the matrix was constructed by an interdisciplinary team, it lends credibility to the process and the resulting recommendations.

4. Because it is a common-source reference base, it permits one to see interrelationships and highlights information gaps. This, in turn, provides valuable input for designing surveys and focus groups to obtain the right information.

5. Because it is a structured process, it becomes an assault on complexity and forces participants to deal with complex issues one piece at a time.

6. When kept up-to-date, and because it is based on functions, the matrix will provide a technology reference base for designing future similar products.

7. The matrix provides the basis for designing a product that meets both customer and company needs.

8. The process highlights features important to the customer.
9. The competitive analysis provides the structure to pinpoint strengths and weaknesses for both company and competitors' product features and functions.
10. The process highlights areas needing improvement and attention.
11. Because it is function based, the process of expanding the technologies allows for greater use of creativity.
12. The two sets of criteria and the technology ratings allow one to choose the best combination of technologies to satisfy both customer and company.
13. Quantifying the matrix also promotes communication because numbers are easily debated and they highlight areas of disagreement.

Comparison of COPC and QFD

In case there is any confusion about what the difference is between COPC and QFD and how they relate to each other, a comparison chart has been assembled (Figure C.9). Also, in Figure C.10, a schematic COPC matrix has been prepared which contains for each section the questions we are trying to answer and the respective output.

CONCLUSIONS

The COPC process has proven to be successful in a wide variety of applications. The reason for many of the successes is that they were also designed and planned politically and had top-down management support and funding. The process as designed and initially presented to management and sponsors had the following attributes that contributed to successful application:

1. There was a perceived advantage to using the process.
2. It was compatible with the existing company/department structure and operating philosophy.
3. The process was based on the existing language and vernacular of the organizations. There were no new threatening terms or fads.
4. The process did not have a high price in terms of anxiety, emotion, and comfort level. It appeared "safe."
5. There was little to lose if the process is terminated before closure.

Finally, the COPC process as well as Quality Function Deployment are vehicles for dialogue. To be able to communicate, people and teams need a structure and a language. The QFD processes like COPC provide the

COMPARISON OF COPC AND QFD

COPC

1. COPC is perceived to be faster than QFD
2. COPC produces a product concept
3. COPC has a clear tangible end point (a concept)
4. COPC is a design process
5. COPC focuses on what the product must do
6. With COPC, you know when you are finished
7. With COPC, you define the market, customer at the start of the process
8. COPC works with the whole product vs. pieces only
9. COPC is an up-front, macro-level, quick hit process
10. COPC title is more understandable than QFD; customer-oriented product concepting is explicit
11. COPC does not take the product to the shop floor
12. COPC results in a product concept that is used as input to start the QFD process
13. COPC is used in conjunction with company mission and business plan and uses VOC to help guide to a focused endpoint; it is outside-in holistic focused

QFD

1. QFD is perceived to take a long time
2. QFD does not produce a design but rather a list of technical requirements
3. QFD is complex and may have a confusing endpoint
4. QFD is a problem-solving process (rusty car door) or sometimes a redesign process.
5. QFD focuses on technical parameters that are not necessarily focused back to a whole product
6. QFD may not have a clear endpoint
7. Market and customer are too often assumed and/or not clearly focused
8. QFD works with pieces (car door) vs. the whole product
9. QFD is a micro-level, drawn out process
10. What is Quality Function Deployment? This may take some explanation
11. QFD will take you to the shop floor IF all four matrices are used
12. QFD takes this concept in whole or in pieces to take it to the shop floor
13. QFD starts in the middle of a problem and uses VOC for direction to a less focused endpoint; it is inside-out focused

Figure C.9 Comparison of COPC and QFD. (From Shillito, M. L., *Advanced QFD Linking Technology to Market and Company Needs*, John Wiley & Sons, New York, 1994. With permission.)

1. What product? Evolutionary or revolutionary? 2. What task is the customer trying to accomplish? 3. What is the basic function?	1. For whom are we designing product?

	FUNCTIONS	CUSTOMER	COMPANY
QUESTIONS	What are the FUNCTIONS necessary to provide the deliverable? What FUNCTIONS are needed to accomplish the BASIC function?	1. What does the customer want? 2. How important are they? 3. How does our current product satisfy customer needs? 4. How does our competition's product satisfy customer needs? 5. Where should we be in the future with product satisfaction? 6. Can marketing get leverage from the specified improvements?	1. What are all the possible technologies we might use to accomplish the function? 2. How well does the technology satisfy a. Customer needs? b. Company needs? 3. What are the company decision criteria used for choosing among technology? How important are they? 4. What are the most likely technology path options? What does that path look like? Will it win? Can it compete? Can we play the game?
OUTPUT	1. Function map/flow	1. Customer needs hierarchy 2. Competitive analysis 3. Target areas for improvement	1. Product concepts 2. Integrated technology path options 3. Weighted decision criteria 4. What it takes to play the game 5. Sourcing strategy

Figure C.10 COPC question/output template. (From Shillito, M. L., *Advanced QFD Linking Technology to Market and Company Needs,* John Wiley & Sons, New York, 1994. With permission.)

structure through the matrices and the format/procedure used to construct them. A language is provided by the numbers that are derived and put into the matrices by the team members. Team members can debate different choices for numerical inputs. Considerable dialogue is required to merely derive the rating scales used to select numerical inputs to the matrix. The combination of the COPC matrix and the numerical language of value measurement provide the basis for enhanced communications. In this respect COPC/QFD will not make decisions but rather structure input for users to make a better, more informed, decision.

ACKNOWLEDGMENT

This appendix was reprinted with permission from Shillito, M. L., *Advanced QFD, Linking Technology to Market and Company Needs,* John Wiley & Sons, New York, 1994.

BIBLIOGRAPHY

Shillito, M. L., Increasing product innovation effectiveness through QFD and value engineering, *PDMA Visions*, 23, 2, April 1999.

Shillito, M. L., and DeMarle, D. J., *Value: Its Meas. Design and Manage.*, John Wiley & Sons, New York, 1992.

Shurig, R., Morphology: a tool for exploring new technology, *Long Range Plann.*, 17, 3, 129-140, 1985.

REFERENCES

1. Cook, T.F., Determine value mismatch by measuring user/customer attitudes, *Proc. Soc. Amer. Value Eng.* 21,145-156,1986.
2. Snodgrass, T.J. and Kasi, M., *Function Analysis: the Stepping Stones to Good Value*, University of Wisconsin, Madison, 1986.
3. Meyer, D.M., Direct magnitude estimation, a method for quantifying the value index," *Proc. Soc. Amer. Value Eng.*, 6, 293-298, 1971.
4. King, R., *Better Designs in Half the Time, Implementing QFD Quality Function Deployment in America*, GOAL/QPC, Methuen, MA, 1987.
5. Shillito, M.L., Function morphology, *Proc. Soc. Amer. Value Eng.*, 20, 119-125, 1985.
6. Pugh, S., *Total Design*, Addison-Wesley, Reading, MA, 1990.

APPENDIX D

The following is taken in its entirety from *Advanced QFD, Linking Technology to Market and Company Needs*, Shillito, M. L., John Wiley & Sons, © 1994 reprinted by permission of John Wiley & Sons.

VOC EXAMPLE

Included in this appendix is a complete example of the VOC process applied to a 3-hole punch. All tools discussed throughout the book are included as completed examples. A template flow chart shows the sequence of activities needed to develop VOC. On the right side of the template are the chapters in which the tools were discussed.

Product Hypothetical Background

Product:	ABC 3-Hole Punch, Model 1.0
Country:	U. S. Only
Market:	Commercial
Segment:	Office/School
User:	Secretaries, Teachers, Engineers
Task:	Organize papers
Basic Function:	Register holes
Yearly Volume:	1M

Project Mission

Improve design — cleaner cuts; increase number of multiple sheet punches.
Cost reduction (low cost producer).

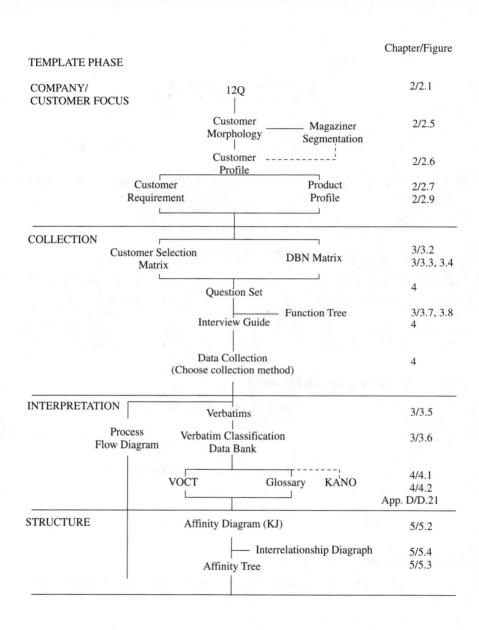

Figure D.1a VOC template and tools.

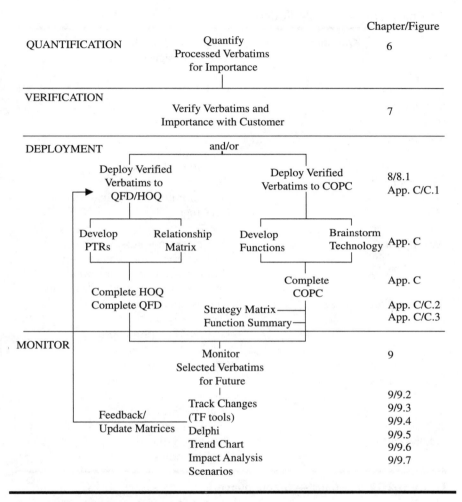

Figure D.1b VOC template and tools.

12 Questions — 3-Hole Punch

Question	Answer
Purpose	VOC + design for customer
Completion	4Q year 19xx
Decision maker	L. Shillito
Scope	Entire punch
Product	Upgrade, model 2.1
Market	
Country	U.S. only
Market	Commercial market
Segment	Office/school segment
User	Sec's, admin., engrs., teachers
CBI	Mtl's mgr
Time Horizon	1Q97
Assumption	Will use same presses
	Will use same mold/machinery
	Will use same metal for body
	Must use same paint/finish facility
Business Plan	Increase market share 10%
	Compete on cost
	High volume producer
	Low cost producer
Team Members	OK, all functions covered
Purchase Drivers	Robust, rugged construction
	Always works — "tank proof"
	"Can punch anything"
Task	Organize materials
Deliverable	Registered material
Function	Register holes

Figure D.2 12 questions — 3-hole punch.

Customer Morphology: 3-Hole Punch

Where used?	Office	School	Home	Exec. Office	Other		
	a units	b units	c units	d units	e units		
	% units	% units	% units	% units	% units		= 100%
Who uses?	Exec	Sec	Teacher	Parents	Technical	Profls	
	%	%	%	%	%	%	= 100%
Buy decision?	Exec	Mtl Mgr	Admin	Teachers	Parents	Pur Agent	
	%	%	%	%	%	%	= 100%
Method?	Single Sheet		Multiple Sheet				
	%		%				= 100%
Format?	8" edge	7" edge	7" edge				
	8x10	5x7	5x7				
	3-hole	3-hole	6 hole				
	%	%	%				= 100%
Material used? (Purchased)	Paper	Bristol	Transpcy	Cardboard			
	%	%	%	%			= 100%

Whose product used?				
OM1 %	OM2 %	OM4 %	OM1	
OM2 %	OM3 %		OM3	
OM3 %			OM5	
OM4 %				
100%	100%	100%	100%	

Note: *Boundary represents the playing field and the players we wish to engage.*

Figure D.3 Customer morphology — 3-hole punch.

Customer Profile — 3-Hole Punch

Customer
 School
Profile
 Used by admin., teachers, students
 Much use
 Much abuse
 Multiple sheets — majority of time
 Punch material other than paper
 Use different 3-hole formats (other than 8 x 10)
 Appearance (paint, etc.) not high priority
Requirements
 Rugged — can take abuse
 Robust — many uses, many materials
 East to adjust
 Multiple detents for punches
 Punches maintain sharpness
Time Horizon
19xx

Figure D.4 Customer profile — 3-hole punch.

Customer Need Matrix: 3-Hole Punch

Needs	Users for 3-Hole Punch				
	Secretary	Teacher	Engineer/ Professional	Executive	Parents
Rugged	√	√			√
Robust (Many uses/materials)	√	√			√
Easy to adjust	√	√			√
Multiple detents for optional punch locations	√	√	√		
Professional appearance				√	

Figure D.5 Customer needs matrix — 3-hole punch.

Product Profile — 3-Hole Punch

Profile
  Stamped metal construction
  Heavy duty springs in punch assembly
  Vacuum painted surfaces
  Heavy duty riveted axle
  Long-lasting punch knife edge
  Fulcrum >x° for high fulcrum leverage to transfer vertical hand force
Time horizon
  19xx

Figure D.6 Product profile — 3-hole punch.

Product Profile : 3-Hole Punch

	Barely Acceptable	Tablestakes	Fully Satisfied		WOW!
VOC	1	2	3	4	5
Punch multiple sheets	1 sheet		≤5 sheets Δo		>10 sheets x
Will not jam	Often	o	Some Δ	x	Never
Easy to align punch assembly	Difficult to see scale	Δo			Easy visual Finger tight x
Punch assembly always stays in place	Comes loose after 100 punch; screwdriver to set	Finger tight o	Loose after 2000 punches; finger tight Δ		Never comes lose; finger tight x
Can pierce transparency material without jamming	0 sheets	1 sheet; some jam Δo	≥2 sheets; no jam x		>5 sheets no jam
Holes will not fall out	Holes fall out when used in hand; fall out when removed	Holes won't fall out when used in hand	Holes won't fall out while removing o	Δ	Holes will not fall out when dropped or when removing x
Etc.	Etc.	Etc.	Etc.	Etc.	Etc.

Current Product   = o   x = 2.3   Less than satisfied
Competition Product = Δ   x = 2.8   Satisfied
Target Product   = x   x = 4.5   More than satisfied

Figure D.7 Product profile — 3-hole punch.

CUSTOMER SELECTION MATRIX
3-HOLE PUNCH

		CUSTOMERS AND CATEGORIES							
CUSTOMER	FUNCTION	Demanding Customer	Satisfied Customer	Unhappy Customer	Lost Customers	New Customers	Paper Only?	Trans. Mat'l.	Geography NE,SE,C, SW, NW
School	Secretary Teacher Pupil Admin.								
Office	Secretary Manager Executive								
Industrial	Secretary Engineer Supervisor								
Home	Parent Child, K-6 Child, HS								

Figure D.8 Customer selection matrix, 3-hole punch.

Magaziner Customer Categories

Planner	Determines consistency of the product with organizational policy
Funder	Pays for the product, its installation, maintenance, and operation
Auditor	Prevents misuse of the product
Installer	Integrates the product into its environment
Maintainer	Repairs the product
Operator	Provides resources and supplies to the product
User 1	Directly benefits from using the product, but is not the final user (e.g., distributor)
User 2	Directly benefits from using the products

Source: Magaziner, E., *Very High Quality Customer Requirements,* Project Linguistics International, Sedona, AZ.

Figure D.9 Magaziner customer categories.

	Segment 1	Segment 2
Planner		
Funder	Sell to	
Auditor	Influence	
Installer	Understand	
Maintainer	Etc.	
Operator	Etc.	
User 1		
User 2		

Sell to   =   "Customers must believe that your product has the ability to fulfill all requirements."

Influence   =   "Customers we must understand who influence those who use the product but their job may not be affected by the product."

Understand =   "Customers we must understand who usually don't directly use the product."

Source: Adapted from Daetz, D. et al., *Customer Integration, the Quality Function Deployment (QFD) Leader's Guide For Decision Making*, Oliver Wright Publications, Essex Junction, VT, 1995.

Figure D.10 Daetz, Barnard, Norman grid (DBN).

DBN Grid for 3-Hole Punch

Product: 3-Hole Punch
Market: Commercial

Viewpoint	Segment 1 Office	Segment 2 School
Distribution channel buyer (User 1)	Sell to	Sell to
Secretary/teacher (User 2)	Understand	Understand
Materials mgr./buyer (Funder)	Sell to	Sell to
Stock clerk (Installer)	Influence	Influence

Figure D.11 DBN grid — 3-hole punch.

Open-Ended Questions

1. What images come to mind when you visualize this product or service?
2. From your experience, what complaints, problems or weaknesses would you like to mention about the product or service?
3. What features do you think of when selecting the product or service?
4. What new features might address your future needs?
5. What are the important _____ of _____?

qualities	product
elements	service
characterization	system
features	

Figure D.12 Open-ended questions.

Some Useful Questions[a]

What would you like to have in a _____?

What concerns would you like to share?

What comments or recommendations do you have for improvement?

Why did you mention _____?

Why is this _____ important to you?

What does that _____ do for you?

What problems do you have with _____?

What works well about _____?

What would work better than this _____?

What is missing in the _____?

If you were to design/redesign the _____, describe its features, performance, _____, _____, _____.

[a] Always ask open-ended questions. Be careful, customers talk more in features than in needs.

Figure D.13 Some useful questions.

Interview Guide

Opening

Thank you for volunteering your time to talk to us today. As we discussed earlier, we want to talk to you about your wants and needs concerning _____. Your data along with interview information from other users of our product, will be combined and used to improve our product in order that we can better meet your needs.

In order to help us, we ask that you be as candid as possible. Please be assured that the contents of this session will be kept confidential and will be used only by our design team.

Main Questions

1. What are problems you face when using a 3-hole punch?
2. What are issues you deal with today in using a 3-hole punch?
3. What is the net end result benefit you would like to receive when you purchase a 3-hole punch?

Backup Probes

1. What problems do you face when punching multiple sheets?
2. What problems do you face when punching material other than paper?
3. Are there any other needs you may have for a punch?
4. What comes to mind when you think about purchasing your next 3-hole punch?
5. What features do you think of when selecting a 3-hole punch?
6. What new features might address your future needs?

Closing

1. Are there any topics we should have discussed?
2. We will most likely contact you again regarding clarification of things we discussed today, i.e., when is best time to call and/or what number is best to reach you?
3. We will be contacting you regarding the importance of needs and features that evolve from interviews.

Figure D.14 Interview guide.

Process Flow Diagram for 3-Hole Punch

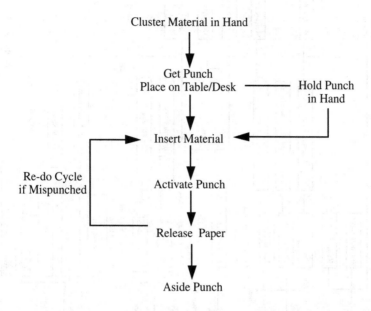

Figure D.15 Process flow diagram — 3-hole punch.

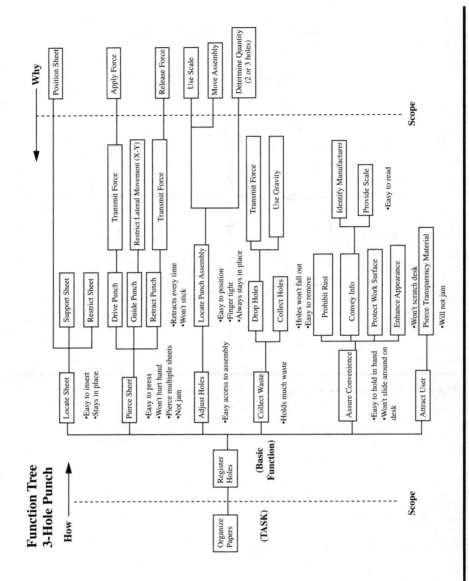

Figure D.16 Function tree for 3-hole punch.

Customer Verbatims — 3-Hole Punch

1. Easy to insert paper
2. Easy to insert multiple sheets
3. Sheet stays in place
4. Sheet is aligned properly for punch
5. Easy to locate sheet(s) and punch with other hand at same time
6. Can pierce multiple sheets
7. Punch will not jam
8. Minimum force to punch
9. Punching does not hurt any hand
10. Clean punch — no wrinkle on sheet
11. Takes less than 10 lb force to activate
12. Punch shaft should be stainless steel
13. Padded punch cover won't hurt any hand
14. Easy access to punch assembly
15. Punch always stays in place
16. Easy to align punch to preset stops
17. Easy to read punch preset locations
18. Can reset punch assembly without screwdriver (loosen and tighten)
19. Holes will not fall out when handling and when unloading
20. Easy to remove back to empty holes
21. Back will not snap out —spewing holes all over
22. Holes will not fall out when punch is dropped
23. Back should be made from plastic
24. Punch will not scratch desktop
25. Can pierce other materials (OH transparency)
26. Punch will not jam when punching OH material
27. Punch will not slide around
28. Punch has professional appearance
29. Punch has plate for engraving

Figure D.17 Customer verbatims — 3-hole punch.

VOC Collection
Verbatim Classification

Product: 3-Hole Punch; Model 2.0

Item	Use	User	Interviewer	Customer	Interviewee Verbatims
1	01	01	01, 03	01	Easy to insert paper
2	01	01	01, 03	01	Easy to insert multiple sheets
3	01	01	01, 03	01	Can pierce multiple sheets
4	03	03	03, 04	02	Easy access to punch assembly
5	03	03	03, 04	02	Punch always stays in place
6	02	02	Etc.	Etc.	Etc.
7					
8					
9					
10					

Product: 3-hole punch Model 2.0

Customer	Interviewer(s)	Use Category	User Type
01 Customer A	01	01 Office	01 Secretary
02 Customer B	02	02 School	02 Teacher
	03	03 Exec off	03 Executive
	04		

D.18 VOC collection verbatim classification — 3-hole punch.

Affinity Tree 2-Level 3-Hole Punch

Locate sheet	Easy to insert paper
	Easy to insert multiple sheets
	Sheet stays in place
	Sheet is aligned properly for punch
	Easy to locate sheet(s) and punch with other had at same time
Pierce sheet	Can pierce multiple sheets
	Punch will not jam
	Minimum force to punch
	Punching does not hurt any hand
	Clean punch — no wrinkle on sheet
	Takes less than 10lb force to activate
	Punch shaft should be stainless steel
	Padded punch cover won't hurt any hand
Adjust punches (holes)	Easy access to punch assembly
	Punch always stays in place
	Easy to align punch to preset stops
	Easy to read punch preset locations
	Can reset punch assembly without screwdriver (loosen and tighten)
Collect waste	Holes will not fall out when handling and when unloading
	Easy to remove back to empty holes
	Back will not snap out — spewing holes all over
	Holes will not fall out when punch is dropped
	Back should be made from plastic
Assure convenience	Punch will not scratch desktop
	Can pierce other materials (OH transparency)
	Punch will not jam when punch OH material
	Punch will not slide around
Aesthetics (please senses)	Punch has professional appearance
	Punch has plate for engraving

D.19 Affinity tree, 2–level — 3-hole punch.

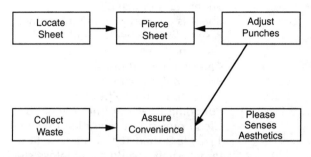

Figure D.20 Interrelationship digraph — 3-hole punch.

VOC Glossary

East to insert paper	Paper lines up easily in the throat of the punch assembly; will not slide under throat
Can pierce multiple sheets	Can punch 10 sheets of 20# paper; can punch 1 sheet of bristol; can punch 1 sheet of transparency
Punch shaft should be made of stainless steel	Shaft maintains its sharpness and will not corrode; material to be determined
Can reset punch assembly without screwdriver (loosen/tighten)	Easy finger access to punch assembly adjustment screw; can loosen and tighten with finger torque and assembly stays in place until next adjustment
Etc.	Etc.

Figure D.21 VOC glossary.

Voice of the Customer Table

Customer Verbatim	Reworded Data	I/E	Need	Solution	Feature	Other →
1. Easy to insert paper	1. OK	E	X			
5. Easy to locate sheet and punch at same time	5a. Easy to hold sheet in place with one hand	I		X		
	5b. Punch/paper won't move during down stroke with other hand	I	'	X	X	
11. Takes less than 10 lbs. force to activate	11a. Easy to activate assy. Force TBD	E		X		
		I		X		

Figure D.22a Voice of the customer table — 3-hole punch.

Voice of the Customer Table

Customer Verbatim	Reworded Data	I/E	Need	Solution	Feature	Other →
12. Punch shaft should be stainless steel						
	12a. Punch shaft retains sharpness	E		X	X	
	12b. Shaft will not corrode	I	X			
			X			
13. Padded punch cover so won't hurt hand						
	13a. Too much force to activate punch; improve leverage	E		X	X	
	13b. Punch spring too stiff	I				
					X	
19. Holes will not fall out when handling and when unloading		E	X			

P.

Figure D.22b Voice of the customer table — 3-hole punch.

Voice of the Customer Table

Customer Verbatim	Reworded Data	I/E	Need	Solution	Feature	Other →
	19a. Holes will not fall out when handling	I	X			
	19b. Holes will not fall out when emptying	I	X			

P. 3

D.22c Voice of the customer table — 3-hole punch.

**Importance Quantification[a] Processed VOC Verbatims —
Nest Hierarchy Process (NHP)**

Item	Wt.[b]	Item	Wt.[b]	Score
Locate sheet	20	1. Easy insert paper	2	0.4
		2. Easy to insert multiple sheets	15	3.0
		3. Sheet stays in place	10	2.0
		4. Sheet is aligned properly for punch	23	4.6
		5. Easy to locate sheet(s) and punch with other hand at same time	50	10.0
			Σ 100	
Pierce sheet	40	6. Can pierce multiple sheets	35	14.0
		7. Punch will not jam	25	10.0
		8. Minimum force to punch	5	2.0
		9. Punching does not hurt any hand	5	2.0
		10. Clean punch — no wrinkle on sheet	20	8.0
		11. Takes less than 10 lb force to activate	10	4.0
		12. Punch shaft should be stainless steel	5	2.0
		13. Padded punch cover won't hurt any hand	5	2.0
			Σ 100	
Adjust punch assembly	15	14. Easy access to punch assembly	30	4.5
		15. Punch always stays in place	30	4.5
		16. Easy to align punch to preset stops	10	1.5
		17. Easy to read punch preset locations	10	1.5
		18. Can reset punch assembly without screwdriver (loosen and tighten)	20	3.0
			Σ 100	
Collect waste	5	19. Holes will not fall out when handling and when unloading	50	2.5
		20. Easy to remove back to empty holes	30	1.5
		21. Back will not snap out — spewing holes all over	10	0.5

**Importance Quantification[a] Processed VOC Verbatims —
Nest Hierarchy Process (NHP) (cont.)**

		22. Holes will not fall out when punch is dropped	5	0.25
		23. Back should be made from plastic	5	0.25
			Σ 100	
Assure convenience	15	24. Punch will not scratch desktop	10	1.5
		25. Can pierce other materials (OH transparency)	40	6.0
		26. Punch will not jam when punch OH material	40	6.0
		27. Punch will not slide around	10	1.5
			Σ 100	
Aesthetics	5	28. Punch has professional appearance	50	2.5
		29. Punch has plate for engraving	50	2.5
	Σ 100		Σ 100	
			Σ Σ 100	

[a] Nested hierarchy process (NHP), two-level tree, to compute score.
[b] Constant sum method used to assign weights.

Figure D.23 Importance quantification, processed verbatims, nested hierarchy process (NHP) — 3-hole punch.

CUSTOMER ORIENTED PRODUCT CONCEPTING (COPC)
3-HOLE PUNCH

PRODUCT: 3-Hole Punch, Model 2.1
TASK: Organize Papers
DELIVERABLES: Registered Material
BASIC FUNCTION: Register Holes

COUNTRY: U.S. Only
MARKET: Commercial
SEGMENT: Office/School
USER: Sec, Teachers
CHIEF BUYING INFLUENCE: Stockhouse Dealer

SATISFACTION
5 - World Class
4 - Best in Class
3 - Average
2 - Disappointing
1 - The Worst

OPERATIONAL FUNCTIONS	FEATURES (NEEDS)	IMPORTANCE (NHP)	US TODAY	OMI	US FUTURE	IMPROVEMENT RATIO	MKT. LEVERAGE	RAW SCORE	%	CRITERIA		TECHNOLOGY / USE ADJUSTABLE STOP
LOCATE SHEET	Easy to insert sheets	0.4	4	4	5	1.0	1.0	0.4	0.9	Cost (mtl) 7.0	1.	0.21	0.027
	Easy to insert multiple sheets	3.0	3	5	5	1.7	1.2	6.1	14.8	Quality 33.0	2.	1.32	0.592
	Sheet stays in place	2.0	3	4	4	1.0	1.0	2.0	4.8	Reliability 40.0	3.	2.00	0.240
	Easy to locate/punch same time	10.0	3	4	5	1.7	1.5	25.5	62.0	Cost (assy) 7.0	4.	0.28	2.480
	Sheet aligned properly	4.6	3	3	4	1.3	1.2	7.1	17.3	Mfg. abil. 13.0	5.	0.53	0.692
								41.1	99.8	100.0		4.33	4.031
PIERCE SHEET	Want sharp clean cut	8.0	3	4	4	1.33	1.0	10.6	12.1	Cost (mtl) 7.0	PNEUMATICS 1.		
	Able to pierce multiple sheets	14.0	2	5	5	2.5	1.5	52.5	60.0	Quality 33.0	2.		
	Will not jam or stick	10.0	3	4	5	1.7	1.2	20.4	23.3	Reliability 40.0	3.		
	Easy to activate	2.0	2	4	4	2.0	1.0	4.0	4.6	Cost (assy) 7.0	4.		
								87.5	100.0	Mfg. abil. 13.0 / 100.0	5.		
ADJUST PUNCHES	Easy to access	30.0	5	5	5	1.0	1.0	30.0	35.2	ETC◇	CLICK STOP-SPRING BALL 1.		
	Easy to locate position	10.0	5	5	5	1.0	1.0	10.0	11.8		2. ETC		
	Punch stays in place when set	30.0	2	3	3	1.5	1.0	45.0	52.2		3. ETC.		
								85.0	99.9		4.		
											5.		
COLLECT WASTE	Don't want punches to fall out	50.0	3	4	4	1.3	1.0	65.0	58.2	ETC.	HINGED DOOR ON END 1.		
	Easy to remove	30.0	5	5	5	1.0	1.0	30.0	26.9		2. ETC.		
	Back will not pop out	10.0	4	4	4	1.0	1.0	10.0	8.9		3. ETC.		
	Don't want punches to spill when handled	5.0	3	4	4	1.3	1.0	6.5	5.8		4.		
								111.5	99.8		5.		
ASSURE CONVENIENCE	Don't want to scratch table top	1.5	4	4	4	1.0	1.2	1.8	1.1	ETC◇	PNEUMATICS 1.		
	Don't want punch to slide around	1.5	4	4	5	1.3	1.2	2.3	1.3		2.		
	Can punch OH transparency	40.0	4	4	5	1.3	1.5	78.0	48.8		3.		
	Will not jam when punch OH	40.0	4	4	5	1.3	1.5	78.0	48.8		4.		
								160.1	100.0		5.		
AESTHETICS	Professional appearance	2.5	1	1	3	3.0	1.2	9.0	54.5	ETC.	BURNISHED STAINLESS 1.		
	Name plate	2.5	1	1	3	3.0	1.0	7.5	45.4		2.		
								16.5	99.9		3.		
											4.		
											5.		

Figure D.24 Customer-oriented product concepting (COPC) — 3-hole punch.

Scoring Matrix
Technology vs. Company Criteria

	1	2	3	4	5
Cost (Mtl.)	>Today		= Today		< Today
Quality	Unsatisfactory	Today benchmark		Best in class	World class
Reliability	MPTF 5000		MPTF 10,000		MPTF 20,000
Cost (Assy.)	2.0	Today 1.50	1.00		0.10
MFG. Abitity	Complex		Today	80% Auto	Total auto

Figure D.25 Scoring matrix, technology vs. company criteria.

VOC Deployment
HOQ
3-Hole Punch

Satisfaction Scale
5 = May exceed needs; wow!
4 = Meets needs very well
3 = Meets needs
2 = Barely meets needs
1 = May not meet needs

Need	Importance (NHP)	Throat clearance/thick	Throat curvature	Angle of slot	Shear angle: punch	Shear force	Shear COF of punch	Shear COF retract	Spring press to retract	Screw tension to set punch	Tightness of fit of back plate	Force to maintain block plate	Force to remove back plate	US today	OMI	US future	Improve ratio	Mkt. leverage	Score–Raw	Score %
Sheet stop in place	21.0	189	21											4	4	4	1.0	1.0	21.0	4.7
Easy to locate sheet	10.0			90										3	4	5	1.7	1.5	25.5	5.7
Pierce melt sheets	14.0				126	126								2	5	5	2.5	1.5	52.5	11.8
No jam	10.0				90	90	90	90	90					3	4	5	1.7	1.2	20.4	4.6
Easy access to pouches	30.0									30				5	5	5	1.0	1.0	30.0	6.7
Punch stop in place	30.0									270				2	3	3	1.5	1.0	45.0	10.1
Holes won't fall out	50.0										450	450	450	3	4	4	1.3	1.0	65.0	14.6
Easy to remove holes	30.0										270	270	270	5	5	5	1.0	1.0	30.0	6.7
Punch trans.	40.0	40			360	360	360	360	360					4	4	5	1.3	1.5	78.0	17.5
No jam with trans.	40.0				360	360								4	4	5	1.3	1.5	78.0	17.5
Σ		229	21	90	936	936	450	450	450	300	720	720	720	=602.2			Σ	Σ	445.4	100.0
Σ%		3.8	0.3	1.5	15.5	15.5	7.5	7.5	7.5	5.0	12.0	12.0	12.0	=100						
Measure		mm	Rad	deg	deg	lbs	lbs	crgs	crgs	torq	torq	lbs	lbs							
Current		3	10	27	85	2	1	5	4	20	2	2.5	2.5							
OMI		2	10	23	90	0.5	0.8	5	3	15	4	5	6							
Target		3	10	30	92	0.5	0.8	5	3	15	2	2.5	2.5							

Correlation
High = 9
Medium = 3
Low = 1

Figure D.26 VOC Deployment HOQ — 3-hole punch.

VOC Trend Matrix 3-Hole Punch

VOC Needs		Current Importance (NHP)	Future Importance	
			5 years	10 years
6.	Can pierce multiple sheets	14	↑	→
7.	Punch will not jam	10	↑	↑
25.	Can pierce other material (OH transparency)	6	↑	↑
26.	Punch will not jam with other material	6	↑	↑

Figure D.27 VOC trend matrix — 3-hole punch.

Interactive Delphi Grid 3-Hole Punch

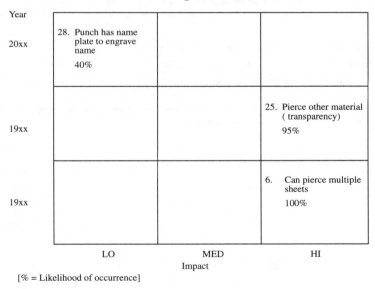

Figure D.28 Interactive Delphi grid — 3-hole punch.

Scenario by Matrix Method

Product: 3-Hole Punch

Scenarios for 19xx: Country, Market, Segment, User

Assumptions: Use current manufacturer and assembly machines

VOC	Areas Affected in Company	Impact on Company			Impact on Product Design		
		O	P	M	O	P	M
Pierce transparency material; no jam	Design Manufacturing Sourcing Assembly	↑	→	↑	↑	↓	↑
Professional line with nameplate	Design Assembly	↑	→	→	→	→	→
Burnished stainless steel punch	Design Sourcing Manufacturing	→	→	→	→	→	→

O = Optimistic   ↓ = Negative impact

P = Pessimistic   ↑ = Positive impact

M = Most likely   → = Neutral; no effort

Figure D.29 Scenario by matrix method.

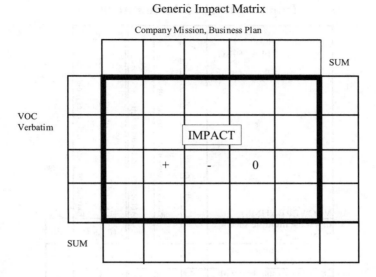

Figure D.30 Generic impact matrix.

Impact Matrix 3-Hole Punch

PLANNING / VOC VERBATIMS	MISSION			BUS PLAN		Σ
	Create superior product value	Focus on customer satisfaction	Achieve market leadership	Expand functionality of punches	Expand into new market segments (exec)	
6. Pierce multiple sheets 7. No jam	+	+	+	0	0	3
25. Pierce transparency 26. Material, no jam	+	+	+	+	0	4
28. Professional line with name plate	0	0	+	+	+	3
Σ	2	2	3	2	1	

+ = Will make it easier to achieve mission and business plan
− = Will make it difficult to achieve mission and business plan
0 = No influence

Figure D.31 Impact matrix — 3-hole punch.

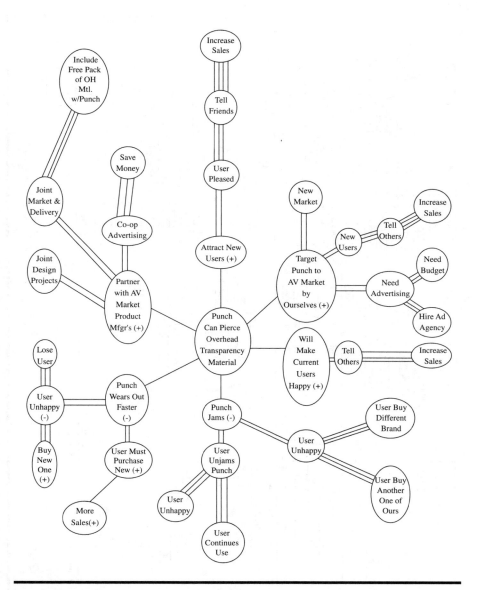

Figure D.32 MEM diagram for 3-hole punch.

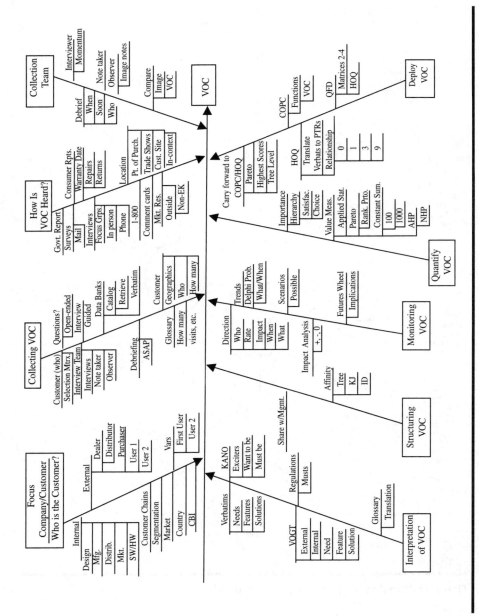

Figure D.33 Ishikawa diagram — VOC.

APPENDIX E

BIBLIOGRAPHY

Akao, Y. (Ed.), *Quality Function Deployment*, Productivity Press, Cambridge, MA, 1990.

Bossert, J. L., *Quality Function Deployment: A Practitioner's Approach*, ASQC Press/Marcel Dekker, New York, 1991.

Cohen, L., *Quality Function Deployment: How to Make QFD Work for You*, Addison-Wesley Publishing, Reading, MA, 1995.

Day, R. G., *Quality Function Deployment*, American Society for Quality, 1993.

Guinta, L. and Praisler, N., *The QFD Book*, AMA Press, New York, 1992.

Hauser, J. R., and Clausing, D., The house of quality", *Harvard Bus. Rev.*, 43-63, May-June, 1988.

King, R., *Better Designs in Half the Time, Implementing Quality Function Deployment in America*, GOAL/QPC, Methuen, MA, 1987.

Marsh, S., Moran, J. W., Nakui, S., and Hoffherr, G., *Facilitating and Training In Quality Function Deployment*, GOAL/QPC, Methuen, MA, 1991.

Revell, J. B., Moran, J.W. and Cox, C., *The QFD Handbook*, John Wiley & Sons, Inc., New York, 1998.

Shillito, M. L., *Advanced QFD, Linking Technology to Market and Company Needs*, John Wiley & Sons, New York, 1994.

Sullivan, L. P., "Quality function deployment," *Quality Progress*, 39-50, 1986.

Terninko, J., *Step-by-Step QFD: Customer Driven Product Design*, CRC Press, Boca Raton, FL, 1997.

APPENDIX F

I have included in this appendix a flow chart connecting all of the activities that have been discussed. They are sequenced in order of their occurrence. It can be used as a roadmap for direction as well as a global positioning system to determine where you are in the process.

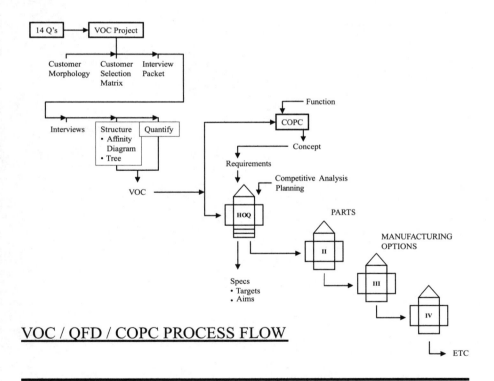

VOC / QFD / COPC PROCESS FLOW

Figure F.01

Index

A

Affinity
    Diagram, 93, 98, 137, 145
    Tree, 139, 253
Alignment, 23
Alternative ranking, 105
Analytical hierarchy method, 115
Assumptions, 27
Attributes, 15
Audit trail, 146

B

Backup probes, 65
Balanced communication, 146
Base case model, product profile, 41, 43
Basic features, 2
Basic function, 5, 12
    of product, 2
    of punch, 4
Benefit, 12
Brainstorming, internal, 57
Business
    case, 43, 224
    plan, 146
        company, 28
        generic, 44
Buzz words, 63

C

Choice criteria, 125
CIDM, see Customer integrated decision
      making
Classification codes, 71
Closed ended questions, 66
Closing, 65
Collecting VOC, 47–77
    background, 47
    qualitative and quantitative VOC, 47–54

customer selection, 50–54
how many customers to talk to,
    50
when to start, 48–49
VOC collection techniques, 54–75
    contextual inquiry, 58–61
    customer panels/councils, 58
    customer visits, 63
    debriefing of visit, 70
    focus groups, 56–57
    function trees, 72–75
    internal brainstorming, 57–58
    Internet, 61
    interview guide, 63–64, 65
    interviews, 56
    interview team, 65–66
    intranet homepage, 75
    location studies, 57
    nominal group technique, 64
    probing, 67–68
    process flow mapping, 61–62
    questions to ask, 66–67
    recording observations, 69–70
    scheduling interview visits, 68–69
    service calls, 58
    surveys, 55–56
    transcribing interview tape
        recordings, 75
    verbatim classification data bank,
        71–72
Collection, 135
    methodologies, common, 54
    technique, questions to help
        determine appropriate, 55
Collective voice (CV), 132
Color coded affinity tree, 139
Commercialization process, 13, 14
Common collection methodologies, 54
Communication, balanced, 146
Company business plan, 28
Company and customer focus, 19–45
    customer chains, 30–32
    QFD starting questions, 20–21

W